Racial Disadvantage and Ethnic Diversity
in Britain

returned on (or before) the last da

EG26276

Racial Disadvantage and Ethnic Diversity in Britain

Andrew Pilkington

© Andrew Pilkington 2003

All rights reserved. No reproduction, copy or transmission of this publication may be made without written permission.

No paragraph of this publication may be reproduced, copied or transmitted save with written permission or in accordance with the provisions of the Copyright, Designs and Patents Act 1988, or under the terms of any licence permitting limited copying issued by the Copyright Licensing Agency, 90 Tottenham Court Road, London W1T 4LP.

Any person who does any unauthorised act in relation to this publication may be liable to criminal prosecution and civil claims for damages.

The author has asserted his right to be identified as the author of this work in accordance with the Copyright, Designs and Patents Act 1988.

First published 2003 by
PALGRAVE MACMILLAN
Houndmills, Basingstoke, Hampshire RG21 6XS and
175 Fifth Avenue, New York, N.Y. 10010
Companies and representatives throughout the world

PALGRAVE MACMILLAN is the global academic imprint of the Palgrave Macmillan division of St. Martin's Press, LLC and of Palgrave Macmillan Ltd. Macmillan® is a registered trademark in the United States, United Kingdom and other countries. Palgrave is a registered trademark in the European Union and other countries.

ISBN 0–333–58931–9   hardback
ISBN 0–333–58932–7   paperback

This book is printed on paper suitable for recycling and made from fully managed and sustained forest sources.

A catalogue record for this book is available from the British Library.

Library of Congress Cataloging-in-Publication Data

Pilkington, Andrew, 1947–
    Racial disadvantage and ethnic diversity in Britain / Andrew Pilkington.
        p.   cm.
    Includes bibliographical references and index.
    ISBN 0–333–58931–9 (cloth)
    1. Great Britain—Race relations.   2. Pluralism (Social sciences)–
    –Great Britain.   3. Race discrimination—Great Britain.   4. Great
    Britain—Ethnic relations.   5. Ethnic groups—Great Britain.
    6. Racism—Great Britain.   7. Blacks—Great Britain.   I. Title.

DA125.A1 P56 2002
305.8′00941—dc21   2002026762

10   9   8   7   6   5   4   3   2   1
12   11   10   09   08   07   06   05   04   03

Printed and bound in Great Britain by J. W. Arrowsmith Ltd, Bristol.

EG 26276
FHWLC
LEARNING CENTRE EALING GREEN

To Jude with love

Contents

List of tables and figures

Tables

Figures

Acknowledgements

It would have been impossible to complete this book without the support and encouragement of a number of people. I am grateful to Professor John Rex for initially encouraging me to write a sequel to *Race Relations in Britain* and to my editor at Palgrave Macmillan, Catherine Gray, for her patience and gentle goading when I periodically wondered whether other work commitments would ever allow me enough time to finish the book. Thanks are also due to Joy Knight, Diane Entwistle, Penny Hubbard and Marie Camillo for their secretarial support and to Magenta Lampson and Anstice Hughes for their invaluable help in editing and indexing the manuscript.

Lord Bhikhu Parekh, Dr Peter Ratcliffe, Dr Anne Monroe, Dr Michael Wyness, Dr Nirmal Puwar, Dr Ali Andrew and Michael Haralambos kindly commented on earlier drafts of specific chapters. I found their advice, along with that of two anonymous reviewers, invaluable, although the final responsibility for what is written clearly rests with me. Thanks are also due to my colleagues at University College Northampton for providing a conducive and stimulating environment to work in, and my students who constituted the original guinea-pigs for the book's main ideas.

Above all, however, I am grateful to my family and friends. Jane and Tim Beer together with Keith Sharp have been constant sources of support, while 'the over the hill club' has only accepted my apologies from 'committee meetings' on condition that I really do finish the book. I owe my mother and (late) father a great deal. They taught me to abhor racism and it is reassuring to find that my own children, Jessica and Katherine, and stepchildren Tobias and Rupert, find it equally abhorrent. On those numerous occasions when pessimism is induced by the horrific behaviour of human beings towards other human beings, my children's intolerance of racism provides grounds for cautious optimism that racial inequality can be overcome. The book is dedicated to my wife, Judith, whom I cherish and without whom this book would never have seen the light of day.

Andrew Pilkington

The author and publishers wish to thank the following for granting permission to reproduce copyright material: the Policy Studies Institute for Tables 3.2, 3.3, 3.4, 3.5, 3.6, 4.1 and 5.4 from the Third and Fourth National Surveys of Ethnic Minorities reproduced from Modood *et al* (1997), Ethnic Minorities in Britain: Diversity and Disadvantage, London: Policy Studies Institute; and Taylor and Francis Ltd for Tables 5.2 and 5.3, reproduced from Demack *et al*, 'Minding the gap: ethnic, gender and social class differences in attainment', *Race, Ethnicity and Education,* Vol. 3 (2000), No. 2 (http://www.tandf.co.uk/journals). Crown copyright material is reproduced with the permission of the Controller of Her Majesty's Stationary Office and the Queen's Printer for Scotland.

Introduction

It is impossible to understand contemporary British society without paying due regard to issues relating to race and ethnicity. This book seeks to present an overview of research in this area and on that basis delineate key features of multi-ethnic Britain at the start of a new millennium. The approach adopted is primarily a sociological one, with recent studies being used to assess a series of key social theories, which both underpin popular understanding of racial and ethnic issues and provide the rationale for many of the policies adopted to promote racial equality. No one discipline, however, can do justice to the wide range of issues relating to race and ethnicity that need to be addressed. It is therefore essential, at a time when the boundaries between disciplines are becoming blurred, to draw on the contributions of a variety of disciplines. While this book is written primarily from a sociological perspective, a range of other disciplinary perspectives, including History, Geography, Politics and Cultural Studies, are drawn upon where appropriate. In this sense the book is inter-disciplinary.

It is possible to detect the emergence in the last decade of a new framework guiding research on issues relating to race and ethnicity in Britain. For much of the post-war period, a particular framework was dominant. This framework can be characterised, in the words of Modood (1992a), as that of 'racial dualism'. Within this framework, which took different forms according to the preferred theoretical leanings of different social scientists, the primary emphasis was on a boundary between people drawn on the basis of skin colour. 'White' people were envisaged as in a markedly more powerful structural position than that of 'Black' people. The role of researchers was therefore primarily to delineate and explain the disadvantages shared in common by Black people. This framework has lost its dominant position, with the development of new theoretical approaches in the social sciences and the inclusion in social research of more sophisticated measures of ethnicity. Theoretically, what has been labelled the 'cultural turn' (S Hall 1997a) has entailed

1

deconstruction of the central categories, White and Black, sensitised us to diversity among members of both the majority group and minority groups, and highlighted how all human beings have multiple and shifting identities. Empirically, a plethora of recent studies has demonstrated that there are significant differences in both the socio-economic position and identities of different minority ethnic groups. In this context, a new framework has emerged, which can be characterised as that of 'racial disadvantage and ethnic diversity'. This framework continues to see a need to delineate and explain the disadvantages shared by groups whose skin colour marks them out in the eyes of the majority group as racially different. At the same time, it highlights the diversity among minority ethnic groups and emphasises that the socio-economic positions and identities of their members are not structurally determined but are (at least partially) formed by their actions. This book draws on this new framework in order to try and illuminate our understanding of issues relating to race and ethnicity in contemporary Britain.

Structure of the book

Chapter 1 introduces the key concepts of race and ethnicity. While it is recognised that these terms are often used interchangeably, it is important to make a conceptual distinction between them. Race entails distinguishing people on the basis of physical markers, such as skin pigmentation, hair texture and facial features, and placing people into distinct categories. Ethnicity on the other hand entails distinguishing people on the basis of cultural markers, such as language, religion and shared customs, and identifying key social groups. While members of a purported race may not identify themselves as sharing a common racial identity, members of an ethnic group necessarily recognise that they share a common ethnic identity with other members of their ethnic group.

The idea of race is a distinctly modern one and only emerged in a fully fledged form in the nineteenth century. Proponents of this idea accept three central tenets: a limited number of fixed and discrete races can be distinguished on the basis of clear physical and visible differences between people; these races are not only physically different but also different in terms of their intellectual capacities and cultural achievements; as a result, they form a hierarchy whereby some are inherently superior to others. Historically, a disparate range of people were identified by Europeans as inferior races, including various disadvantaged groups within Europe as well as non-European peoples. In this way, as Malik (1996) argues, the idea of race constituted an ideology in a society purportedly valuing equality, by depicting the manifest global and local inequalities between people as fixed by nature.

While, at one stage, belief in the idea of race was given legitimacy by (Western) science, the advent of genetics has thoroughly discredited the idea: the visible differences between people are now recognised to be biologically of trivial significance and (the more significant) genetic differences are acknowledged to be more variable within purported races than between them. Despite the lack of any intellectual support for the idea of race, evident for example in the common contemporary employment of the word 'racism' to describe the old idea of race, it still remains the case, however, that the idea lives on in popular consciousness and that people defined as racially different are often differentially treated and thereby disadvantaged. Whether we should continue to use the concept of race in the social sciences, given that the central tenets of the idea of race lack any credibility, remains a disputed issue. Some writers prefer not to use the term since its continued employment misleadingly seems to imply, and thus give credibility to, the notion of distinct and naturally occurring populations. Others argue that we cannot avoid using the term, or some derivative such as racial, on the grounds that many people continue to believe that race is real and that belief has real consequences. Whatever position is taken on this issue, there is agreement that the idea of race lacks any intellectual credibility and that it is morally repugnant for people to be treated differently because they have been *socially* defined as members of a race.

The concept of ethnicity does not carry the same problematic connotations associated with the idea of race and is much more readily employed by contemporary social scientists. An ethnic group comprises a group whose members believe they share a common ancestry, history and culture, and who are recognised by others to be a distinctive group. While it is not uncommon for ethnic groups to be depicted as primordial groupings, and in this sense to be seen as not unlike the image of races as distinct and naturally occurring populations, social scientists have demonstrated that the boundaries between ethnic groups shift considerably. They change over time and may be drawn differently on different occasions. The boundaries between groups are influenced by a range of social processes. These include the (changing) ways in which members define themselves and external constraints exerted by other powerful groups. While people's communal affiliations are often central to their identities, we need to be careful, however, not to be seduced by a discourse which refers to people's membership of ethnic groups into reifying the concept of ethnicity and thereby overstating the boundaries between groups and exaggerating the cultural distinctiveness of each. We need in short to recognise that ethnic identities are socially constructed and that in contemporary Britain ethnic identities may be becoming increasingly overlapping, dynamic and fluid.

While it is important to make a conceptual distinction between race and ethnicity, this distinction is not always evident in social research. While the term ethnicity is more readily used by social scientists than that of race, social surveys often do not do justice to the fluidity of people's identities. The primary concern has been to delineate how those socially defined as non-White are faring relative to those socially defined as White. Given this concern, the majority ethnic group has been identified on the basis of a physical marker, while minority ethnic groups have been distinguished from each other on the basis of a cultural marker, geographical/national origin.

Issues relating to race and ethnicity are now recognised to be central to an understanding of contemporary British society. Chapter 2 seeks to address the question as to why these issues have moved from the periphery to the centre of social scientific discourse in the post-war period. Two factors are identified as responsible for this shift. The first relates to immigration after the Second World War, especially from the Caribbean and the Indian subcontinent. While immigration is not a new phenomenon in British society, there is little doubt that the arrival of substantial minorities clearly distinguishable in terms of skin colour and cultural traditions from the majority of the population has made Britain a more ethnically diverse society. The second factor relates to racial discrimination. Contradicting Britain's image as a tolerant society, immigrants from the Caribbean and the Indian subcontinent experienced racial discrimination of both a direct and indirect kind. The persistence of such discrimination, and consequent disadvantage, indicated that alongside a long-recognised class division and a newly appreciated gender division, attention needed to be given to a third social division within British society, namely a racial division. While none of these divisions was in fact new, it took social scientists some time to acknowledge the significance of each and the need to examine how they interact to influence people's life chances.

What struck most social scientists initially as central to an understanding of the impact of substantial minorities settling in most major towns and cities was one distinguishing feature which the minorities shared, notably their skin colour. It was this that defined them in the eyes of the vast majority of the population as a race apart. While social scientists employed a diverse range of theoretical approaches and adopted somewhat different problematics in order to explore a range of issues relating to race and ethnicity, a particular framework became increasingly, albeit never completely, hegemonic. This framework centred on race rather than ethnicity and has been characterised as that of 'racial dualism'. In the last decade, this framework has come under mounting criticism and a new framework has emerged which acknowledges the continuing need to delineate and explain racial disadvantage, but adds to this the need to acknowledge and account for ethnic diversity. While this new framework, which can be characterised as that of 'racial disadvantage and ethnic diversity', has thus far been primarily concerned to stress the diverse experience of different minority ethnic groups, there is increasing recognition that attention needs to be given to the ethnic diversity evident within the majority group (Parekh 2000). The tendency in this book to focus on (visible) minority ethnic groups rather than groups such as the Irish should not be misconstrued as implying that the latter do not also experience significant disadvantage (Mac an Ghaill 1999; Hickman and Walter 1997).

The following three chapters use this new framework to explore the position of ethnic groups in three institutional areas critical to people's life chances, notably those of employment, housing and education. Three main sources of data are drawn upon to delineate and explain the socio-economic position of minority ethnic groups: the 1991 Census; the 1994 Policy Studies Institute (PSI) survey; and the 1999–2000 Labour Force Surveys (LFSs). In addition, the 1995 Youth Cohort Survey (YCS) is drawn upon to explicate the position of ethnic groups in the education system. All of these sources concur in pointing to evidence within each of these institutional areas of both racial disadvantage and ethnic diversity.

Minority ethnic groups continue to face racial discrimination in the employment and housing markets, and within the education system. Partly, but not wholly, as a result of such discrimination, they face some common disadvantages in comparison to the majority ethnic group. They face within the labour market a higher risk of long-term unemployment and a glass ceiling in relation to elite positions. In addition, they are more likely to experience poverty and, within the housing market, are more likely to live in the less popular and more overcrowded housing in deprived areas.

At the same time, there is evidence of considerable diversity in the socio-economic position of different minority ethnic groups. While the patterns here depend partly on which ethnic groups are distinguished and what indicators are used for comparative purposes, the PSI survey demonstrates that a contrast can be drawn between African Asians and especially the Chinese, on the one hand, and Pakistanis and especially Bangladeshis, on the other hand. While the former tend to be performing above or at much the same level as Whites, the latter tend to be severely disadvantaged across the board. Indians, who are catching up fast, are closer to the former, while Caribbeans (especially the men) are closer to the latter.

Until recently, sociologists concerned with explicating the socio-economic position of minority ethnic groups have been more struck by racial disadvantage than ethnic diversity. Chapters 3 and 4 address two interrelated theses, which have been put forward by theorists who believe that the implications of extensive racial disadvantage are far reaching. The first thesis detects the emergence of a racialised underclass, while the second thesis sees the emergence of minority ethnic social exclusion. Chapter 3 challenges the first thesis on the grounds that the position of minority ethnic groups in the labour market is highly variable, that in only one case are any of the indicators for an underclass manifest at all, and that over time minority ethnic groups have narrowed the gap in job levels and earnings. Chapter 4 challenges the second thesis on similar grounds, drawing on evidence relating to poverty, health, residential location and housing.

These two chapters also explore alternative explanations for the socio-economic position of minority ethnic groups. While it is recognised that the recently rediscovered concept of institutional racism sensitises us to the subtle, and sometimes unintentional, ways organisations engage in discriminatory practices and thus reproduce racial disadvantage, it is argued that the latter cannot simply be seen as the outcome of the former. Inasmuch as social exclusion is envisaged as a social process (rather than an outcome), this concept at least enables us to recognise that factors other than discriminatory practices can also play a role in explaining the socio-economic position of minority ethnic groups. Theorists who highlight institutional racism or social exclusion share, however, a tendency to emphasise the way external structural forces impact on us and thus underplay the role of agency. In the process they tend to neglect the way minority ethnic groups draw on the cultural capital of their own communities to resist discriminatory practices and exclusionary processes, and thus improve their situation.

Many of the themes developed in Chapters 3 and 4 are taken up again in Chapter 5, which examines the experience of minority ethnic groups in the education system. When we look at ethnic differentials in educational attainment, we discover, as we did in Chapters 3 and 4, that there is no simple White/Black divide. Rather, Indian, African Asian and Chinese pupils are performing at least on a par with Whites, while at the other extreme Pakistani and Bangladeshi pupils along with Caribbean boys are underachieving. When we seek to explain such underachievement, we again find a complex range of factors involved. These include socio-economic factors, which stem in part from racially discriminatory practices; cultural factors; ineffective schools, which themselves are often located in deprived areas; and some (often unintentional) discrimination in educational institutions.

What again comes out clearly is the concern of minority ethnic groups to improve their situation. They are more likely than Whites to invest in education and continue their studies after compulsory schooling. While the rate of return on this investment is less than that of Whites, at least partly because of racial discrimination, investing in education does have its payoffs and has helped minority ethnic groups close the gap in socio-economic terms, albeit to varying degrees, between themselves and the majority ethnic group.

Chapter 6 represents a move away from the institutional analysis undertaken in the previous three chapters and addresses a set of issues relating to the question of identity. The cultural turn in social theory has entailed increasing attention being paid in recent years to this question. Many, but not all, social scientists concerned with race and ethnicity now recognise the need to complement their traditional focus on material inequalities by paying due regard to matters relating to culture and identity.

While the trajectory of Chapters 3–5 entailed moving from a consideration of the structural factors which account for the position of minority ethnic groups in different institutional areas to an appreciation of the way these groups use the resources of their communities to effect change, the trajectory of Chapter 6 entails a move in the opposite direction, from agency to structure.

It is now widely recognised that we do not have one fixed identity but rather multiple shifting identities. While this may suggest that we can don whichever identity we prefer, identities are socially constructed and we learn to identify with particular representations of, say, our ethnic group. Over time collective identities can solidify in this way and become established. Globalisation, however, tends to destabilise established collective identities so that we can no longer take our identity for granted but are obliged to choose who we are, albeit within social constraints. In this context, very different responses are evident. Some, feeling threatened by other cultures, may opt to return to their cultural roots, and retreat to the familiar certainties of the past. Identifying with an ethnically exclusive representation of the nation or opting for religious fundamentalism constitute two examples. Others, aware that we cannot but live with difference and need to come to terms with it, may draw on different cultural traditions and seek to produce new identities. Identifying with an ethnically inclusive representation of the nation or opting for hyphenated identities such as Black British constitute two examples. While we are able to choose with which representations to identify, their plausibility and appeal depend at least in part on the experience of members of different ethnic groups within key institutional areas. The concerns evident in Chapter 6 are intimately connected to those explored in previous chapters.

Chapter 7 explores the state's response in the post-war period to issues relating to race and ethnicity. For much of this period, successive British governments have pursued a two-pronged strategy. This has involved, on the one hand, increasingly restrictive immigration controls and, on the other hand, measures designed to combat racial disadvantage and integrate minority groups who have settled in the country. The two prongs rest on contrary principles, with the first presaged (in practice) on racist assumptions and the second presaged on liberal assumptions.

While some convergence is evident in the ways West European governments have addressed issues surrounding migration, not least in the common concern to control immigration, a comparison with other regimes helps to bring out some distinctive characteristics in the response of the British state. In contrast to Germany, Britain has been less reluctant to grant citizenship rights to immigrants while, in contrast to France, Britain has been less wedded to assimilationism. We should not, however, exaggerate these differences. There is evidence that members of Britain's minority groups do not always enjoy effective citizenship rights, and an examination of state policy confirms the analysis of education policy in Chapter 5, notably that only hesitant moves have been made towards pluralism. That there have been some moves is, at least in part, testament to the agency of minority ethnic groups who have engaged in diverse forms of political activity in pursuit of racial equality.

Chapter 8 briefly summarises the key themes of the book before seeking to draw out the policy implications of the analysis. The latter has been made easier by the publication of the Parekh report, which identifies five tasks which need to be undertaken in order for Britain to become a genuine multi-ethnic society: the need to re-imagine Britishness in an inclusive way; the need to strike a balance between social cohesion, equality and diversity; the need to combat different forms of racism; the need to reduce inequalities; and the need to build a pluralist human rights culture. The hostile media coverage of the report indicates that there is fundamental opposition to some of these ideas. The appropriate response is to acknowledge contrary tendencies in British society and for all of us to reinforce those tendencies that will enable Britain to become a vibrant multi-ethnic society.

1 The social construction of race and ethnicity

Race and ethnicity are both categories which involve drawing boundaries between people. Racial boundaries are normally drawn on the basis of physical markers, such as skin pigmentation, hair texture and facial features, while ethnic boundaries are normally drawn on the basis of cultural markers such as language, religion and shared customs. Contrary to the expectations of the founding fathers of Sociology, the force of race and ethnicity shows no signs of diminishing at the beginning of a new millennium. Indeed, given the persistence and power of racial/ethnic ties and identities across the globe, and the conflicts which they can engender, we may be tempted to believe that the division of people into racial and ethnic groups is in some sense natural or 'primordial'. What we need to recognise, however, is that the strength of racial/ethnic ties and identities changes over time and varies across the globe. This suggests that racial/ethnic divisions can only be understood when located in their social and historical context. Sociologists take this position and argue that both race and ethnicity are socially constructed. Let us deal with each in turn.

The social construction of race

There have always been physical differences between groups of human beings as a result of 'population inbreeding' (Giddens 1997: 212), but it is only within the last two centuries that these differences have been conceptualised as racial (Banton 1997). 'The word, "race", as used in Western languages, is of extremely recent origin' and 'it was not until the late seventeenth century' that it began to 'have the meaning we attach to it now'. Indeed, 'it was not until after the French and American Revolutions and the social upheavals which followed that the idea of race was fully conceptualised and became deeply embedded in our understandings and explanations of the world' (Hannaford 1996: 4–6). In

11

other words, the idea of race is distinctively modern and only emerged in a fully fledged form in the nineteenth century.

The idea of race developed to account for the manifest physical and cultural differences between people. We can distinguish three main theories (Banton 1987). The first, which was dominant in the seventeenth and eighteenth centuries, conceptualised race as lineage. Human beings belong to the same species, being ultimately descendants of Adam and Eve. As a result, however, of divine intervention, they were dispersed around the world. This allowed distinct lineages or lines of descent (races) to develop in different environments, which in turn helped to account for why people were both physically and culturally different. This theory was marred, however, by its inability to 'explain how environment affected the transmission of inherited characters' (Banton 1987: 168).

A second theory emerged – eventually to become dominant in the middle of the nineteenth century – which conceptualised race as type. Human beings do not belong to the same species because since time immemorial distinct types have existed. These types are permanent and comprise a limited number of fixed and discrete races. In contrast to the theory of race as lineage, this theory of race as type not only helped to explain physical and cultural differences between, for example, Europeans and Africans, but also 'fostered the beliefs that whites were *permanently* superior to blacks and that the two groups were not two varieties of a common species but two species of a common genus' (Banton 1997: 33). Negative stereotypes, which depicted 'the Negro [as] peculiarly sexual, musical, stupid, indolent, untrustworthy and violent' (Walvin 1987: 60), can be found three centuries earlier. And 'there was nothing remarkable about belief in racial superiority in the eighteenth and early nineteenth centuries' (Banton 1997: 33). What distinguished the theory of race as type was its insistence that such superiority was not a product of environmental factors but was part of the natural order of things. Scientifically, this theory was soon discredited, however, by its failure to account for evolution.

A third theory was born which conceptualised race as subspecies. Human beings belong to the same species because they can breed with one another and have fertile offspring. However, because species are constantly evolving, it is possible for a subdivision of a species (a subspecies), which is geographically isolated and therefore does not bre͏̵ ͏̵outside the subdivision, to develop distinctive characteristics. Through a process of natural selection, whereby those members best adapted to their environment are most likely to breed and have fertile offspring, subspecies (races) can diverge and become physically different.

Although Darwin's theory of evolution effectively refuted the notion of permanent differences between races, the belief that there are inherent racial differences lived on. Social Darwinists, such as Spencer, who focused on social rather than biological change, characterised the evolutionary process as a struggle between groups for survival. Adopting a conceptualisation of race as subspecies, some races were seen as fitter and therefore able to evolve further. In the process, 'racial science married the idea of a fixed hierarchy with that of progress – those at the top of the hierarchy [being] there on merit, because of their natural superiority in the struggle for existence' (Malik 1996: 91).

By the end of the nineteenth century, the idea of race had fully crystallised. The truth of its central tenets seemed to many Europeans to be self-evident: a limited number of fixed and dis-crete races could be distinguished on the basis of clear physical differences between people; these races were not only physically different but also different in terms of their intellectual capacities and cultural achievements; as a result, they formed a hierarchy whereby some were inherently superior to others. Although there was no point when one theory of race proved 'acceptable to all scholars', none the less 'by the time the century ended very many people identified themselves and others in racial terms' (Banton 1997: 34). The idea of race could thus be rou-tinely drawn upon to account for the observed physical and cul-tural differences between people and the assumed superiority of the West. As one writer in 1900 put it:

> There is in the world a hierarchy of races . . . those nations which eat more, claim more, and get higher wages, will direct and rule the others, and the lower work of the world will tend to be done by the lower breeds of men. This much we of the ruling colour will no doubt accept as obvious (Charles Murray, quoted in Fryer 1984: 173).

The idea of race continued to hold many people in thrall in the twentieth century. Indeed it underpinned one of the world's greatest atrocities, the extermination of Jews in Nazi Germany. Disquiet with the idea did, however, grow, culminating in its complete repudiation by most scholars after the Second World War. Intellectually, two arguments were compelling.

Firstly, the essential condition for race is that populations remain isolated from each other so that interbreeding does not occur. This condition, however, has not been met for centuries, especially since the expansion of Europe from the sixteenth century onwards. As a result the possibility for distinct subspecies to consolidate has not materialised. Secondly, the focus on visible or 'phenotypical' differences has been shown to be misplaced since the discovery by Mendel of the unit – the gene – upon which natural selection operates. A new specialism, genetics, has resulted in the realisation that visible differences between people are biologically trivial and that there is far greater genetic variation within than between groups previously defined as races (S Jones 1996).

This raises a paradox. On the one hand, we now have good scientific evidence that there is no such thing as race. On the other hand, we know that classifying people in racial terms has real effects. The paradox is solved once we realise that, as W I Thomas put it, 'if men [*sic*] define things as real, they are real in their consequences'. This means that physical differences such as skin colour can become significant because of the importance attached to them by people's beliefs. Let us take a particular example. Below is a short extract from the diary of a man who describes an experience he had travelling through the southern states of America in the 1960s:

> I walked up to the ticket counter. When the lady ticket seller saw me, her otherwise attractive face turned sour, violently so. This look was so unexpected and so unprovoked that I was taken aback. 'What do you want?' she snapped. Taking care to pitch my voice to politeness, I asked about the next bus to Hattiesburg. She answered rudely and glared at me with such loathing I knew I was receiving what the Negroes call 'the hate stare'. It was my first experience with it. It is far more than the look of disapproval one occasionally gets. This was so exaggeratedly hateful I would have been amused if I had not been so surprised. I framed the words in my mind: 'Pardon me, but have I done something to offend you?' But I realised I had done nothing – my colour offended her (Griffin 1972: 481).

Griffin was in fact white, but had artificially darkened his skin so as to give the appearance of a 'Negro'. Because of the way he was defined, he endured a catalogue of humiliations from people who, if they had known he was White, would have treated him with courtesy. Being Black was here considered to be significant and as a result was. Differences in complexion of course constitute a continuous distribution, with some people being lighter and some darker. In the United States a clear colour line was drawn between White and Black. Societies do not always, however, divide up the colour continuum in this way. For example, 'in Spanish-speaking parts of America no sharp line is drawn between black and white' (Banton 1997: 54). This is crucial. The significance of colour has nothing to do with biology but instead depends on the meaning given to it at a particular time and place.

We must not assume, however, that historically skin colour has been the only indicator of race. Here is Charles Kingsley, author of *The Water Babies*, writing to his wife during a visit to Ireland in 1860:

> But I am haunted by the human chimpanzees I saw along that hundred miles of horrible country. I don't believe they are our fault. I believe that there are not only many more of them than of old, but that they are happier, better, more comfortably fed and lodged under our rule than they ever were. But to see white chimpanzees is dreadful; if they were black one would not feel it so much, but their skins, except where tanned by exposure, are as white as ours. (Kingsley, quoted in Husband 1987: 12).

During the nineteenth century, the combination of a rising population and bad harvests encouraged a major movement of population from Ireland. As the quotation above indicates, the Irish who came to Britain – though white – moved to a society in which they were already seen as an inferior race. And the same fate awaited a later immigrant group at the turn of the century – Jews – who were seeking to escape violent anti-semitism in Eastern Europe.

The concept of an inferior race was not, however, restricted to people in the colonies or immigrants. During the nineteenth century, an analogy was often drawn between sexual differences and race so that white indigenous women were also represented as an inferior race. As one writer puts it:

Women it was observed, shared with Negroes a narrow childlike and deli-
cate skull, so different from the robust and rounded heads characteristic
of males of 'superior' races. Similarly, women of higher races tended to
have slightly protruding jaws, analogous to, if not as exaggerated as, the
apelike jutting jaws of lower races. Women and lower races were called
innately impulsive, emotional, imitative rather than original, and incapable
of the abstract reasoning found in white men ... in short, lower races
represented the female type of the human species, and females the lower
race of gender.

And indeed the concept of inferior race was extended even further: 'By analogy with the so called lower races, [not only]
women [but also] the sexually deviate, the criminal, the urban
poor, and the insane were ... constructed as biological "races
apart" whose differences from the white male, and likeness to
each other, explained their different and lower position in the
social hierarchy' (Stepan 1990: 39–41).

The idea of race entails a particular representation of the One
and the Other, us and them. What above all marks the difference
are certain (alleged or real) biological features which signify inherent superiority and inferiority. Races themselves do not exist;
rather, during a particular period – the last two centuries – groups
have been represented as races. It is revealing to note what the
vast range of groups represented above as inferior races have in
common: they are all groups who are disadvantaged in various
ways. Representing these Others in racial terms – 'both the "lower
orders" in European society and non-European peoples' (Malik
1996: 99) – justifies the inferiority of both. The justification takes
a particular form. In a society purportedly valuing equality,
inequalities are pictured as fixed by nature and therefore unalter-
able. The idea of race therefore provides 'a means of reconciling
the conflict between the ideology of equality and the reality of the
persistence of inequality. Race account[s] for social inequalities by
attributing them to nature' (Malik 1996: 6).

The idea of race has been thoroughly discredited. In view of
this, the question arises as to whether we should continue to
employ the term in Sociology on the grounds that many people
continue to believe that race is real and that belief has real consequences. Is it still legitimate to define a race as 'a group of
human beings socially defined on the basis of physical characteristics' (Cornell and Hartmann 1998: 24)? Typically, the answer

has been 'yes'. Recently, however, this answer has met with vigorous opposition.

One highly influential view has been put forward by Miles. The continued employment of the term is, he stresses, misleading since it seems to refer to, and thus give credibility to, the notion of naturally occurring populations, when in fact it constitutes a false representation of reality. Instead, he enjoins us to abandon the term and utilise the concept of 'racialisation' to refer to the 'process of defining an Other' in terms of (alleged and real) biological characteristics (Miles 1989: 75). There is some merit in this view. Take, for example, the implicit assumptions underlying legislation on 'race relations'. 'By incorporating into the law . . . the idea that there are "races" whose relations . . . must be regulated' (Miles 1993a: 6), the law (however helpful it is in combating discrimination) reifies the concept of race. It implies that there really are races to which people belong. To acknowledge this danger in the use of the term does not, however, mean that we can banish it. The concept of racialisation itself presupposes a concept of race (Anthias 1990) and, given this, it is perhaps not surprising that the term continues to appear in sociology books. The term is now often placed in inverted commas to signal to the reader the danger of reification involved in an unreflective use of the term. As this practice becomes routinised, however, it is likely to lose its impact. This is especially likely if other problematic concepts are also signified in this way. Is there another way of using the term without falling into the trap of reifying it?

An alternative position has been put forward by Mason. Taking his cue from the fact that the idea of race was inherently hierarchical – concerned not merely 'to divide the human species into categories on the basis of phenotypical characteristics' but to link 'those categorisations to personal, social and cultural competencies' (Mason 1994: 847) – he argues that race does not refer to categories (even socially defined ones) but to a social relationship. This 'relationship presumes the existence of racism', which, for Mason, means ideas and beliefs 'which emphasise the social and cultural relevance of biologically rooted characteristics' (Mason 1995: 9–11). Such a definition of race is able to avoid reifying the concept. For there are no races, just the social relationship, race.

To acknowledge a debate about whether and, if so, how to employ the term 'race' should not blind us to the more fundamental points of agreement between sociologists. Whether we seek to banish the term, problematise it, refer to socially defined groups or a social relationship, there is widespread consensus that the idea of race which came to fruition in the nineteenth century has been thoroughly discredited and that we are talking about a phenomenon which is socially constructed. 'Racial categories are created, inhabited, transformed, and destroyed' by human action and therefore are a product of society and not nature (Omi and Winant 1994: 55).

The social construction of ethnicity

Although the concept of race has by no means disappeared from the lexicon of sociologists and policy makers, the concept of ethnicity is now more readily employed. The widespread use of the term stems at least in part from the realisation that 'it does not suffer from the historical association of error in the way that the concept of race does' (Fenton 1999: 6). It avoids biological determinism and identifies groups primarily in terms of the self-definitions of their members (Mason 1995).

Ethnicity is a term with a longer ancestry than race. Deriving from the Greek word, 'ethnos', meaning people, it still retains in its contemporary usage the sense of 'belonging to a particular group and sharing its conditions of existence' (Anthias and Yuval-Davis 1992: 8). What distinguishes an ethnic group from most other groups is the 'belief' shared by its members 'in their common descent' (Weber 1997: 18). The crucial issue here is not whether members actually do have a common ancestry but that they believe that they do and share common memories and on that basis claim a common identity. An ethnic group can therefore be defined as 'a population whose members believe that in some sense they share common descent and a common cultural heritage or tradition, and who are so regarded by others' (M Smith 1986: 192).

Ethnic groups are not dissimilar in this respect to nations, and indeed on occasions they may become nations. There are differences as well as similarities, however. In contrast to nations, which are modern groupings with a distinctively political agenda concerned above all with the establishment of political sovereignty over a territory, ethnic groups are a recurrent feature of human history, comprise sub-populations within a larger society and have multifarious concerns. At the same time they share with nations the fact that they are more extensive than kinship groups or even neighbourhood groups and consequently are 'imagined communities' – imagined because members 'will never know most of their fellow members, meet them, or even hear of them, yet in the minds of each lives the image of their communion' (Anderson 1983: 15).

Crucial to the formation of ethnic groups as imagined communities is socialisation into a distinct subculture, whereby members learn to differentiate themselves from others and recognise which cultural features symbolise their difference. The degree to which ethnic groups are in fact culturally distinctive varies enormously, but typically particular cultural practices are highlighted to signify a group's identity. Different imaginings are of course possible, with the result that the boundaries between ethnic groups may change over time or be drawn differently on different occasions. Although ethnic groups entail a sense of belonging in their members, we should not, however, assume that the boundaries between one group and another depend wholly on processes internal to a particular group and result purely from the power of some members to persuade other members of their imagining. Ethnic groups always coexist with other ethnic groups. Some are more powerful than others and therefore are in a strong position to exert an external influence on where group boundaries are drawn.

The position of Black people in the United States can serve to illustrate the process of ethnic group formation. Black people were forcibly taken from diverse ethnic groups in West Africa to become slaves in America. Their previous ethnic identities counted for nothing and instead they were assigned a common racial identity. Over time, however, Black people have formed themselves into an ethnic group and asserted their own identity. Members therefore typically identify themselves as sharing a common descent (an African ancestry); share common memories (slavery and continuing racial disadvantage); and, despite often not being very culturally distinctive from the wider society, draw upon a variety of cultural features (from language to music) to signal their difference and common identity. Within this group different imaginings have been evident. The term 'Black', which at one stage had negative connotations and was a term of abuse aimed at Black people, was subverted in the 1960s and made into a positive source of identity: 'Black is beautiful'. For many this is still the favoured identity; hence the use of the term 'Black' above to identify a group previously described as Negro or coloured. Different names, however, have been preferred at different times. 'African-American' is now a preferred term for some to signal the fact that Black people are in a comparable position to other groups that migrated to the United States, such as the Irish. They are American, but like other Americans are proud of their roots in another country and thus have a hyphenated identity. 'People of colour' is a preferred term for others to signal the fact that Black people share a disadvantaged position with other non-White groups and point to the need for a wider grouping to combat such disadvantage. Although continuing racial discrimination limits possible imaginings, the choice of these different names to describe the group's self-identity indicates different imaginings and different group boundaries.

The persistence of ethnic attachments

Contrary to the expectations of the founding fathers of Sociology and many of their successors, ethnic attachments show no signs of erosion. Why? Two main answers have been forthcoming.

The first – known as primordialism – argues that ethnic attachments are 'primordial', in other words 'fixed, fundamental, and rooted in the unchangeable circumstances of birth' (Cornell and Hartmann 1998: 48). For theorists who take this line, such as the Soviet ethnos theorists, ethnic identities are enduring with 'a stable core of ethnicity – the ethnos or ethnicos – persist[ing] through all social formations' (Banks 1996: 18). While only a few social scientists adopt this line and think that 'ethnicity... really is a fundamental aspect of the human condition', typically, explanations 'in the mass media' of major ethnic conflicts, such as those in Rwanda and Bosnia, 'tend to rest on primordialist understandings of ethnicity' (Banks 1996: 186, 165). The major appeal of primordialism is that it explicitly addresses the issue of the power of ethnic ties and provides a simple explanation for the emotional charge, which they often carry. What is at stake in many conflicts are fundamental identities, which are pictured by the participants as rooted in blood ties.

Despite the appeal of primordialism, most social scientists are critical of its inability to account for change and variation in ethnic attachments. Ethnic identities are not always more salient than other identities. In fact, historically religious identities have often taken precedence over ethnic identities. What is more, some people may have a range of ethnic identities, which they draw upon in different contexts, without prioritising any one. Sometimes entirely new ethnic groups, such as Latinos in the United States, emerge. And even seemingly ancient ethnic groups often turn out on inspection to be modern. The Yoruba of Nigeria, for example, did not exist as a distinct ethnic group in the early nineteenth century. The term 'Yoruba' was initially used by Europeans as a label to designate a range of 'groups that shared certain linguistic practices' (Cornell and Hartmann 1998: 51). Over time, however, the label has been taken up by the people themselves and now carries considerable power.

In view of the problem primordialism has in explaining ethnic change and variation, most social scientists have turned to an alternative approach to ethnicity and put forward a second answer to the question of why ethnic attachments show no signs of erosion. This approach – known as circumstantialism or instrumentalism – argues that ethnic attachments have practical uses (they are instrumental) and that they are the products of concrete social and historical situations (they derive from the circumstances people find themselves in). In contrast to primordialism, which conceptualises ethnicity as fundamental and fixed, circumstantialism/instrumentalism conceptualises ethnicity as 'contingent on circumstance and therefore fluid' (Cornell and Hartmann 1998: 71). Which ethnic groups we identify with therefore depends on what suits our interests in a particular context. The result is that groups, which may be in competition at one time, may be in alliance at another time.

Wallman (1986) gives two examples from her fieldwork in London of the way ethnic boundaries can be drawn differently in different contexts. In one ethnically mixed residential area, where the local authority had placed homes in a 'housing action area', the boundaries between the ethnic groups were less significant than between 'us', the locality, and 'them', the local bureaucracy. In another area, she discovered among the Asians a variety of boundaries in operation between Indians, Pakistanis, Bangladeshis and Kashmiris, between Hindus, Sikhs and Muslims, and between Punjabi, Gujerati and Urdu speakers. However, faced by a common form of discrimination in which they were all treated as Asians, the separate groups developed a common identity as Asians – 'us', as against the ethnic majority group, 'them'.

The circumstantialist/instrumentalist approach emphasises the socially constructed nature of ethnicity and provides a convincing explanation of ethnic change and variation. It has been criticised, however, for its failure to account for the power of ethnic ties and their stubborn persistence in contexts where they do not seem to have an obvious practical use. Building upon the circumstantialist/instrumentalist approach, some writers have sought to remedy this deficiency.

Cornell and Hartmann's constructionist approach is particularly noteworthy. While they accept that circumstances play a critical role in the construction of ethnic groups, they emphasise the creative role of people in fashioning their own identities. Ethnic identities therefore are 'highly variable and contingent products of an ongoing interaction between, on the one hand, the circumstances groups encounter – including the conceptions and actions of outsiders – and, on the other, the actions and conceptions of group members – of insiders'. This approach 'makes ethnic groups active agents in the making and remaking of their own identities, and...views construction not as a one-time event but as continuous' (Cornell and Hartmann 1998: 85).

The power of ethnic ties does not derive from the fact that they really are primordial but 'from the rhetoric and symbolism of primordialism that are so often attached to them' (Cornell and Hartmann 1998: 90). In some contexts, individuals may internalise an ethnic identity in the course of 'primary socialisation, along with many of the markers of ethnicity such as language, religion, non-verbal behaviour, etc.' As a result, ethnicity may be experienced as fundamental and therefore 'be character-isable as a *primary,* although not a primordial, dimension of individual identity' (Jenkins 1997: 47). Where this is prevalent, ethnicity may indeed exhibit a stubborn persistence, 'all the more so when it is embedded in established relationships and institutions, cultural practices, and ways of seeing the world' (Cornell and Hartmann 1998: 100).

Recognition of the social construction of ethnicity makes it easier to avoid the pitfall of reification. When we study ethnic groups, there is the very real danger that the boundaries between them will be overdrawn and the cultural distinctiveness of each exaggerated. The very language we use – for example, our reference above to people's 'membership' of ethnic groups – tends to imply that ethnic groups are distinct things. As a result of such reification, it is often believed that 'ethnicity [is] typically – or even only – an attribute of the Other' (Jenkins 1997: 14). This failure to recognise the ethnicity of the majority group implicitly assumes that the latter comprise the norm from which minority groups deviate. And the consequence all too often is that minority ethnic groups in turn are represented as distinct, static and 'distinguished by a social and cultural essence' (Eade 1996: 61). By alerting us to the social processes by which ethnic identities 'are born, persist, change, and disappear' (Cornell and Hartmann 1998: 96), the constructionist approach sensitises us to the danger of such reification and encourages us to explore the possibility that ethnic identities are overlapping, dynamic and fluid. How far they are, of course, cannot be prejudged but can only be assessed in the light of empirical investigation.

Race and ethnicity in official statistics

Although a conceptual distinction can be drawn between race and ethnicity, these terms are often used interchangeably. This is evident both in the classifications that people use in everyday life and the groupings that research organisations distinguish when they undertake surveys.

In this book, we shall draw upon three major sources of data: the four national surveys of ethnic minorities undertaken by the Policy Studies Institute (PSI) in 1966 (Daniel 1968), 1974

(D Smith 1977), 1982 (Brown 1984) and 1994 (Modood *et al.* 1997), known collectively as the PSI surveys; the Labour Force Surveys carried out from 1984 to 1991 (T Jones 1993) and in the late 1990s (Owen *et al.* 2000), known collectively as the LFS data; and the decennial Census, of which the most recent one to be analysed was conducted in 1991 (Coleman and Salt 1996; Peach 1996; Ratcliffe 1996; Karn 1997).

Only the PSI surveys have been expressly designed to explore the situation of ethnic minorities, but all three data sources are based on large samples and enable us to compare different groups. What allows such a comparison is the inclusion in these surveys of an ethnic question. The PSI surveys were the first to incorporate such a question, followed by the LFS and for the first time in 1991 the Census. Without an ethnic question we would have to rely on surrogate measures of ethnicity, such as people's country of birth, as we did in earlier Censuses. These measures were always unreliable, resulting in 'up to 15 per cent of those classified' in 1981 as ethnic minorities being '"white", belonging to families who had returned from former colonies, especially India' (Fenton 1996: 150). And they have become increasingly unreliable, as the proportion of the minority ethnic population born in Britain has increased.

The ethnic question used in the 1991 Census, and subsequently adopted by the LFS and the 1994 PSI survey, asked respondents to tick one of nine boxes – White; Black Caribbean; Black African; Black other; Indian; Pakistani; Bangladeshi; Chinese; Any other ethnic group – and, if appropriate, to specify which other group they belonged to. Where the PSI survey differs from the Census and recent LFS is in restricting coverage to England and Wales rather than Britain; in not covering Black Africans and 'Others'; and in allocating people to ethnic groups on the basis of the ethnicity of their family of origin rather than their own self-assigned ethnicity. The use of family of origin as the basis of allocation allows the PSI survey to make a distinction between Indians and African Asians and to include in their Caribbean group 'not only those who called themselves Caribbean in the Census but also others, who described themselves in the Census as "Black other"' (Modood *et al.* 1997: 16).

Whether we look at the Census, the LFS or the PSI survey, 'the one thing the ethnic group question does not measure is "ethnicity"' (Karn 1997: xix). It may be the case that ethnicity and the associated idea of ethnic group are too complex to be 'amenable to investigation in essentially fact gathering exercises' (Ratcliffe 1996: 7). What is clear, however, is that the groups which respondents are asked to select from have been distinguished in terms of a curious mix of criteria, notably skin colour and geographical/national origin. Whether these criteria enable significant ethnic groups to be identified is debatable. The White group (which is by far the largest) certainly is not an ethnic group and indeed conflates a range of groups, such as the Irish and Cypriots of both Greek and Turkish origin, which do believe that they have a distinct ancestry and comprise ethnic groups. The other groups are all non-White and differentiated in terms of geographical/national origin. How significant these distinct origins are to people's ethnic identities probably varies. It is evident, however, that all of these groups are heterogeneous, with many containing people with different cultures and religious traditions.

On inspection it is apparent that the primary purpose of the ethnic group question is not to delineate the major ethnic groups in society but to monitor how non-White groups are faring. 'And if it is the case that material disadvantage applying to broadly defined groups is the key issue...then rather cruder divisions of the population may suffice' (Karn 1997: xix–xxi). In terms of our earlier distinction between race and ethnicity, the ethnic question in the British Census (and other surveys) is not dissimilar in intent to the race question in the United States Census. It is concerned predominantly with race. The concern with ethnicity arises from the realisation that non-White people are not in the same situation and thus entails differentiating only minority groups. Hence it is that the majority ethnic group is identified on the basis of a physical marker, skin colour, and the minority ethnic groups are distinguished from each other on the basis of a cultural marker, geographical/national origin.

While the delineation of distinct ethnic groups in social research does not do justice to the fluidity of people's identity choices and tends to lead to the reification of ethnicity, we cannot do without categories of identity and need to identify broad groupings in order to be able to monitor and measure inequalities. What is crucial, however, is that we remain self-critical about the categories we employ and the groupings we identify, and are sensitive both to the commonalities and differences within these categories/groupings (Calhoun 1994; Bonnett 2000).

It is interesting in this context to note how the ethnic groups identified in the 2001 Census have changed in response to criticisms of the previous ethnic classification used in the 1991 Census. Although the results of the most recent Census are not yet available, it is significant that the new ethnic classification recognises the significance of hyphenated identities such as Black British, acknowledges people of dual heritage, namely 'Mixed', and explicitly distinguishes among Whites an Irish ethnic group. The new ethnic classification will enable researchers to compare the socio-economic position of 16 groups in total rather than the 9 distinguished in the previous Census. The full ethnic question is illustrated in Figure 1.

What is your ethnic group?

Choose one section from A to E, then tick the appropriate box to indicate your cultural background.
A White
British
Irish
Other white
B Mixed
White and Black Caribbean
White and Black African
White and Asian
Other Mixed
C Asian or Asian British
Indian
Pakistani
Bangladeshi
Other Asian
D Black or Black British
Black Caribbean
Black African
Other Black
E Chinese or Other Ethnic Group
Chinese
Other Ethnic Group

Figure 1   Census 2001: What is your ethnic group?

Conclusion

Race and ethnicity both involve drawing boundaries between people. A conceptual distinction can, however, be made between race and ethnicity. While racial boundaries are drawn on the basis of physical markers, ethnic boundaries are drawn on the basis of cultural markers. Nevertheless, the two may empirically overlap, with people defined as a race becoming over time an ethnic group. Sociologists stress the social construction of both race and ethnicity, challenging any notion of race as a naturally occurring population or ethnic group as a primordial grouping. We need to recognise, however, that the distinction between race and ethnicity is not always evident in everyday life or indeed in social research.

2 Migration, race and ethnic diversity

The three writers who above all others established the principal frames of reference of Sociology – Marx, Durkheim and Weber – were remarkably prescient in identifying the characteristics of the modern world. Although they conceptualised the transition to modernity – which they saw emerging in their lifetimes – in different ways, they all recognised that the world which was being ushered in represented a significant break from the past. The major features of this new world can be grouped under three headings – the economic; the political; and the cultural. 'Economically, modernity involves the dominance of industrial capitalism; politically, it involves the consolidation of the nation state and typically liberal democracy; culturally, it involves a stress on reason as opposed to tradition' (A Pilkington 1997a: 22).

Despite their perceptiveness in identifying the central features of modernity, Marx, Durkheim and Weber were remarkably silent about race and ethnicity. They were aware of the significance of race and ethnicity as sources of identity and generators of conflict in particular societies, but their emphasis on those features that are characteristic of all capitalist or industrial societies led them to discount race and ethnicity as of central importance (Lockwood 1970). Indeed all three social theorists tended to regard race and ethnicity as spent forces (Parkin 1979). This applies both to Marx, who pointed to capitalism as the key factor behind the erosion of racial and ethnic identity and conflict, and to Durkheim and Weber, who regarded features of industrial society as the central variables underlying the declining significance of race and ethnicity (Giddens 1982).

While appreciating and indeed fulminating against the dehumanising consequences of capitalism, Marx considered the system to be a progressive stage in the history of mankind. Its expansion over the whole world and its destruction of what

Marx considered to be archaic attachments to particular ethnic groups was therefore thought to be a necessary prelude to human emancipation. Durkheim and Weber likewise thought that certain features of industrial society were inimical to race and ethnicity, with the need for efficiency, for example, demanding the replacement of ascription by achievement and rationalisation entailing the erosion of traditional attachments.

The expectations of Marx, Durkheim and Weber on the declining significance of race and ethnicity have not been borne out. It has therefore been left to a later generation of sociologists to develop their ideas in order to account for the continuing salience of race and ethnicity. Some have found their thoughts on imperialism, slavery and nationalism perceptive (Stone 1977), while others have taken up and developed specific ideas – such as Marx's analysis of colonialism, Durkheim's critique of biological reductionism and Weber's account of ethnicity. It has been, however, less the substantive ideas of classical sociologists in this area so much as their general approaches which have been utilised by the successors of Marx, Durkheim and Weber and applied to race and ethnicity (A Pilkington 1984).

The first sociologists to recognise the continuing importance of race and ethnicity in the modern world were predominantly American. This is not altogether surprising since the United States is a multi-ethnic society, formed through successive waves of immigration, and has long been characterised by a racial division between white and black. The study of race and ethnicity took longer to emerge in Britain (and other European societies) and it has only been in the last decade that it has moved from the margins to the centre of the discipline (Mason 1996; Bulmer and Solomos 1999). What prompted initial interest in this area were two interlinked phenomena – the post-war immigration of people from the Caribbean and Indian subcontinent and evidence of racial discrimination. While immigration signalled greater ethnic diversity, discrimination pointed to the intensification of a significant racial division. The combined impact of these phenomena obliged sociologists to reconsider the nature of British society, which has led over time to a recognition that race and ethnicity are central to an understanding of contemporary Britain.

Migration in a global age

Population movements have always been part of human history. There is little doubt, however, that European colonialism, which emerged in the sixteenth century, accelerated such movements (Castles and Miller 1998). Colonialism entailed in turn the migration of European colonisers to the colonies; the transfer of slaves from Africa to the Caribbean and the Americas; the employment of indentured servants from India and China in other colonies; and, in the period 1850–1914, the mass migration of Europeans to North America and Australasia and considerable migration within Europe.

The Spanish and Portuguese were the first to establish colonies in the Caribbean and the Americas, and faced with labour shortages began importing slaves in the sixteenth century. In the seventeenth century, however, their monopoly of the 'New World' was challenged by the British, French and Dutch, with the British becoming dominant in the eighteenth century, the centre of a triangular trade. This involved the purchase of Black people in Africa with British manufactures, their carriage to the Caribbean and the Americas for work on the plantations, and the transport of cotton, sugar and tobacco back to Britain for processing. The slave trade, which entailed the shipment of some 15 million Africans, lasted for three and a half centuries. Following the abolition of slavery during the nineteenth century, the British turned more towards indentured servants – people contracted to work for their employers for a number of years – and recruited over 30 million people from the Indian subcontinent to work in East Africa, the Caribbean and other countries. Population movements were not, however, restricted to non-Europeans. Indeed from the middle of the nineteenth century to the outbreak of the First World War, there was both large-scale migration from Europe to North America and Australasia and significant migration within Europe. The impetus behind such migration was industrialisation and economic growth, with those countries that were expanding proving increasingly attractive as destinations.

In the inter-war period, migration slowed down in tandem with economic stagnation, but since 1945 has accelerated again. Two main phases can be distinguished, according to Castles and

Miller. The first, which lasted until the 1970s, involved significant migration to Western European countries and North America. These societies faced a labour shortage after the war and recruited labour either from former colonies or from neighbouring countries to allow significant economic growth to occur. A serious recession in the early 1970s, however, entailed – especially in Europe – a reduced demand for labour and therefore falling recruitment of new migrant labour. Migration did not, however, slow down. Rather a second phase began. 'Gaining a momentum in the 1980s and the 1990s', it entailed not only the permanent settlement of earlier migrants as they were joined by family members and had children in the countries to which they had migrated but also 'new forms of migration' (Castles and Miller 1998: 67, 79). Migration has increased in volume in response to upheavals in the former Soviet bloc and elsewhere and steadily involved all regions of the world. Indeed 'the hallmark' of what has been labelled 'the age of migration is the global character of international migration' (Castles and Miller 1998: 283). The result is that virtually all countries are becoming more ethnically diverse.

Post-war immigration to Britain

Our concern here is with a series of migrations after the Second World War, which involved significant numbers of people emigrating from Britain's former colonies to settle in Britain. There have, of course, been significant waves of immigration before. Thus in the nineteenth century, the combination of a rising population and bad harvests encouraged a major movement of the population from Ireland, and around the turn of the century virulent anti-semitism prompted the movement of Jews from Eastern Europe (T Rees 1982). What is more, population movements have not been one way. Millions of people have emigrated from Britain in the last two centuries to settle in new lands and indeed, except for relatively short periods, emigration exceeded immigration. Migration, therefore, is nothing new. Nor is the presence of Asian and Black communities in Britain. Asian people came to Britain, both as servants or 'ayahs' and 'lascar' seamen, as early as the seventeenth century (Visram 1986), while Black people, who first arrived during Roman times, have been a continuous presence since the sixteenth century (Fryer 1984).

To recognise continuity should not, however, blind us to change. While migration to Britain has a long history and 'the presence in Britain of small, isolated Asian and black communities (is) of very long standing', especially in a small number of dockland areas such as Cardiff and Liverpool, nevertheless 'the appearance in most major towns and cities [in] Britain of permanently settled, substantial minorities – clearly distinguishable by appearance, traditions and customs and practice from the very large majority of the population – is a development of the very recent past, of the late 1950s and succeeding decades' (I Spencer 1997: 4). It is a consequence in fact of a series of migrations from Britain's former colonies since the Second World War.

Although during the 1960s and 1970s emigration continued to exceed immigration, as it did in the first three decades of the twentieth century, net migration has consequently grown, with migration in the 1990s becoming the main engine of population growth. The combination of increased net inward migration and a falling birth rate has thus increased the proportion of the British population born overseas. While the majority of people migrating to the United Kingdom (UK) neither seek nor are granted permanent settlement, 'the simultaneous global expansion of migration flows, accompanied by cheaper and rapid air transport, means that the range of ethnic groups arriving . . . has greatly expanded' (MacMaster 2001: 217). At the same time the number of people accepted for settlement since 1997 has increased, with 'high percentages of acceptances from Asia and Africa in recent years . . . mainly asylum-related, but also reflecting the increase in spouses of those already accepted for settlement from South Asia' (ONS 2001: 38). In short, inward migration since the war has made Britain not only a more ethnically diverse society but also one that contains minority ethnic groups who are permanently settled.

Immigration from the Caribbean and Indian subcontinent

While post-war immigration has involved a wide range of groups, including the highly differentiated groupings of Chinese and Black Africans, research has focused predominantly on the most numerous groups, notably Caribbeans and South Asians.

People from the Caribbean were the first to migrate to Britain, with the majority coming from one island, Jamaica. Like other Caribbean islands, Jamaica had been colonised by white people from Western Europe. By the time Britain captured Jamaica from the Spanish in the seventeenth century, the original inhabitants, the Arawak Indians, had been wiped out, so that the population of the island comprised mainly immigrants from England, who managed the plantations, and people imported from Africa, who worked as slaves. The economy was geared to the needs of Britain: sugar was exported to Britain, and with it the profits from the trade. Starved of investment, the Jamaican economy was unable to develop. This underdevelopment still persists, in spite of the country becoming self-governing in 1944 and independent in 1962: the economy continues to be dominated by plantation agriculture and dependent on a few multinational corporations (Pryce 1986). Despite the abolition of slavery in 1833, the majority of Jamaicans saw little improvement in their economic situation. The paucity of adequate farmland and the lack of sufficient jobs subsequently encouraged many Jamaicans – and other Caribbeans – to consider emigration to South America, North America or Britain as a way of improving their situation (Foner 1979).

In India a similar process of underdevelopment occurred. After the setting up of trading posts by the East India Company in the seventeenth century, the British gradually took power. With the defeat of the French in the eighteenth century and recognition by the British government of the importance of India in the nineteenth century, the stage was set for the British Raj. As in Jamaica, the economy was made to serve the needs of Britain. The local textile industry was destroyed, being seen as a competitor to the Lancashire-based one; indeed India became a key market for cotton goods from Britain. Since a large market is necessary for industrialisation to take place, as Hobsbawm (1969) has argued, the possession of India and other colonies was critical for Britain's Industrial Revolution. There seems little doubt that as the nineteenth century wore on, India became 'the jewel in the Imperial diadem' (Barratt Brown 1970), which Britain increasingly leant on as other countries caught up economically. This is not to say that Britain did not invest in India. In the course of the nineteenth century significant investments were made, for example in communications, but these did not prevent the Indian economy from becoming underdeveloped and dependent on British society. The resulting inability of the economy to generate enough jobs to meet the needs of a rapidly increasing population encouraged people to look to migration as a solution. Some migrated to other parts of the British Empire under a system of indentured labour, whereby they were contracted to work for a particular employer for a number of years. In some cases, they stayed when the contract had expired and brought their families over to join them, to be followed later by other immigrants. In this way, Indian settlements developed, for example, in East Africa. Migration is, therefore, not a new phenomenon for South Asians. Indeed, independence itself, which was only achieved in 1947 after a long struggle, entailed further migration. The struggle between the two major religious groups, the Hindus and Muslims, resulted in the partition of India to create, on the one hand, Pakistan, which comprised two territories at the eastern and western extremities of northern India, and was predominantly Muslim, and, on the other hand, India, which was predominantly Hindu. Not surprisingly, given the intensity of the preceding struggles, many people migrated to join their co-religionists. The countries have remained relatively poor so that some people have continued to look to emigration as a way of improving their economic situation. It is in this context that migration to Britain needs to be seen.

Under the British Nationality Act of 1948, citizens of the British Commonwealth were allowed to enter Britain, to seek work and settle here with their families. Some took the opportunity to do so. Caribbeans were the earliest to come, but were soon followed by South Asians – Indians, Pakistanis and Bangladeshis (East Pakistan became the independent state of Bangladesh in 1972) – and East African Asians, from countries such as Kenya and Uganda, who had opted on the independence of these countries for British citizenship. All in all, immigration since the Second World War from the New Commonwealth (which includes all Commonwealth countries except Australia, Canada and New Zealand, which had gained their independence much earlier) and Pakistan (which left the Commonwealth in 1972) has brought a

Table 2.1 Ethnic group composition of the population, Great Britain, 1999

Ethnic group	Great Britain	Per cent of GB
Total persons	56 879 400	100.0
White	53 074 200	93.3
Black-Caribbean	490 100	0.9
Black-African	376 200	0.7
Black-Other	308 400	0.5
Indian	929 600	1.6
Pakistani	662 900	1.2
Bangladeshi	267 900	0.5
Chinese	136 700	0.2
Other-Asian	206 400	0.4
Other-Other	408 900	0.7
Total minorities	3 787 200	6.7

Source: Labour Force Survey 1999, adapted from Owen *et al.* (2000).

significant increase in the proportion of people of colour in Britain. Some notion of the extent of ethnic diversity and the impact of this process of migration can be gleaned from Table 2.1. According to this table, which relates to 1999, the minority ethnic population of Britain is now well over three and a half million or 6.7 per cent of the total population. It should be noted that fifty years earlier it amounted to less than 80,000 (I Spencer 1997).

The minority ethnic population comprises a range of ethnic groups, which 'differ somewhat in the timing of the arrival of their primary immigrant groups'. If we again concentrate on people from the Caribbean and Indian subcontinent, we find that 'the bulk of the immigrants from the Caribbean arrived in the period between 1955 and 1964, while the main time of arrival of the Indians and Pakistanis was between 1965 and 1974. Bangladeshi arrivals peaked in the period 1980–84' (Peach 1996: 9). Although there has been a significant growth in the minority ethnic population, as a result of immigration and a higher birth rate consequent to a large extent on their being relatively young, we need, however, to get matters in perspective. People from the New Commonwealth and Pakistan comprise well under half the overseas-born population in Britain (Skellington 1996) and none of the 'non-White' minorities is as large as the Irish (Peach *et al.*, 2000). What is more, immigration from the New Commonwealth and Pakistan is to all intents and purposes at an end. It reached a peak in the 1960s, but has been, with the odd temporary increase caused by the expulsion of East African Asians, on a downward trend since. Immigration Acts, beginning with the 1962 Commonwealth Immigration Act, have made it increasingly difficult for people from the Caribbean and Indian subcontinent to emigrate to Britain, with the result that the vast majority of those from the New Commonwealth and Pakistan now accepted for settlement are dependants, that is, mainly wives and children, or (increasingly) refugees.

A note on terminology

In the course of discussing the entry of immigrants from the New Commonwealth and Pakistan into Britain, three terms have been used interchangeably to refer to them and their children – 'non-White people', 'people of colour' and 'minority ethnic groups'. All these terms try to pick out colour because this has been a salient feature of their immigration for many of the indigenous population and has resulted, as we shall see, in non-White people/people of colour/minority ethnic groups to some extent sharing a common experience. None of the terms, however, is uncontested. In much of the literature, 'Black' is used in preference to non-White to refer to both Caribbeans and South Asians in order to identify groups distinguished by their colour in a positive rather than negative way. The problem here is that while Caribbeans often define themselves as Black and see this as a positive source of identity, many Asians prefer to define themselves in religious and other ways (Modood 1992a). 'People of colour' has become a popular term in the United States, where there have been attempts to create an alliance between diverse ethnic groups who feel excluded because of their colour, since it more successfully includes Chinese and Hispanic groups, for example, than the word 'Black'. The term has not yet caught on here, however, and does not wholly escape the criticism previously levelled at the term 'coloured people' – aren't we all people of colour? 'Minority ethnic group' is the term used in Table 2.1, but, in terms of our earlier discussion of ethnicity, there is no good reason why the term should necessarily exclude White minorities such as people of Italian or Polish origin. In view of the essentially contested nature of these terms, I shall refer to specific groups as much as possible and – to avoid the tedium of continual translation – shall use the different terms adopted by researchers in different places. Where there is a need to point to the common experience of groups which are defined as non-White/people of colour/ethnic minorities, I shall with some hesitancy refer to 'minority ethnic groups' in order to highlight not only their difference from the majority group but also their diversity (Mason 1995/2000).

Causes of post-war immigration to Britain

What, then, caused some people from the Caribbean and Indian subcontinent to migrate to Britain after the Second World War? It is convenient to distinguish here between push factors and pull factors (Banton 1972). Push factors refer to those which encourage people to leave their country of origin and pull factors refer to those which encourage people to come to Britain (or to other developed economies). The principal push factor relates to poor opportunities in the countries of origin where, for instance, the population may have grown at a pace which their underdeveloped economies could not sustain. This is not to say that there is a mechanical association between the degree of poverty and emigration. Most of those who emigrated have been people with some wealth from areas with a tradition of migration. Most initially expected their stay to be temporary and have maintained close contacts with their homelands, including sending back remittances (Watson 1977). The other major push factor relates to the East African Asians, who were in most cases forced to leave Africa as a result of the adoption of an 'Africanisation' policy by some governments. To point to these push factors does not, however, explain why people came to Britain. In order to understand this, we need to turn to pull factors. The first has been the closing of other avenues and, particularly for Caribbeans, the difficulty of gaining admission into the United States as a result of the McCarren-Walter Act of 1952.

This meant that those who wished to migrate had to go elsewhere. They chose to migrate to Britain because of two further pull factors – the connection with Britain which stems from the fact that their countries had been part of the British Empire, and, most importantly, Britain's labour shortage at the time.

Although there was, immediately after the war, a substantial group of Polish immigrants and other refugees and displaced persons who came as European Volunteer Workers, the labour shortage which Britain, along with other West European countries, experienced when the economy began to expand, was met primarily through immigration from the New Commonwealth and Pakistan. In a few cases, people were recruited for specific jobs. More often they came to Britain having heard that jobs were available. Although the period of migration was generally a time in which the economy was booming and there was a consequent shortage of labour, there were occasions when the demand for labour fell. Remarkably, Caribbean movement to Britain seems to have responded with extraordinary sensitivity to the demand, with net migration tending to go down as unemployment went up in the period for which appropriate figures are available (Peach 1968 and 1978/9). The only exception seems to have been from 1960 to 1962, immediately prior to the first Commonwealth Immigration Act, when anxiety about impending immigration control led some to 'beat the ban'. What is true of Caribbean migration has also been shown to be true, although to a lesser extent, of Asian migration (V Robinson 1980). Labour demand has been an important determinant of Asian immigration into Britain too.

Racial discrimination in Britain

Immigration from the New Commonwealth and Pakistan since the Second World War has resulted in the formation of distinct minority ethnic communities within British society, and in the process made Britain a more ethnically diverse society. The question which arises is how these communities have been received. While there is general agreement that their reception has been generally unwelcoming, two different answers have been put forward for this. One emphasises that minority ethnic groups are relatively new to British society, typically being either immigrants or now more commonly children of immigrants; the other emphasises that minority groups are different in outward appearance from the native White population. The first answer sees the newness of ethnic minorities as central to an understanding of their negative reception, while the second answer sees the colour of ethnic minorities as central to an understanding of their negative reception.

The immigrant–host framework

The first position is well exemplified by Patterson (1965) but hints of it can be found in much of the early post-war writing on race and ethnicity in Britain. Immigrants, it is argued, have to go through two processes before they can be absorbed or assimilated into the society they have entered: they have to adapt themselves to and at the same time be accepted by the host society. Neither of these two processes is likely to take place in the life span of one generation, with the result that the reception minority groups meet is at least temporarily a negative one. On the one hand, some immigrants find difficulty in making what is often a move from a rural to an urban existence and in many cases a transition from one culture to another, with all that this implies in terms of language, religion and family structure. On the other hand, the host society finds difficulty in coming to terms with people who do not show an understanding of the implicit norms governing behaviour and therefore seem strangers.

Although most of the writers who have expounded the 'immigrant–host' framework recognise that there is a degree of cultural antipathy to ethnic minorities in Britain which makes what they call 'absorption' more difficult, the overriding mood is one of optimism. It is assumed that the discrimination which 'dark strangers' presently confront will, with the passage of time, and a new generation, be transcended. As support for this thesis, attention might be drawn to the experiences of immigrant groups generally in the United States. Although later generations still tend to retain traces of their roots (Glazer and Moynihan 1970), the two key processes pointed to – namely adaptation on the part of the immigrants and acceptance on the part of the host society – have been to a large extent completed and the earlier hostility and discrimination overcome.

The immigrant–host framework derives from a theoretical perspective – functionalism – which has its roots in the writings of Durkheim. This pictures society as held together by common values – the shared customs and traditions of 'community' and 'nation' – so that immigration, inasmuch as it involves groups with different customs and traditions, constitutes a potential threat to social order. Assimilation or 'absorption' is therefore considered crucial. According to this framework, Britain is characterised as having been culturally homogeneous prior to the Second World War. Although post-war immigrants from the New Commonwealth and Pakistan may initially have seemed strange, it is argued that there are no significant barriers (given, it is assumed, traditional British tolerance) to prevent their gradual assimilation, a process thought important for social stability.

The assumptions built into the immigrant–host framework are problematic and have been challenged. Has Britain ever been a culturally homogeneous society? Has it not been characterised, for example, in the last two centuries by social classes with different customs and traditions and has there not been significant conflict between these social classes? Have there not, in addition, been significant national and regional differences which have persisted over a considerable period? Is assimilation into a uniform culture, in fact, desirable? Does the coexistence of a plurality of cultures not make a society more vibrant and allow its members more options? Is not the demand that ethnic minorities assimilate 'asking for conflict and destabilization and the fragmentation of communities that are currently the sources of stability, group pride and self-esteem?' (Modood 1992a: 5). And, anyway, are there not significant barriers to assimilation? Does not the evidence that 'even the relatively small-scale black settlements that took shape in the inter-war period were perceived as "alien" and a possible threat to the British way of life' suggest that the British are not so tolerant after all (Solomos 1993: 51)? While some immigrant groups have indeed been assimilated, they were White in skin colour, so that later generations are not easily distinguishable from the indigenous White population. The children of immigrants from the New

Commonwealth and Pakistan do not share this physical similarity to the indigenous population. If skin colour is seen as an indicator of difference, are they not liable, therefore, to experience more lasting patterns of hostility? This brings us on to the second account of how immigrants from the New Commonwealth and Pakistan and their children have been received in this country.

The imperialism–racism framework

The second account stresses the high status attached to being White in British society and is the view found in much recent writing on the subject. Attention is drawn, in this approach, to imperialism, which involved the domination of people with a different skin colour by Whites from European countries. The development of the West not only facilitated exploration of the world, but also enabled it to control what were for Europeans newly discovered lands. In the 'New World', such colonialism involved the mass transfer of people from Africa to work as slaves on the plantations. Needing to reconcile their treatment of slaves as mere objects with their dimly recognised humanity, beliefs emerged which classified such people as inferior. Such beliefs spread from situations of slavery to other situations of colonialism, so that the image of the inferior slave tended to be stamped on all who were colonised. In the process, White domination was justified. These beliefs, it is argued, are still endemic in British culture, so that the arrival of people with a different skin colour from countries which had formerly been part of the British Empire was met with a degree of hostility which would not have been triggered by the entry of White immigrants. Indeed, White Australians, South Africans, Canadians and New Zealanders, for example, have been readily absorbed into British society.

For those who point to the prevalence of such beliefs, the passing of time and a new generation will not necessarily entail a dramatic diminution in racial discrimination. As support for this more pessimistic outlook, attention might again be drawn to the United States, but this time to an early immigrant group forcibly taken there, notably Black people. Unlike other immigrant groups, most of which arrived later, Black people in the USA have found that, over one hundred years after the abolition of slavery, it still remains extremely difficult to receive equitable treatment.

Evaluating the two accounts: newness or racism?

The two accounts, which we have considered, of the reception met by immigrants from the New Commonwealth and Pakistan in Britain, involve a process of intellectual abstraction. They pick out and focus on what are taken to be the really significant issues and they ignore a great deal of detail. Both accounts agree on picking out discrimination as significant in the reception met by the first generation, but they differ in their choice of what constitutes the basis for this discrimination. In the one case, the status of these immigrants as newcomers is highlighted and in the other case their status as non-White people is highlighted. Although we might have an intuitive preference for one or other of these two accounts, to assess which, if either, is better supported, we need to look at some empirical data.

Direct racial discrimination

The best evidence comes from three PSI studies directed by Daniel (1968), D Smith (1977) and Brown and Gay (1985). Together these studies provide, over a 20-year period, the most systematic data we have on the extent of discrimination. To ascertain the level of discrimination and whether it was based on newness or colour, Daniel conducted a series of situation tests in which actors applied for jobs, housing and commercial services in a series of carefully controlled circumstances. Here, a non-White immigrant (Caribbean or Asian), a White immigrant (Hungarian) and a White native, matched in terms of age and claiming equivalent occupational qualifications or housing requirements, applied (in that order) for a job, a house, or a commercial service on offer to the public. Discrimination was defined as a case in which one tester was made an offer or a better offer, and the other(s) none or a worse one. What Daniel discovered was that the non-White immigrant met by far the most discrimination. Despite legislation since then, designed to combat racial discrimination, the later studies reveal that it still remains considerable and is based predominantly on colour. While Smith detected a fall in the level of discrimination between 1967 and 1973, Brown and Gay – utilising both actor testing and a form of situation test, pioneered by Smith, known as correspondence testing, in which matched written applications were sent in reply to advertised vacancies – found little evidence to suggest that the level of racial discrimination (found in 1984–85) had decreased since 1973. At least a third of employers still discriminated against non-White applicants for jobs.

We do not have comparable national test data on the extent of discrimination since 1985. The 1994 PSI survey chose instead to examine people's beliefs and attitudes. 'The belief that employers discriminate is much more widespread than the experience of discrimination' (Modood *et al.* 1997: 132). While 90 per cent of White respondents and 75 per cent of minority ethnic respondents believe in the existence of discrimination, approximately one in five of minority ethnic respondents claim to have had direct experience of it. The difference between the two is not surprising. For discrimination is often covert and it is therefore difficult for individuals to know whether they have been discriminated against. What is perhaps more surprising is that both the belief in discrimination and (to a lesser extent) reported experience of it have risen since 1982. Whether discrimination itself has actually risen is more debatable. The intervening period witnessed the advent of equal opportunity policies and increased competition for jobs. In this context, discrimination may not actually have increased but instead have become a more salient issue, with people becoming more aware of it.

In contrast to previous PSI studies, the most recent PSI survey suggests that there is 'a religious component of racial discrimination' (Modood *et al.* 1997: 352). Two arguments are put forward. Firstly, a significant proportion of ethnic minorities, especially Asians, who report experiencing discrimination believe it to be a result of both their race and religion. Secondly, 'there is now a consensus across all groups that prejudice against Asians is much the highest of any ethnic, racial or religious group; and it is believed by Asian people themselves that the prejudice against Asians is primarily a prejudice against Muslims' (Modood *et al.* 1997: 133). These arguments do not, however, convincingly demonstrate that discrimination in employment and housing is no longer based primarily on colour. A far higher proportion of those reporting discrimination see it as based primarily on race and, although there is evidence of greater prejudice, especially among young White people, against Asians and in particular Muslims than other minority ethnic groups, prejudicial attitudes are not equivalent to discriminatory behaviour (A Pilkington 1984). To ascertain both the prevalence and basis of discrimination, we need to turn to other evidence.

The most recent tests of discrimination at the local level (CRE 1996; Simpson and Stevenson 1994) continue to point to racial discrimination. Take those conducted in Nottingham in 1992. Repeating the format of an earlier study conducted between 1977 and 1979, which used letters of application from three fictional applicants (White; Asian; Caribbean), matched in terms of age and qualifications, to prospective employers, the authors discovered 'that, much as in 1979, a white applicant's chances of getting an interview were twice as high as those of either the Asian or Afro-Caribbean applicant' (Simpson and Stevenson 1994: 15).

An alternative way of approaching racial discrimination is through an examination of whether people from different ethnic origins, with the same educational qualifications, have equal chances of attaining the most desirable occupational destinations, for example managerial and professional occupations, and avoiding the least desirable occupational destinations, for example unemployment. If members of minority ethnic groups, with the same educational qualifications as native-born Whites, do not have the same opportunities, we can conclude that they face an ethnic penalty. An ethnic penalty is 'a broader concept than that of discrimination', since it refers 'to all the sources of disadvantage that might lead an ethnic group to fare less well in the labour market than do similarly qualified Whites' (Heath and McMahon 1997: 91). Analysis of the 1983–89 LFS revealed 'the absence of ethnic penalties for the Irish and Chinese and their presence among Indian, Pakistani and West Indian men' which 'suggests strongly that discrimination along the lines of skin colour' is occurring (Cheng and Heath 1993: 164). This analysis focused on minority ethnic members who were born overseas, the first generation, some of whom held overseas qualifications and were not fluent in English. More recently, Heath and McMahon have drawn on the 1991 Census to compare the situation of this generation with that of the second generation, born and brought up in Britain, who have gained British qualifications and are fluent in English. A comparison of the two generations, matched in terms of age and qualifications, indicated that 'for both men and women . . . the second generation experience the same pattern and magnitude of ethnic penalties in the British labour market as did the first generation' (Heath and McMahon 1997: 108). This suggests even more strongly than the previous analysis that racial discrimination is occurring. It is true that minority ethnic groups incur different ethnic penalties, which suggests that discrimination on the basis of colour is not all that is going on, but interestingly, in view of Modood's suggestion that discrimination has a religious component, it is Black Africans and not Pakistanis who face the biggest ethnic penalty.

Both the local evidence, which involves testing whether Asians and Caribbeans face discrimination in employment, and the national analyses of ethnic penalties point to continuity rather than change and suggest that the extent of discrimination has not changed significantly since 1984–85. What is more, the Nottingham study indicates that Caribbeans and Asians face the same level of discrimination, and analyses of ethnic penalties reveal a complex pattern, in which Asian groups, including Muslims, do not stand out as in a worse position than other minority groups. In view of this, there seems no good reason to question the main conclusion of the extensive research available, namely that the basis for the discrimination met by minority ethnic groups is primarily colour and not, as some had thought, newness or indeed, as Modood suggests, a mixture of religion and colour.

Indirect racial discrimination

What we have examined so far, however, is only one form of discrimination – direct discrimination. There is, however, a more subtle form of discrimination, sometimes labelled 'institutional racism', but which we shall call here indirect discrimination. This refers to institutional practices which, however unintentionally, have the consequence of systematically operating to the disadvantage of groups seen as racially different. Here are a few examples:

- a school uniform policy which has the consequence of prohibiting the wearing of turbans;
- the practice of allocating apprenticeships in an informal way to the 'lads of the dads', a practice which clearly disadvantages people who are not part of this network;
- restrictions on the size of council houses, a policy which may particularly affect groups who wish to live together as an extended family;
- immigration rules which do not give British citizens the automatic right to be joined by their wives/husbands and children;
- using behavioural as well as academic criteria to allocate pupils to streams, a practice which (if, for instance, teachers stereotype Caribbean pupils as less well-behaved) may disadvantage a group seen as racially different;
- a colour-blind approach to the selection of juries, which can result in black defendants being judged by 'all-White' juries;
- recruitment to a workforce via old universities, which have disproportionate numbers of White graduates, or through informal networks to which minority groups may have less access;
- the routine use by the police of stop and search powers within areas of high minority ethnic settlement, which may 'disproportionately expose people from these minorities to an infringement of their liberty and disadvantage them' (Holdaway 1996: 20).

These are only a few examples from the research literature, but they do indicate that indirect discrimination is pervasive (Braham *et al.* 1992). Inevitably, however, when we look at specific cases, problems arise. And we find that the distinction between direct and indirect discrimination is less clear-cut in practice. Many of these practices, it is now known, are indirectly discriminating and yet persist. What is more, some of them may, on examination, turn out to have been motivated by racial considerations. Nevertheless, the distinction between direct and indirect discrimination is a useful one and, when we take account of both forms, what is clear is that racial discrimination is still extremely common.

Changing conceptualisations of race and ethnicity

The issue of race and ethnicity has only become central to Sociology relatively recently. What initially prompted interest in Britain was the post-war migration of people from the New Commonwealth and Pakistan and the realisation that migrants and their children faced racial discrimination. Early recognition of the difficulties minority groups faced in assimilating did not generally, however, lead British sociologists to follow their American counterparts and highlight the issue of ethnic diversity as well as racial disadvantage. Instead they tended to conceptualise the key issue as one of race rather than ethnicity.

The race relations problematic

Drawing on the pioneering work of Park and other American sociologists, 'what Banton and others have called "the race relations problematic" became the dominant approach' during the 1960s (Solomos and Back 1996: 6). Race relations are pictured as a specific form of social relationship, in which relations between groups are predicated on people's belief in the existence of race. Accordingly, the relationship in Britain between the majority ethnic group and minority ethnic groups is characterised as an example of race relations, one structured in terms of the significance attached to differences in skin colour. The role of the sociologist is to study such relations, paying attention to both the power of the majority ethnic group to discriminate and the struggle by minority ethnic groups to resist domination (Rex 1970). Although the race relations problematic remained dominant in the 1970s and still has its adherents (Banton 1991), it was subject to mounting criticism in the 1980s. In particular, use of the term 'race' was considered misleading since it legitimised a discredited idea and implied that there are naturally occurring populations between whom there are relations.

The racism problematic

An 'alternative problematic of racism' emerged to become dominant until very recently (Miles 1993a: 6). This approach rejected any notion of race as given but sought instead to understand the process of racialisation whereby particular populations are identified as races within the capitalist world economy. Accordingly, the relationship in Britain between the majority ethnic group and minority ethnic groups is characterised as an inherently unequal one, with the minorities being subject to racism. The role of the sociologist is to analyse the origins and consequences of forms of racism within modernity, paying attention to both the power of the majority group to racialise others and the struggle by minority groups to combat such racism. Recently, the racism problematic has been challenged, with critics arguing that it fails to account for ethnic diversity (Modood 1992a).

Moving beyond racial dualism: racial disadvantage and ethnic diversity

Despite the differences between the race relations and racism problematics, what is more evident, in the light of developments in social theory which sensitise us to acknowledge diversity, and recent data from the LFS, the Census and the PSI survey which highlight ethnic diversity, is what they share. Both recognise that race is socially constructed; both realise that the relation between the majority ethnic group and minority ethnic groups is unequal, with ethnic minorities subject to (but also resistant to) both racism and discrimination; both emphasise as a result the racially defined/racialised nature of this relation. Such an approach tends to foreground a colour division between Whites and the Rest and to downplay ethnic diversity. The prevalence of this approach is apparent in the title of the first three PSI surveys: *Racial Discrimination in England; Racial Disadvantage in Britain;* and *Black and White Britain.* By contrast, a new problematic has emerged in the 1990s which, while acknowledging continuing racial disadvantage, also focuses on ethnic diversity. A form of dualism persists since the ethnic diversity of Whites continues to be ignored or at least downplayed, but this no longer entails seeing minority ethnic groups as in the same position. Far from it. Ethnic diversity is fully recognised and is evident in the title of the most recent PSI survey: *Ethnic Minorities in Britain*.

Conclusion

Sociologists have only relatively recently been concerned with social divisions centred upon race and ethnicity in Britain. The concern arose from the post-war wave of immigration from the New Commonwealth and Pakistan and the reception met by the newcomers and their children. The arrival of widely different groups from former colonies has made Britain a more ethnically diverse society. These groups share one attribute in common – they differ in skin colour from the White indigenous population and have been subject to discrimination as a result of being defined as racially different. Such discrimination has resulted in a significant racial division opening up in British society. Until recently the primary concern of sociologists has been with this racial division between the majority group and minority groups, but this focus is increasingly being complemented by one which acknowledges ethnic diversity.

3 Institutional racism and the underclass thesis: minority ethnic groups in the labour market

Sociology does not operate in a vacuum. Concepts developed by sociologists to illuminate social reality can be, and sometimes are, taken up by politicians and journalists and thus gain a wider currency. One such concept is that of the 'underclass', which has been extensively employed in the last decade to point to what many consider a major new social division between what Galbraith (1992) calls the 'contented majority' and the rest. The concept, however, is highly contested.

Firstly, the concept is rather nebulous. The term is used in a variety of ways 'by conservatives, liberals and radicals alike' (Peterson 1992: 3) but tends to carry with it particular connotations, representing the underclass as pathological. One writer, for example, describes its use as an example of the language of disease and contamination, which encourages a view of the underclass as the Other (Lister 1996). Secondly, the groups which are deemed to constitute the underclass vary enormously – minority ethnic groups or a particular minority ethnic group; the poor or a subgroup of the poor; and (occasionally) women or a 'fraction' of women (Gallie 1988). In short, the concept has been used to prioritise not only social divisions based on race, but also social divisions based on class and gender. Thirdly, the explanations proffered for the emergence of this new division are radically divergent. Those writing from a conservative position typically emphasise cultural factors and see the underclass developing as the result of the adoption by some people of deviant values and corresponding deviant patterns of behaviour. Those writing from a liberal or radical position typically stress structural factors and see the underclass developing in response to structural changes such as the growth of long-term unemployment and the persistence of racism.

A racialised underclass in America?

The claim that it is possible to identify a racially defined underclass was first made in the United States and is still more likely to be invoked by American than European writers (Andersen 1999). Aware that 'racialised minorities have tended to suffer the most privation in times of economic hardship...the pattern of this deprivation...has been described as the formation of a new underclass' (Bhattacharyya *et al.* 2002: 40). The term was first coined in the United States to refer to 'an unprivileged class of unemployed, unemployables and underemployed who are more and more hopelessly set apart from the nation at large and do not share in its life, its ambitions and its achievements' (Myrdal, 1963, quoted in Gans 1996: 142–3). The popularity of the term, however, stems from a book written by an American journalist, Auletta, in 1982. Myrdal's structural definition of the underclass is jettisoned and in its stead we are presented with 'a new social stratum, identified by a set of interlocking behaviours, not primarily by poverty' (Katz 1993: 5). For Auletta, the underclass refers to people who 'do not assimilate' and comprises 'four distinct categories: (*a*) the *passive* poor, usually long term welfare recipients; (*b*) the *hostile* street criminals who terrorise most cities, and who are often school dropouts and drug addicts; (*c*) the *hustlers*, who, like street criminals may not be poor and who earn their livelihood in an underground economy, but rarely commit violent crimes; (*d*) the *traumatised* drunks, drifters, homeless shopping bag ladies and released mental patients who frequently roam or collapse on city streets' (Auletta 1982: xvi). Although Auletta expresses sympathy for the plight of the underclass, his categorisation of them as dependent and deviant carries 'an implicit moral judgement. Each of his groups can potentially be condemned for their behaviour; the welfare dependant for their passivity, and the rest for their illegality, or lack of self-discipline' (Morris 1994: 81). The central issue at the heart of the American debate on the underclass, however, has not so much been Auletta's characterisation of the underclass as its genesis. Two very different accounts have been put forward.

Explaining the American underclass: Murray and Wilson

According to Murray, a Black underclass emerged in the late 1960s and has subsequently grown substantially. As evidence for this, he points to the rise in the proportion of Black (female) never-married single parents and the fall in the proportion of Black (male) youth participating in the labour market. Such changes cannot be accounted for in terms of reduced economic opportunities since they initially took place at a time of economic expansion. For Murray, the explanation for these changes lay in the growth of social welfare, which made 'it profitable for the poor to behave in the short term in ways that were destructive in the long term' (Murray 1984: 9). Thus Aid to Families with Dependent Children (AFDC) acted as a disincentive on young women to get married, by giving single mothers financial security, and thereby reduced the incentive on young men to work to support their families. With the introduction of further welfare benefits, the value of self-sufficiency is further eroded and the stigma associated with dependence diminishes. The welfare system for working-aged persons in short encourages dependency and therefore facilitates a growth in the number of people defined as poor. In addition, because 'poor, uneducated single teenaged mothers are in a bad position to raise children, however much they love them' (Murray 1984: 127), poverty is transmitted across the generations as children internalise the deviant values of their parents. The answer for Murray is to scrap the welfare system which breeds both dependence and delinquency and thus reaffirm the values of the work ethic and the nuclear family.

The major liberal response to Murray's conservative account has come from Wilson. He acknowledges the existence since 1970 of an urban underclass, consisting primarily of black and Hispanic Americans, and indeed agrees that their 'behaviour contrasts sharply with that of mainstream America' (Wilson 1987: 7). Where he differs from Murray is in his explanation for the emergence and growth of the underclass.

The presence in the post-war period of large numbers of Black people in the cities of the Midwest and Northeast and their concentration in non-skilled manufacturing work stems from discrimination in the past. Racial discrimination prompted migration from the rural South but these migrants continued to face racial discrimination when they applied for jobs in the urban North. Since 1970 their situation has further deteriorated not so much because of continuing racial discrimination but as a result of economic changes. Manufacturing industry declined and where it survived was relocated outside inner cities. Services took its place but work in the service sector often demanded skills which Black and Hispanic residents did not possess. At the same time those who were, with the advent of civil rights legislation, upwardly mobile moved away to the suburbs. The combination of high levels of unemployment and 'out migration has sharply concentrated poverty in inner-city neighbourhoods'. And the result is that 'today the ghetto features a population, the underclass, whose primary predicament is joblessness reinforced by growing social isolation' (Wilson 1991: 461–2). Their concentration in the inner cities exacerbates social problems. Black women, 'facing a shrinking pool of "marriageable" (i.e. economically stable) men' (Wilson 1987: 91), increasingly remain single, have children out of wedlock and rely on welfare benefits, while Black men, facing declining employment opportunities and with no suitable role models in the vicinity, increasingly turn to crime. The answer for Wilson is not race-specific policies, which in his view tend to favour the more advantaged and anyway are unlikely to generate widespread support, but 'targeted and universal initiatives' which improve 'the life chances of truly disadvantaged groups' and 'to which the more advantaged groups of all classes and races can positively relate' (Wilson 1991: 478).

The competing explanations put forward by Murray and Wilson for the rise of an American underclass have generated considerable debate. While sociologists have generally found Wilson's account more persuasive, both have been subject to criticism. Murray's contention that social welfare lies at the root of the growth of female-headed households and youth (male) unemployment has been challenged because 'the value of

AFDC benefits declined in the 1970s while the numbers of single-parents were growing' (Devine 1997: 226) and the 'young unemployed are one group in American society who have no claim to state support as of right' (Morris 1994: 74). Wilson's claim that economic restructuring rather than racial discrimination lies at the root of ghetto poverty has been questioned for failing to recognise 'the continuing significance of race' which entails for urban Blacks 'segmentation into low-wage employment' and means overall that while 'the black poor are sinking economically...the black middle class is not rising' (N Fainstein 1992: 276–7).

Despite these criticisms which have been levelled at both Murray and Wilson, 'there does...seem to be general agreement that [a] black underclass' can be detected 'in deteriorating areas of the city' (Morris 1994: 90), whose members suffer economic marginality and extreme social isolation and live in a culture where criminality, dependency and family breakdown increasingly become the norm. Whether those living in such high poverty areas are appropriately conceptualised as an underclass, however, has been challenged. The hijacking of this concept by the New Right, where it constitutes a victim-blaming discourse which sees irresponsible behaviour as causing deprivation, has prompted many liberals and radicals to abandon 'the notion of the *Underclass*' since it 'explicitly erases the exclusionary experiences of racisms from social science analysis while silently enthroning the demeaning impact of race-based insinuations and considerations' (Goldberg 1993: 172). Even Wilson himself no longer talks of an underclass, preferring instead to talk of the 'ghetto poor'. Despite this dispute over terminology and continuing disagreement on the genesis of this grouping, there is consensus that there has been an 'increase in the number of residents in high-poverty areas...and especially black ghettos' (Wilson 1999: 35). Although it has been argued that this grouping 'comprises only a small minority of the poor' (Fainstein 1996: 154) and that the social problems often associated with poverty have not uniformly 'gotten worse for people at the bottom of the social pyramid since 1970' (Jencks 1991: 96), there is little doubt that the plight of this urban underclass or the ghetto poor, as Wilson now prefers to label them, is serious and deteriorating.

A racialised underclass in Britain?

When the underclass concept crossed the Atlantic in the 1970s, it was most readily applied to minority ethnic groups, whether in Western Europe as a whole (Giddens 1973, 1981) or Britain in particular (Rex and Tomlinson 1979). Although the concept has subsequently been extended to refer to a (predominantly) White group, and the underclass debate has typically not focused on race and ethnicity, the identification of a racially defined underclass is still on occasions evident (Lister 1990). According to one writer, minority ethnic groups – in America and Western Europe – form 'the greater part of the underclass' and 'are needed to do the work that the more fortunate do not do and would find manifestly distasteful, even distressing' (Galbraith 1992: 31, 33). Although most British sociologists would find this too sweeping a statement, many, however, still continue to maintain that ethnic minorities are 'at the bottom of the occupational scale' (Anthias and Yuval-Davis 1992: 62), 'are still predominantly part of the lower socio-economic groups with all the well-documented disadvantages of these groups' (Tomlinson 2000: 23) and that they 'are becoming increasingly locked into an underclass' (R Hudson and A Williams 1995: 192). The conclusion of a recent investigation into racial disadvantage in Britain supports this view, characterising Britain, like other European countries, as 'having a disadvantaged ethnic underclass' (Leslie 1998: 9).

This association of the concept of the underclass with minority ethnic groups is not surprising since its origins in America, where it is a 'code word' for Black people in the inner cities (F Robinson and Grigson 1992; Heisler 1991), cannot easily be escaped. In this context, it is noteworthy how in the wake of inner-city disorders, one newspaper editorial warned that 'there are alarming signs that Britain is well on the road to creating a new black underclass' (*Sunday Times*, 15 September 1985), how in reaction to a research report 'the highly respected series *Panorama*' applied the concept to other minority groups in their 'programme on Muslims in Bradford entitled *Underclass in Purdah* (1994)' (Alibhai-Brown 1998: 120) and how more recently in response to another research report 'Foreign Office Minister Peter Hain has warned that Britain is creating a black underclass similar to that which has emerged in South Africa', black here being used to refer to the 'vast pool of ethnic minority citizens who are doing extremely badly in comparison... with mainstream society' (*Independent*, 16 October 2000).

Although proponents of the underclass thesis characterise the underclass in different ways, there is widespread agreement that members live in households where joblessness is rife. How true is this of minority ethnic households in Britain? According to one recent source, 'the labour market disadvantage of minority ethnic groups is evident across a range of indicators... but is particularly marked in terms of unemployment. On average, minority ethnic groups suffer unemployment rates twice as high as those for white people' (Owen and Green 2000: 581). The LFS, for example, indicates that 'in 1998 5.8 per cent of people of working age were unemployed on average, but among people from minority ethnic communities it was more than double at 13 per cent' (Cabinet Office 2000: 25). In the light of this evidence, the question arises as to whether there is any substance to the media portrayals above of a racially defined underclass and whether either of the two versions of the underclass thesis delineated above is applicable to Britain.

Evaluating American versions of the underclass thesis: Murray and Wilson

For Murray, the higher rate of minority unemployment is to be explained primarily by cultural factors. An increase in welfare benefits and an increasing reluctance to condemn deplorable behaviour underlie the emergence of an underclass. These two phenomena have bred a culture of dependency and thus created a situation which allows deviant values to be transmitted across the generations. This culture, it is argued, generates a reluctance among members of minority ethnic groups to undertake relatively low-paid menial jobs that otherwise similar White people are willing to accept. While few British studies have explicitly addressed this (racialised) version of the underclass thesis, reference should be made to one study, which expressly asked whether there is a connection between job aspirations and minority ethnic unemployment. On the basis of an analysis of the 1987–88

Survey of Incomes In and Out of Work, Thomas found no support for 'the proposition that systematically higher ethnic minority job aspirations underlie their higher unemployment rates' (Thomas 1998: 195). What is more, differences between groups in their likelihood of possessing qualifications, being previously employed in manual work, and residing in the inner city, only partially account for the differential levels of unemployment (Modood *et al*: 1997). Taken together, these findings suggest that racial discrimination, rather than cultural factors, plays a pivotal role in explaining the higher rate of minority unemployment. Murray's version of the underclass thesis is not supported, at least in relation to minority ethnic groups in Britain.

This should come as no surprise, since Murray himself in a series of highly contentious but influential articles in the *Sunday Times*, argues that while 'Britain does have an underclass' which 'is growing rapidly', this underclass is different in one respect to that in the United States. In Britain, he believes the growing underclass to be a primarily White phenomenon (Murray 1996: 25). Murray's articles have been subject to blistering critique by many sociologists (A Pilkington 1997b, 1999a). This critique has taken two forms: (*a*) dismissal of the cultural version of the underclass thesis as merely the most recent manifestation of a victim-blaming discourse (Dean 1991; K Mann 1992) and (*b*) challenge to the central tenets of the thesis as uncorroborated by empirical research (D Smith 1992; R MacDonald 1997). It is none the less interesting that the foremost advocate of the cultural version of the underclass thesis acknowledges that this version of the thesis cannot account for racial disadvantage. In view of this we shall only be concerned below with assessing the adequacy of the structural version of the thesis in accounting for racial disadvantage.

Wilson provides one example of the structural version of the underclass thesis. Does this fare any better than Murray's? For Wilson (1987), the higher rate of unemployment among members of minority ethnic groups stems from their concentration in poor inner-city neighbourhoods which have witnessed a decline in manufacturing industry. To assess this version of the underclass thesis, we need to examine therefore whether the spatial concentration of minority ethnic groups in Britain amounts to ghettoisation.

We shall defer a fuller consideration of patterns of settlement to Chapter 4. Suffice it to say, at this stage, there is little evidence for the formation of racially segregated ghettos on the American model in Britain. Wilson pictures the underclass in the United States 'as nonwhite ethnic minority populations living in the inner city ghettos'. In Britain, however, 'the association of the underclass with inner city ethnic minorities self-evidently makes far less sense, given the absence of such racially segregated inner city neighbourhoods' (S Fainstein and Harloe 1992: 11). This is not to say that the (continuing) concentration of minority ethnic groups in large urban areas is of no significance in accounting for the higher minority unemployment rate. Indeed Census data indicate that between 1981 and 1991, 'employment has tended to decentralise from large urban centres to smaller cities, towns and rural areas' which implies that many people from minority ethnic groups are in the "wrong places" to benefit from net employment growth' (Owen and Green 2000: 602). Nevertheless, it cannot be argued that Wilson's thesis is applicable to minority ethnic groups in Britain.

The British version of the underclass thesis

To argue that neither Murray's cultural version of the underclass thesis nor Wilson's structural version of the underclass thesis fits the situation of minority ethnic groups in Britain does not mean that an alternative (structural) version cannot fare better. The American debate has been concerned with accounting for the extreme deprivation experienced by those living in deteriorating inner-city areas, with Murray and Wilson providing contrasting explanations for the plight of (predominantly) racialised minorities 'isolated in growing urban ghettos of despair and joblessness' (Wilson 1999: 127). The British debate by contrast has

concentrated on the *class position* of minorities. Therefore when we have asked if ethnic minorities constitute an underclass, it has been a question about just that: are they part of the working class, a class fraction, or a class *under* the working class and in part exploited by it?…When we have…used the term underclass it has been part of a debate with Marx and/or Weber – about class position, not total social exclusion (Moore 1999: 5).

Two phenomena have in fact suggested to many British sociologists that minority ethnic groups comprise an underclass. Firstly, fundamental economic changes entail a process of social polarisation, whereby those at the bottom of the class structure become cast adrift and experience increasing social exclusion (Roberts 2001). Secondly, evidence continues to accumulate that minority ethnic groups in Britain still face considerable racial discrimination of both a direct and indirect nature (Wrench and Solomos 1993). In the light of these phenomena, it is plausible to suppose that the class position of minority groups will indeed be distinct from that of the indigenous population. Of the two major European theoretical traditions on class – the Marxist and the Weberian – it is the latter which has been more willing to depict minority ethnic groups as an underclass.

For Weber, inequalities in power and advantage take three main forms – those of class, status and party. Our concern here is with the first two. Class pertains to inequalities in power and advantage which have their source in the workings of the capitalist market. As such, class refers to an aggregate of people who share a similar market position and therefore similar life chances, and social classes are characterised as struggling with each other to improve their position. By contrast, status pertains to inequalities in power and advantage which have their source in the way people evaluate each other and express respect for some human attributes and contempt for others. The result is the existence of prevalent beliefs and values concerning the criteria for social worth or esteem which some groups are able to exploit to their advantage. Drawing on Weber's conceptual distinction between class and status, Weberian theorists argue that 'racial inequality comprises an example of status inequality and as such can be as significant as class inequality' (A Pilkington 1993).

During the colonial era, skin colour was seen as a significant human attribute and a signifier of status. This belief, which became prevalent with the advent of the idea of race, still persists and underlies a status division between the White majority group and minority groups. This division is in turn reinforced when social groups (including the White working class) attempt to maximise their rewards by restricting the access of other groups, who are defined as racially different, to resources and opportunities (Parkin 1979). If racial discrimination results in minority ethnic groups being restricted to those occupations that are characterised by low pay, poor job security and few promotion prospects, status disadvantages are being translated into class disadvantages and we can then talk of the formation of an underclass comprising ethnic minorities.

Just such an outcome was detected as early as the 1970s by Rex and Tomlinson. They argued that in Handsworth, Birmingham, 'immigrants are employed predominantly in less attractive industries and in less rewarding jobs' (Rex and Tomlinson 1979: 121). Hence it is that both the West Indians and Asians tend to suffer a higher rate of unemployment, work longer hours often involving shifts, receive lower than average earnings and are offered fewer chances of promotion relative to White workers. The authors concluded that two kinds of job situation can be distinguished, with White people 'predominant' in one and West Indians/Asians in the other. As a result these minority ethnic groups, who also face disadvantage in both housing and education, constitute an underclass. A similar conclusion has been reached about minority ethnic groups more generally in Western Europe. Thus Giddens has argued that 'in many European societies migration has led to a "transient underclass" (which turns out not to be so transient after all) being imported from the outside' (Giddens 1981: 220), while Moore has suggested that Europe's migrant workers 'by virtue of differential citizenship' are 'perhaps more similar to one another than they are to those of indigenous working classes. To that extent this "fraction" of the European labour force may approximate to a class' (Moore 1989: 166).

While some Marxists detect the formation of an underclass resulting from the presence of 'the third world within the first' under 'multinational capitalism' (Sivanandan 1995: 21), most are reluctant to talk of an underclass. Following Marx, they highlight the primacy of class and especially the division between capital and labour in capitalist societies and therefore locate ethnic minorities in the working class. Some indeed go so far as to argue that members of minority groups are integral members of the working class. Critical of research which has been so 'preoccupied with the disabilities that attach to colour' that it fails to recognise that it has been 'rediscovering what are in fact common disabilities of class', Westergaard and Resler (1976: 359) see 'racial discrimination' as merely increasing the impact of otherwise common disadvantages. In similar vein, Callinicos (1993: 47) points out that 'the overwhelming majority of blacks are in employment, as wage labourers, part of the same working class as their white brothers and sisters'. Most Marxists, however, who have addressed the issue of racial disadvantage believe that this position underestimates the significance of racism and instead highlight divisions within the working class which migration accentuates.

Two studies in particular have been extremely influential in propagating such a view. The first involved a study of migrant workers to Western Europe and reached the conclusion that the new ethnic minorities comprise 'a lower stratum' of the working class (Castles and Kosack 1985: 504). Like other workers, they do not own or control the means of production and are therefore members of the working class with the same long-term interests, but they are not spread across the working class. They constitute a 'reserve army of labour', recruited during the boom to fill jobs which typically are characterised by 'low pay, poor working conditions, little security and inferior social status' (Castles and Kosack 1985: 112) and the first to be dismissed with the onset of recession. Such a disadvantaged economic situation is matched by a corresponding low political and social position. Migrant workers politically do not have full citizenship rights and socially are subject (even when White) to racism. The persistence of two distinct strata within the working class, with the indigenous workers in a more favourable position than migrant workers, means that their short-term interests diverge. The result is 'a split in the working class of Western Europe' which 'weakens the working class and hence increases the power of the ruling class' (Castles and Kosack 1985: 480).

The suggestion that migrants constitute a distinct part of the working class in Britain is taken up in another study by Phizacklea and Miles. Although critical of Castles and Kosack for seeing migration as bringing about a split in the working class because, as the authors put it, 'the working class was not, prior to the migration of labour, first united and then divided by its arrival' (Phizacklea and Miles 1980: 12), they acknowledge that migration entailed a new division within the working class. Rather than see the working class as divided into two strata, they prefer to see it as comprising a number of fractions. From this view, 'migrant labour constitutes a fraction of the working class' (Phizacklea and Miles 1980: 14). It occupies a specific economic position being 'not only concentrated within the manual working class but in semi- and unskilled sections of the working class' with 'a parallel position in the housing market' (Phizacklea and Miles 1980: 14). In addition to its inferior economic position, migrant labour occupies a subordinate political position, with few effective rights, and finds that it is the target of racist ideologies. Although Phizacklea and Miles recognise that there are differences between the position of migrant labour in Britain and on the Continent, their stress is on the similarities. 'Black migrant labour', like its counterpart in other countries in Western Europe, constitutes a distinct fraction of the working class.

While the Weberian thesis that ethnic minorities in Britain constitute an underclass may seem very different from the Marxist thesis that they comprise either a lower stratum of the working class or a fraction of the working class, what is more noteworthy is the similarity of their analyses (Sarre 1989). On four key issues, they are in accord. Firstly, they agree that the economy generates disadvantaged positions in the class structure, and racial discrimination ensures that members of minority ethnic groups continue to fill them. Secondly, they concur in recognising that racism is extremely pervasive, affecting the position of the minorities not only in the labour market but also in other areas, especially housing. Thirdly, they share the view that, in locating ethnic minorities in the class structure, particular attention needs to be given to their subordinate position in the labour market. Fourthly, they are in accord in acknowledging that the distinctive position of ethnic minorities is likely to lead them to develop distinct forms of consciousness and action.

To discover similarities between the Weberian and Marxist theses does not mean that there are not significant differences between them. Although there is considerable agreement that minority groups still constitute a 'replacement population' – employed (if at all) in predominantly non-skilled manual work; with few chances of promotion; subject to poverty; and substantially segregated from the White working class – Weberian and Marxist theorists conceptualise the class position of minority groups differently. The former, who are not tied to the notion that there are two major classes, readily identify a new class – the underclass – with different interests from the working class. The latter, who identify the conflict between capital and labour as fundamental, are reluctant to identify a new class with different (long term) interests from the working class and therefore point to a new division within the working class. Whether to characterise the class position of minority ethnic groups as an underclass or a fraction/stratum of the working class, in short, depends on one's preferred definition of class (Moore 1977).

Evaluating the British version of the underclass thesis

To acknowledge the plausibility of the underclass thesis and to recognise that its substantive predictions are shared by a substantial number of sociologists of different theoretical persuasions does not mean that it is well corroborated. In order to evaluate the thesis we need to operationalise the somewhat elusive concept of underclass and examine pertinent empirical data. Since the primary concern in the British debate has been with the class position of minority groups and, for sociologists, 'all concepts of class group together people with similar ways of making their livings, that is, people in similar occupations' (Roberts 2001: 21), we shall restrict ourselves in this chapter to an examination of the position of minority ethnic groups in the labour market. While it is recognised that underclass theorists often go further, in characterising members of the underclass as overwhelmingly poor and concentrated in the least desirable housing in poor and increasingly segregated areas (issues examined in the next chapter), these characteristics tend not to be seen as fundamental as persistent disadvantage in the labour market.

The underclass thesis, which we shall be assessing, will be operationalised as claiming that members of minority ethnic groups overwhelmingly live in households where adults are concentrated either in non-skilled work or among the long-term unemployed, and face severe barriers to upward social mobility. In the light of this, we shall focus on two key questions. Firstly, what is the current position of minority ethnic groups in the labour market? Are they, as the underclass thesis suggests, overwhelmingly concentrated in the non-skilled sector or among the long-term unemployed? Secondly, what changes have taken place in relation to their position in the labour market? Are they, as the underclass thesis suggests, finding it well nigh impossible to be upwardly mobile and therefore remain over time concentrated in the non-skilled sector or among the long-term unemployed?

Three major sources of data will be drawn upon to answer these questions: the Census, the LFS and the PSI survey. All three have their merits. The Census provides the most complete coverage and thus allows us to analyse data at the level of small areas; the LFS offers us the most regular data and thus enables us to trace trends over time at frequent intervals; the PSI survey explores the experiences of ethnic minorities in the most depth and thus is able to examine a wider range of issues. All three have their corresponding deficiencies. The Census is designed for self-completion and in practice is often completed by one person in the household on behalf of others. This means that the quality of data may be lower than in interview surveys. The LFS is a general purpose survey of a sample of the population, with interviews conducted in English. Although it has a comparatively high response rate, the number of minority respondents is often low and there is evidence that some minority groups, including poorer Blacks and those, like Bangladeshis, with relatively few English speakers, are underestimated. The PSI survey is a sample survey, expressly designed to analyse the position of minority ethnic groups, with respondents generally interviewed by a member of the same ethnic group as themselves and, where appropriate, in a language other than English. Although there is evidence that the sample includes members of minority ethnic groups whom the Census, and especially the LFS, found 'hard to find' (Coleman and Salt 1996), it has a lower response rate than the LFS and there are some discrepancies between its findings and the Census.

While our three sources all have weaknesses, and some of their detailed findings are not congruent, they comprise the most reliable national data we have and their conclusions point in the same direction. Although they acknowledge the persistence of racial disadvantage, they emphasise – in comparison to most previous studies – ethnic diversity. Hence it is that the major authors conclude that 'the socio-economic position of the nine [Census] ethnic categories differs significantly' (Peach 1996: 22); that 'growing differences between the position of different ethnic minorities' are evident (T Jones, 1993: 151); and that the 'study of the six main groups of immigration-based minorities shows that the differences are even more important' than any similarity in their circumstances (Modood *et al.* 1997: 356). As such, the Census, LFS and PSI survey concur in challenging the notion that minority ethnic groups *en bloc* constitute a racialised underclass.

We shall draw predominantly on the PSI survey below because – relative to the Census and the LFS – it includes in its sample 'hard to find' respondents, employs the most appropriate ethnic categorisation and provides a wider range of information, but we shall supplement this survey by drawing on the other two sources, especially the more recent LFS from the late 1990s (Owen *et al.* 2000). Our confidence in the PSI as a data source is enhanced by the fact that the other data sources present a broadly similar picture of the broad contours of racial disadvantage and ethnic diversity.

The current position of minority ethnic groups in the labour market

Ethnicity and economic activity

What is evident when we examine the proportions from different ethnic groups who are economically active (i.e. of working age in employment or seeking employment) is the higher rate of economic activity among Whites, a function at least to some extent of the higher rate of participation by minority ethnic groups in further and higher education. Activity rates vary with age and gender in all ethnic groups, tending to peak among the 25–44-year-olds and being higher among men than women. The difference between the economic activity rates of White people and those from minority backgrounds is much greater among women than men in all age groups. We should not ignore, however, significant differences between the economic activity rates of minority ethnic groups. These are most marked among women, with Black Caribbeans being in a not dissimilar position to Whites and with Pakistanis and Bangladeshis having extremely low rates of activity. The position of Black Caribbean women may 'reflect the cultural construction of femininity in communities where gender roles are more equal, and male and female roles characterised by relative autonomy' (Mason 2000: 45), while the position of Pakistani and Bangladeshi women may be a product of Muslim cultural norms relating to the role of women, 'the generally low degree of economic activity among women with unemployed husbands (since unemployment rates are high for Muslim people), and the high percentage of women from these groups with poor English language skills' (Owen *et al.* 2000: 73). Data about rates of economic activity do not, however, enable us to tell whether people have been successful in gaining employment or what kind of jobs they do. Let us therefore turn to the most recent data on unemployment and job levels.

Ethnicity and unemployment

Unemployment is, arguably, 'the major [economic] problem that faces the ethnic communities', with 'young non-white unemployment [being] particularly severe' (Leslie 1998: 206). The most recent data on unemployment rates is outlined in Table 3.1.

The table demonstrates that the unemployment rates of minority ethnic groups are on average over twice as high as those for Whites. This applies to both men and women. While in all ethnic groups those with better skills and qualifications are more likely to be employed, 'being from a minority ethnic background reduces people's chances of employment at all levels of qualification' (Cabinet Office 2000: 25). This suggests that racial discrimination is a significant contributory factor. Other evidence supports this conclusion. For example, the Social Exclusion Unit points to the fact that rates of unemployment are higher for people from minority ethnic backgrounds regardless not only of their qualifications but also their place of residence,

Table 3.1 Unemployment rates for Great Britain by ethnic group and gender (all persons aged 16 and over), 1999

	All	Men	Women
White	6	6	5
Minority ethnic groups	13	13	13
Black Caribbean	13	15	12
Black African	17	15	18
Black Other	19	22	17
Indian	8	8	8
Pakistani	16	15	20
Bangladeshi	24	21	–
Chinese	10	–	–
Other Asian	9	–	–
Other Other	15	16	13

Source: Labour Force Survey, mean of spring 1999 to winter 1999/2000, adapted from Owen *et al.* 2000.

gender and age (Cabinet Office 2000), while 'early evidence from the New Deal suggests that individuals from minority ethnic groups are less likely than their White counterparts to move into (unsubsidised or subsidised) employment' (Owen *et al.* 2000: 96).

Such a finding needs to be placed in context, however. Minority ethnic unemployment tends to be 'hyper-cyclical' (T Jones 1993: 112), rising faster and further during economic contraction and falling quicker during economic recovery than among White people. As it is, the unemployment rate of minority groups is not uniformly higher. In the PSI survey

> among men under retirement age around 15 per cent of whites were unemployed. The proportions of Chinese, African Asians and Indians were within the same range (9, 14 and 19 per cent respectively). By contrast, Caribbean men had an unemployment rate double that of whites, 31 per cent, [Black African rates according to the Census were three times as high] and Bangladeshi and Pakistani rates were even higher at 42 and 38 per cent respectively. Female unemployment rates were generally lower than men's. The same ethnic pattern occurs as for men, but the differences are smaller (Modood *et al.* 1997: 89).

Differences between groups in their likelihood of possessing qualifications, being previously employed in manual work and residing in the inner city, only partially account for the differential levels of unemployment. Some groups may well therefore be incurring an ethnic penalty.

Central to an evaluation of the underclass thesis is not unemployment *per se* but long-term unemployment. What is disturbing here is that 'members of all the main minority groups, men and women, experienced much longer periods of unemployment than white people' (Modood *et al.* 1997: 97–8). While White men had been typically unemployed for nine months, the duration of unemployment of minority men was usually over a year and for both Pakistani/Bangladeshi and Caribbean men typically two years. Among women, unemployment tended to be shorter but the gap was even more striking, with White women typically unemployed for six months and minority women for 18 months. Such differences, which can only be partially explained in terms of non-ethnic factors, clearly point to considerable racial disadvantage. Even so, when we take the most disadvantaged groups and calculate the proportion of the economically active among them who were long-term unemployed, we find that only about a quarter of Caribbean men and a third of Pakistani/Bangladeshi men had been out of work for a year or more and that the proportion unemployed for three years or more falls to 11 per cent in the case of the former and 15 per cent in the case of the latter. While these figures testify to considerable disadvantage, they do not indicate by themselves, even among the most disadvantaged groups, the formation of an underclass – in the sense of a group who are more or less permanently unemployed – comprising a majority of any minority ethnic group. It is possible, however, that this preliminary judgement on the adequacy of the underclass thesis will be overturned when account is also taken of the position of members of minority ethnic groups who are in employment. Let us therefore turn our attention to those with jobs.

Ethnicity and employment

When we turn to the occupational breakdown of employment, ethnic diversity is much more evident than racial disadvantage. A comparison of the job levels of people in work indicates that there is no longer any simple White/Black divide, with the job

Table 3.2 Job levels of men by ethnic group, 1994 (%)

Socio-economic group	White	Caribbean	Indian	African Asian	Pakistani	Bangladeshi	Chinese
Prof./managers/employers	30	14	25	30	19	18	46
Employers & managers (large establishments)	11	5	5	3	3	0	6
Employers and managers (small establishments)	11	4	11	14	12	16	23
Professional workers	8	6	9	14	4	2	17
Intermediate and junior non-manual	18	19	20	24	13	19	17
Skilled manual and foreman	36	39	31	30	46	7	14
Semi-skilled manual	11	22	16	12	18	53	12
Unskilled manual	3	6	5	2	3	3	5
Other	2	0	3	2	2	0	5
Non-manual	48	33	45	54	32	37	63
Manual	50	67	52	44	67	63	31

Source: PSI survey, adapted from Modood *et al.* (1997).

levels of minority ethnic groups uniformly skewed towards lower levels so that – relative to the job levels of the majority ethnic group – they all tend to be under-represented in non-manual jobs, especially the higher ones, and over-represented in manual jobs, especially the lower ones. Table 3.2, which is derived from the PSI survey, compares the job levels of men from seven ethnic groups. Five main occupational categories are distinguished, with the highest (professionals, managers and employers) subdivided into three. While Whites, along with Indians and African Asians (and according to the Census, Black Africans), are evenly divided between manual and non-manual work, two-thirds of Chinese are in non-manual work and in contrast two-thirds of Caribbeans, Pakistanis and Bangladeshis are in manual work.

While Table 3.2 challenges what has been called 'racial dualism' (Modood 1992a), it also demonstrates that racial disadvantage is not restricted to those who are unemployed. All the minority groups are under-represented among employers and managers of large establishments, which suggests the presence of a glass ceiling inhibiting upward mobility beyond a certain point. What is more, a comparison of the educational qualifications of ethnic groups at comparable job levels reveals that possession of qualifications does not always allow minority groups to have access to the more desirable jobs on the same terms as Whites. This points to the likelihood of persistent racial discrimination which prevents members of minority ethnic groups receiving the same rate of return on their investment in education. While it has to be acknowledged that the occupational breakdown of employment does point to racial disadvantage, even more striking is ethnic diversity. Thus, to give one example, while nearly half the Chinese are professionals, managers or employers, over half the Bangladeshis are in semi-skilled jobs.

What is apparent when we turn to Table 3.3 and compare the job levels of women from six ethnic groups (the number of Bangladeshi respondents in jobs being too small to be included) is that roughly half the women in each ethnic group are concentrated in intermediate or junior non-manual work and, partially because of this, the occupational distribution of women from minority groups is broadly similar to that of Whites.

'The differences between women of different ethnic origins [are] considerably less than the differences among men, and

Table 3.3 Job levels of women by ethnic group, 1994 (%)

	White	Caribbean	Indian	African Asian	Pakistani	Chinese
Professionals, managers and employers	16	5	11	12	12	30
Intermediate non-manual	21	28	14	14	29	23
Junior non-manual	33	36	33	49	23	23
Skilled manual and foreman	7	4	11	7	9	13
Semi-skilled manual	18	20	27	16	22	9
Unskilled manual	4	6	4	1	4	2
Other	0	1	1	1	0	0
Non-manual	70	69	58	75	64	76
Manual	29	30	42	24	35	24

Source: PSI survey, adapted from Modood *et al.* (1997).

there [is] not the division between minorities. This suggests that gender divisions in the labour market may be stronger and more deeply rooted than differences due to race or ethnicity' (Modood *et al.* 1997: 104). This may indeed be the case, but it is also possible that an occupational classification, designed to 'differentiate finely between levels of male work' obscures 'differences in the actual employment position of women' (Breugel 1989: 53). As it is, there are clear ethnic differences between women in their propensity to work full or part time, with minority ethnic women much more likely to be employed full time than majority ethnic women. What is more, and like their male counterparts, minority groups tend to be under-represented in the top occupational category, especially when a comparison is made which focuses on employees and excludes those who are self-employed, In addition, and again like their male counterparts, they find that their qualifications do not always allow them access to the more desirable jobs on the same terms as Whites. Even when we acknowledge these qualifications, however, it still remains the case, as analysis of the LFS in the late 1990s indicates, that 'the occupational distibution of women from minority ethnic groups is similar to that of white women' (Owen *et al.* 2000: 81).

Central to an evaluation of the underclass thesis is location in what has been called 'the secondary market' (Giddens 1981). Is it true, as a recent analysis claims, that 'black and Asian workers [are] largely restricted to secondary labour markets where jobs are low paid, unskilled and subject to severe unemployment during periods of recession' (Moon and Atkinson 1997)? If we use non-skilled work (comprising both semi-skilled and unskilled jobs) as an indicator of location in the secondary labour market, we discover in fact only one group where the majority of workers are mainly in this market: Bangladeshis. Among this group, almost three-quarters of men are either doing non-skilled work or are unemployed. An analysis of the LFS reaches a similar conclusion. 'Using a rough definition of the secondary sector...only one of the ethnic minority groups (Bangladeshis) is markedly concentrated there; the proportions of the other ethnic minority groups that are within the secondary sector are either about the same as for whites, or lower' (T Jones 1993: 86). What both these pieces of evidence challenge is any notion that minority groups *en bloc* constitute a racialised underclass. It is only among one minority ethnic group, notably Bangladeshis, that there is any evidence for the possibility of the formation of an underclass – defined as households concentrated in the secondary labour market. What is most striking, however, when we compare the occupational distribution of men and (especially) women from minority ethnic groups overall is its lack of dissimilarity to that of Whites (Owen *et al.* 2000). The underclass thesis does not seem to be well corroborated.

Disaggregating the data

Our analysis in the previous section was confined to a comparison of job levels. It is possible, however, that the occupational classification on which we have relied is so crude that 'the aggregate data are ... deceptive' and camouflage key differences between occupations which are grouped together (R Hudson and A Williams 1995: 184). To ascertain whether this is the case, we shall compare ethnic groups in terms of their distribution by industry, their likelihood of being supervisors, their earnings from employment and their reliance on self-employment.

Analysis of the industrial distribution of ethnic groups reveals that 'different minority groups have quite distinct distributions. None is quite like any other' or for that matter quite like Whites (Modood *et al.* 1997: 108–9). Nevertheless, there is only one (small) industrial sector – agriculture – in which all minority groups are consistently under-represented; 'there is no evidence' from the Census that ethnic minorities as a whole are 'concentrated in "declining" industries' (A Green 1997: 89); and there is only one group with over half its employees in one sector – Bangladeshis, who are concentrated in catering. Although the PSI survey indicates that among men each minority ethnic group has 'a more restricted distribution than white[s]' (Modood *et al.* 1997: 109) and the Census indicates that some minority groups are over-represented in declining industries, their spread across different industrial sectors does not point to significant segregation and does not qualify our earlier argument, on the basis of a comparison of job levels, that there is no longer any simple White/Black divide.

When we turn to supervisory responsibilities and earnings, we find as expected that those in non-manual jobs are more likely to be supervisors and earn more than those in manual jobs and that, within these broad job levels, men are more likely to be supervisors and earn more than women. There are, however, differences between ethnic groups. Among men, Whites are more likely to be supervisors than members of any minority group in non-manual work and, with the exception of Caribbeans, manual work. The advantaged position of Whites is reinforced when qualifications are taken into account, with one analysis in the late 1990s indicating how at a time when 'the proportion of minority ethnic employees with higher level qualifications increased ...the difference between the proportion of minority ethnic and white employees in managerial and supervisory positions widened' (Cabinet Office 2000: 29). White men are also likely to earn more as professionals/managers/employers or other non-manual workers, though not as manual workers. Among women, however, there is not a uniform tendency for Whites to be more likely to be in supervisory positions than ethnic minorities and indeed, when we compare full-time employees, the latter, with the exception of Pakistanis/Bangladeshis, tend at each job level to be earning more than Whites.

While the greater likelihood, at least among men, of Whites having supervisory responsibilities at different job levels suggests that members of minority ethnic groups may be disadvantaged compared to Whites who are seemingly at the same level, we cannot be confident that the same can be said of earnings. Here the evidence is somewhat contradictory. While an analysis of the economic position of young men from different ethnic groups indicates that ethnic differentials in earnings remain even when educational qualifications and other factors have been taken into account (Berthoud 2000), the PSI survey argues that different ethnic groups, with the exception of Bangladeshi men, 'with similar qualifications doing the same types of jobs in the same areas are paid the same amounts' (Modood *et al.* 1997: 120). While it is not possible to be definitive, the evidence on supervision and earnings overall suggests that a simple comparison of job levels does understate the extent of racial disadvantage but at the same time does not substantially qualify our contention that ethnic diversity is as significant as racial disadvantage.

Ethnicity and self-employment

Self-employment among Asians has grown substantially in the last two decades with the result that in 1994 'about a third of Pakistani, Indian, African Asian and Chinese men who were in paid work were self-employed [while] for Whites and Bangladeshis it was about a fifth, and for Caribbeans it was nearer one in eight' (Modood *et al.* 1997: 122). Given the significance of self-employment for Asian groups, its inclusion in Tables 3.2 and 3.3 warrants serious consideration.

Academic approaches to minority ethnic self-employment differ considerably. For some researchers, entry into self-employment is a response to racism in the labour market and self-employment itself is an economic dead-end, entailing long hours for very little return (Aldrich *et al.* 1981; Ram 1992). For other researchers, concern for status in their own ethnic community motivates people to move into self-employment and the resultant business is often successful, providing a healthy economic return and some independence for family members (Srinivasan 1992; Werbner 1992). Most research on minority ethnic self-employment, however, has tended to focus on specific geographical areas and assume that its findings are generalisable to Asians as a whole. The most recent PSI national survey of ethnic minorities in 1994 and the follow-up survey of South Asian self-employed people in seven areas across the country a year later in 1995, by contrast, point to 'different kinds of self-employment among South Asians' (Modood *et al.* 1997: 129).

There are differences between the ethnic majority and ethnic minorities. While half of White self-employment is in construction, agriculture and manufacturing, half of minority self-employment is in retail or catering. Among minorities, businesses have therefore tended to spring up 'in particular niches, such as restaurants, clothing and textiles, and retailing... rather than in the growing service sector and high technology industries' (Owen 1997: 66).

We must not assume, however, that self-employment for minorities is invariably a second-best option and 'disguises the continuing reality of economic disadvantage' (Ward and Cross 1991: 129). For Asian self-employment is more likely than White self-employment to involve having no supervisor, having employees and having separate business premises. What is more, not only do self-employed members of minority groups generally earn more than their employed counterparts but, 'taken as a whole, self-employed ethnic minority men' and women earn 'more than whites' (Modood *et al.* 1997: 121). While it is true that some forms of self-employment are dependent on a niche market, which comprises primarily members of their own ethnic community in the inner city, this is exceptional. The highest rate of self-employment for ethnic minorities is not in the inner city but in areas of below average ethnic minority density and 'most minority businesses are more dependent on customers from outside than from within their ethnic group' (Modood *et al.* 1997: 126). All in all, comparison of ethnic majority and minority self-employment does not warrant revision of our earlier conclusion that ethnic diversity is as significant as racial disadvantage.

Evidence that the financial rewards from self-employment differ among Asians confirms the importance of ethnic diversity. For the differences in earnings between different groups indicate that Pakistanis and especially Bangladeshis gain fewer financial rewards from self-employment than other groups, thus reinforcing their disadvantaged position in unemployment and paid employment.

The PSI surveys highlight, in contrast to previous research, such differences and suggest that there are 'two kinds of self-employment among South Asians: one closely related to the contraction in employment opportunities for those with few or no qualifications but with the resources of kin and community networks, the other having more the character of a small business' (Modood *et al.* 1997: 129). The Pakistanis (and Bangladeshis) are more likely to be in the first category. 'Driven into self-employment' without adequate capital, they are 'least successful in terms of growth in turnover'. The Indians (and African Asians) are more likely to be in the second category; entering 'self-employment for positive reasons' and with better initial funding, they are 'more business-like' and successful (Metcalf *et al.* 1996: 75, 134).

Our analysis of the current position of minority ethnic groups in the labour market, drawing predominantly on the most recent PSI survey, confirms analyses of previous PSI surveys (A Pilkington 1984, 1997b), the Census (Karn 1997) and the LFS (Modood 1992a) in casting serious doubts on the notion that minority groups constitute a racialised underclass. Empirical evidence instead indicates that some minority ethnic groups are not even confined to the working class, as Miles (1982) recognises, but are now well represented in the middle class. At the same time, 'the overall picture is one not of unconditional entry to the middle class, but of reluctant admission' (Phillips and Sarre 1995: 82). It is noteworthy, for example, that all the minority ethnic groups are under-represented in senior positions and that 'Britain's elite remains virtually impregnable to non-whites' (Adonis and Pollard 1997: 248). This is now widely recognised and has even been highlighted as a problem by the Prime Minister: 'Not one Black high court judge; not one Black chief constable or permanent secretary; not one Black army officer above the rank of colonel. Not one Asian either. Not a record of pride for the British establishment' (Tony Blair, 1997, quoted in Denscombe 1998: 14).

Dismissal of the underclass thesis and recognition of ethnic diversity does not entail denial of continuing racial disadvantage. Our analysis instead indicates that members of minority ethnic groups, whatever their class position, are still clearly subject to racial disadvantage. Tables 3.4 and 3.5 outline in summary form the extent of employment disadvantage faced by ethnic minorities.

The position of Whites is treated as a baseline and represented as 1. A minority ethnic group score above or below 1 indicates therefore over- or under-representation relative to Whites. The extent of disadvantage varies, tending to increase as one moves from left to right. At one extreme stand the Chinese and to a lesser extent African Asians, whose disadvantage pertains predominantly to access to elite jobs. At the other extreme stand Pakistanis and especially Bangladeshis whose disadvantage is severe across the board. And between these two extremes stand the Indians and Caribbeans, with the former clearly subject to less relative disadvantage than the latter, especially when the focus of attention is on men rather than both men and women. While these differences in the position of minority ethnic groups are generally more evident among men than women, both tables clearly point to ethnic diversity. Nevertheless, the fact that all minority ethnic groups face some employment disadvantage (and as we saw earlier suffer some ethnic penalty and experience some racial discrimination) points in addition to racial disadvantage.

Table 3.4 Employment disadvantage of minority ethnic men, 1994

	Chinese	African Asian	Indian	Caribbean	Pakistani	Bangladeshi
Employers and managers in large establishments	0.5	0.3	0.5	0.5	0.3	0.01
Professionals, managers and employers	1.5	1.0	0.8	0.5	0.6	0.6
Supervisors	0.9	0.8	0.6	0.7	0.4	0.4
Earnings	1.0	1.0	0.9	0.9	0.7	0.6
Unemployment rates	0.6	0.9	1.3	2.1	2.5	2.8
Long-term unemployed*	—	(1.6)	3.1	5.9	7.7	7.7

*Those unemployed for more than two years as a proportion of economically active in the ethnic group, relative to White men.

Source: PSI survey, adapted from Modood *et al.* (1997).

Table 3.5 Employment disadvantage of minority ethnic women, 1994

	Chinese	African Asian	Indian	Caribbean	Pakistani	Bangladeshi
In paid work[*]	1.1	1.0	1.0	0.9	0.3	0.1
Professionals, managers and employers	1.9	0.3	0.8	0.7	0.8	–
Higher and intermediate non-manual	1.4	0.9	0.7	0.8	1.1	–
Supervisors	1.1	1.1	0.8	0.6	0.6	–
Earnings	–	1.1	1.0	1.0	–	–
Unemployed	0.7	2.0	1.3	1.3	4.3	4.4

[*]Proportion in paid work based on all women aged 16–60 not in retirement.
Source: PSI survey, adapted from Modood *et al.* (1997).

The changing position of minority ethnic groups in the labour market

Although empirical evidence challenges the notion that minority ethnic groups are overwhelmingly unemployed or concentrated in non-skilled work, the question arises as to whether their situation has deteriorated over time so that they increasingly find themselves in a disadvantaged class position. Ethnic minorities may not currently constitute an underclass, but is there any evidence that they are forming an underclass?

Studies on the changing position of ethnic minorities in the labour market generally involve a comparison of the relative position of ethnic groups at different points in time. Although such data are fraught with difficulties, especially when comparisons are made over a long period, there is widespread agreement that migration initially entailed downward mobility but that the employment position of ethnic minorities has not deteriorated since (V Robinson 1990a).

An analysis, which relied predominantly on Census data, for the 20-year period from 1961 to 1981 in fact concluded that 'West Indians' and 'Asians' had improved their employment position. We need to be careful, however, not to paint too rosy a picture. This period also witnessed an improvement in the position of Whites, and when this is taken into account, it seems that 'the amount of relative progress' was small (Field *et al.* 1981). A subsequent analysis, which involved drawing on the second and third PSI surveys and comparing the position of ethnic groups in 1974 and 1982, reached a similar conclusion: despite some indications that ethnic minorities were moving into white-collar work, 'there [were] few signs overall of any substantial narrowing of the gap between their position and that of whites' (Field 1986: 34).

While these studies are hesitant about detecting a significant improvement in the employment situation of ethnic minorities relative to Whites, the same cannot be said of more recent studies, which point unequivocally to declining differentials between the majority and minority ethnic groups. One analysis, which mainly uses LFS data to examine the pattern of change over a quarter of a century from 1966 to 1991, argues that the three main minority ethnic groups distinguished – West Indians;

Table 3.6 Job levels of male employees, 1982 and 1994(%)

	White 1982	White 1994	Caribbean 1982	Caribbean 1994	Indian 1982	Indian 1994	African Asian 1982	African Asian 1994	Pakistani 1982	Pakistani 1994	Bangladeshi 1982	Bangladeshi 1994	Chinese 1994
Professionals/managers/ employers	19	30	5	11	11	19	22	26	10	14	10	7	41
Other non-manual	23	21	10	20	13	28	21	31	8	18	7	22	26
Skilled manual and foremen	42	31	48	37	34	23	31	22	39	36	13	2	5
Semi-skilled manual	13	14	26	26	36	22	22	17	35	28	57	65	20
Unskilled manual	3	4	9	6	5	7	3	3	8	4	12	4	8

Source: PSI surveys, adapted from Modood *et al.* (1997).

Indians; and Pakistanis/Bangladeshis – have all experienced upward collective mobility and 'have made considerable progress over this time-span relative to whites' (Iganski and Payne 1996: 113). Other studies are keener to emphasise that 'within the ethnic minority population there is an increasing disparity between the circumstances of specific groups' (T Jones 1993: 151), with 'the Indians' achieving 'a considerably greater degree of upward social mobility' than most other groups (R Ballard 1996: 140). Nevertheless, there is widespread agreement that the 1980s witnessed significant progress being made by at least some minority ethnic groups in the labour market in comparison with Whites.

The most recent data available in this area derives from the PSI and involves a comparison of the job levels of ethnic groups in 1982 and 1994. Table 3.6 compares the job levels of men. To enable like to be compared with like, the self-employed are not included and the focus is therefore on male employees. Table 3.6 indicates that all groups have improved their occupational position over the period. While the Chinese (for whom there are no 1982 data) and African Asians have moved to a position where their profile is not dissimilar to Whites, the group which made the most progress over this period were Indians. Although the position of minority ethnic groups still does not generally match that of the majority ethnic group, disadvantage has lessened over time.

Analysing improvements in the job levels of female employees in the same way is more difficult because we do not have comparable data for two of these groups in 1982. When we compare those for whom we have information, we find that Caribbean women made the most progress, closely followed by Whites and African Asians, with Indians lagging a little behind. Minority ethnic groups did not all then make progress in comparison with Whites. We need to bear in mind, however, the fact that, among male employees, Indians made the most progress. Once this is taken into account and the overall picture is examined, we discover that minority groups did make important advances, both absolutely and relative to Whites. A decline in the earnings differential over the same period, coupled with a growth in self-employment, which further reduces the earnings gap (albeit at the cost of working longer hours than employees), confirms this picture of declining disadvantage.

Before we can conclude that minority groups are experiencing collective upward mobility, however, we need to consider whether this pattern of declining disadvantage is 'the artefactual product of other social processes' and therefore misleading (Iganski and Payne 1996: 121). In particular we need to explore whether the apparent improvement in the position of minorities is a result of including in the comparison recent well-qualified immigrants and excluding the unemployed. Perhaps the inclusion of the former camouflages the continuing disadvantage of earlier immigrants and their children, while the exclusion of the latter – formerly non-skilled workers in the main – artificially inflates the proportions in higher-level jobs? These phenomena may indeed make a difference but do not account for declining differentials (Iganski and Payne 1996). For recent immigration has been too small, and unemployment rates in 1994 (Sly 1995) were somewhat lower than 1982 (T Jones 1993). While therefore some members of minority ethnic groups remain seriously disadvantaged (especially among Pakistanis, Bangladeshis and Caribbean young men), overall minority ethnic groups have made progress and 'are returning to their pre-migration occupational levels' (Modood *et al.* 1997: 141).

If it is inaccurate 'to characterise Asian and black immigrants as an imported underclass of unskilled labour' (I Spencer 1997: 161), it is even more inaccurate to picture their children in this way. The evidence in short not only challenges the claim that minority ethnic groups already constitute an underclass, but also questions the contention that the position of such groups is deteriorating and that they are therefore in the process of forming an underclass. Within each of the minority groups as within the majority group, there are of course significant divisions. These have tended to grow sharper, as economic restructuring has enabled some to become upwardly mobile but at the same time entailed for others an increasing risk of unemployment. A process of class polarisation in short seems to be occurring within all ethnic groups, with some people moving 'upwards into white collar work at the same time as...others are experiencing downward mobility into unemployment' (V Robinson 1990a: 284). Since 'it appears that that the second-generation have closed the gap on the White British with respect to occupational attainment but not with respect to unemployment' (PIU 2002: 52), this process of class polarisation may be particularly pronounced among minority ethnic groups. The disadvantaged position of unemployed people, if persistent, could arguably lead to the formation of a multi-ethnic underclass – although this would need to be demonstrated – but this is a far cry from arguing that minority ethnic groups *en bloc* already form an underclass.

Institutional racism in the labour market?

A concept which has made something of a comeback in the late 1990s, and has been used to account for the position of minority ethnic groups in the labour market, is that of 'institutional racism'. The term was coined by Stokely Carmichael, an American Black Power activist, in 1967 and has been championed subsequently in Britain by the Institute of Race Relations. The term owes its current popularity, however, to a judge, Sir William Macpherson, who chaired the official inquiry on the police investigation into the murder of Stephen Lawrence, a Black teenager, by five White youths. Although the primary focus of the inquiry was on the police, the report suggested that all major organisations in British society are characterised by institutional racism. This was a remarkable admission since 'for 30 years British officialdom had consistently denied that it had any meaning when applied to Britain' (Parekh 2000: 72).

While the Macpherson report agreed with the earlier report of Lord Scarman into the Brixton disorders that the police, and other organisations, do not 'knowingly, as a matter of policy, discriminate against black people' (Scarman 1981: 11), it did not accept what was for Scarman a corollary, notably that 'institutional racism does not exist in Britain' (Scarman 1981: 135). For Macpherson, the concept of institutional racism does not imply that the policies of organisations are racist. The term is instead defined as

> the collective failure of an organisation to provide an appropriate and professional service to people because of their colour, culture or ethnic origin. It can be seen or detected in processes, attitudes, and behaviour which amount to discrimination through unwitting prejudice, ignorance, thoughtlessness and racist stereotyping which disadvantage minority ethnic people (Macpherson 1999: para. 6.34).

We have argued above that racial discrimination is a contributory factor behind racial disadvantage in the labour market. Such discrimination, it is commonly assumed, is in turn the product of racial prejudice. While a simple cause-and-effect pattern along these lines may on occasions be operative, with individuals acting out their personal prejudices in overt acts of discrimination which result in racial disadvantage, the notion of institutional racism reminds us 'that, to thrive, racism does not require overtly racist individuals, and conceives of it rather as arising through social and cultural processes' (Parekh 2000: 71). The source of differential treatment in terms of race may not lie with a few 'rotten apples' who let the organisation down, but may be the product of a pervasive occupational culture or taken-for-granted organisational practices which, albeit unintentionally, result in racial disadvantage. The failure of the police investigation into the murder of Stephen Lawrence was not, for Macpherson, attributable to overt acts of discrimination by individual officers acting out their personal prejudices, but stemmed instead from the occupational culture of the police in which 'both negative racial categorisations of black youth and the apparent irrelevance of race to incidents that require its recognition are features' (Holdaway 1999: para. 8.2).

The Macpherson report has generated a renewed interest in institutional racism (Solomos 1999) and has been adopted by some social scientists to explain racial disadvantage in the labour market and other arenas. A recent report highlights 'various interacting components of institutional racism' (Parekh 2000: 73): Is there evidence of 'indirect discrimination' in the services provided for members of minority ethnic groups? Are 'employment practices' racially inequitable? Is the 'occupational culture' ethnically inclusive? Is the 'staffing structure' one in which senior staff are disproportionately White? Is there a 'lack of positive action' in involving members of minority ethnic groups in decision-making? Do 'management and leadership' consider the task of addressing institutional racism a high priority? How widespread is 'professional expertise' in inter-cultural communication? Is there evidence of relevant high quality 'training'? How much 'consultation' is there with representatives from minority communities? Is there a 'lack of information' on the organisation's impact on minority communities? (Parekh 2000: 74–5).

While such questions are clearly pertinent for organisations to ask as a first step towards the pursuit of racial equality, it should be noted that they address issues which can and need to be analytically distinguished. Thus they concern, among other things, beliefs which legitimise racial inequality ('occupational culture'), racially discriminatory practices ('indirect discrimination') and patterns of racial disadvantage ('staffing structure'). It is arguable that characterising all of these as components of institutional racism glosses over important distinctions and is not helpful in identifying the complex mechanisms which result in racial disadvantage. While the concept of institutional racism may be a politically useful rallying cry to encourage organisations to reconsider their practices and take positive action to promote racial equality, 'we must also be aware of the dangers of using such terminology very loosely and rhetorically' (Solomos 1999: para. 2.7).

'In the aftermath of the publication of the Scarman report, there was a wide ranging discussion about both the concept of institutional racism, and its various meanings, as well as the way in which it could be applied to specific institutions' (Solomos 1999: para. 2.4). For critics of the concept, institutional racism represented a form of 'conceptual inflation' (Miles 1989): the concept of racism loses any specificity and its value as an analytical tool diminishes as important distinctions, such as that between beliefs which legitimise racial inequality (both biological and cultural), racially discriminatory practices (both direct and indirect) and patterns of racial disadvantage, are obscured. There is a very real danger in this context of 'allowing the phrase to mean all things to all accusers' (P Barker 1999). While the jury is still out on the question as to whether the notion of institutional racism is a useful sensitising concept in making sense of patterns of racial disadvantage or alternatively a blunderbuss concept which glosses over key distinctions (D Green 2000), grave doubts can be raised about its analytical utility in explaining the position of minority ethnic groups in the labour market.

To point to racial disadvantage in the labour market as evidence of institutional racism at best presupposes what needs to be investigated and at worst is tautological, being tantamount to saying that that institutional racism causes institutional racism. To point to institutional racism, in the sense of discriminatory practices, as – at least in part – responsible for racial disadvantage in the labour market is, by contrast, a substantive claim, which, as we saw earlier, has corroborating support. Matters are not, however, that simple. Racial disadvantage coexists with significant ethnic diversity, and this too needs to be explained. While it cannot be said that we yet have satisfactory explanations for the ethnic diversity to be found in the labour market, we need to recognise that the impact of discriminatory practices is mediated by the cultural resources of minority ethnic communities. Some groups, notably the Chinese, African Asians and Indians, prior to migration to Britain, were economically more successful than others and these have been the ones who have been most successful in drawing on the cultural capital of their own communities to resist racial discrimination and as a result 'are returning to their pre-migration occupational levels' (Modood *et al.* 1997: 141). Although all minority ethnic groups face racial discrimination and gain a poorer rate of return on educational qualifications than Whites, there is no doubt that some minority ethnic groups, including the Chinese, African Asians and Indians, 'have used the education system to improve their job prospects', while others, notably the Africans, have found that their substantial investment in education has had a minimal payoff (Berthoud 2000: 411).

It is conceivable that the groups which have been least successful in the labour market experience more severe discrimination than other groups. If this were the case, it would be possible to argue that institutional racism, in the sense of discriminatory practices, plays a key role in accounting both for the disadvantage faced by all minority ethnic groups in the labour market and the divergent experiences of different groups. The authors of the PSI survey hint at this possibility. They suggest that Islamophobia has become increasingly significant, that Muslims therefore are more likely than other groups to be subject to prejudice and that as a result there now is 'a religious component of racial discrimination' (Modood *et al.* 1997: 352). Since Pakistanis and Bangladeshis are typically Muslim, it is not surprising, the argument goes, that they are the groups most disadvantaged in the labour market. This is a plausible argument, but not entirely convincing. To argue that Muslims face more prejudice than other groups is one thing; to demonstrate that they face more discrimination in the labour market is quite another. The best evidence available relates to ethnic penalties, which is 'a broader concept than racial discrimination' and refers to 'all the sources of disadvantage that might lead an ethnic group to fare less well in the labour market than similarly qualified Whites' (Heath and McMahon 1997: 91). Calculations by Heath and McMahon, based on data from the Labour Force Survey, reveal, however, as we pointed out in the previous chapter, that it is Black Africans rather than any Muslim groups who face the most severe ethnic penalties and, by implication, the most severe racial discrimination.

Given the significance we attached above to cultural factors in accounting for the relative success of some Asian groups, it may seem plausible to explain the markedly disadvantaged position of Pakistanis and Bangladeshis in the labour market in terms of 'Islamic traditions'. A comparison of the Ismaili Muslims from East Africa, who 'had an urban and educationally sophisticated background', and the Sylhetis from Tower Hamlets, who came from poorer rural backgrounds, reveals, however, a marked contrast, and suggests that 'the rural background of many of the original migrants is a more important variable' (Peach *et al.* 2000: 155). Pakistanis and Bangladeshis may not have the same cultural resources to be able to resist racial discrimination as other Asian groups, but this does not seem to be because their members typically adhere to Islam.

Account also needs to be taken of other factors, and not least their geographical location: 'Pakistanis are heavily concentrated in those industrial areas that have been decimated by the decline in manufacturing...[while] Bangladeshis are...the most recent victims of concentration in areas of extremely poor housing, schools and opportunities' (Cross 2000: 364). To point to the role of geographical location in accounting for the position of minority ethnic groups in the labour market queries the overriding importance attached to institutional racism, in the sense of discriminating practices. It may be argued, however, that the geographical location of minority groups is itself a consequence of earlier institutional racism which constrained the housing choices open to minorities. While there is some truth in this suggestion, as we shall see in the next chapter, we should not ignore the role of agency in settlement patterns (Ratcliffe 1996) and we need to acknowledge the difference between explaining the position of minority ethnic groups in the labour market in terms of the discriminating practices of employing organisations, and other factors.

It is interesting in this context to note the range of factors that influence the demand and supply for minority ethnic labour identified by the Performance and Innovation Unit (PIU 2002). Factors that may reduce the demand for minority ethnic labour include lower levels of business activity where minorities live, a function to some extent of poorer levels of public infrastructure in these areas; economic restructuring which changes the range of skills demanded; and racial discrimination. Factors that may negatively impact on the supply of minority ethnic labour include in some instances lower levels of human capital (lower qualifications and skills, and less fluency in the English language); poor access to childcare; unpopular and difficult-to-sell housing which inhibits geographical mobility; and an over-reliance on public transport which inhibits the possibility of commuting to work in adjacent areas. While the PIU recognises that discriminatory practices in the labour market 'have negatively influenced the achievements of both first- and second-generation ethnic minorities in the labour market in significant and often detrimental ways', they argue that 'many other factors are also likely to be important' (PIU 2002: 128). These factors are interrelated and are compounded by discriminatory practices in different institutional areas. It is not helpful, however, to see these factors merely as the result of such practices, when a primary concern is to devise policies in order to change labour market outcomes and promote racial equality.

The danger with being seduced by the concept of institutional racism is that we may overlook the complex mechanisms which produce the current position of minority ethnic groups in the labour market. An analysis of first generation men, based on the General Household Survey for the years 1985–92, reveals 'quite complex' patterns 'and at the very least suggest[s] that any blanket conclusion about ethnic minority disadvantage will be a half-truth' (Heath and McMahon 2000: 23). Here different processes seemed to be operating in different labour markets. While educated members of the Chinese, Indian and Irish minorities appeared to compete on equal terms with British-born whites of similar back-grounds and educational levels in trying to gain access to the salariat [professionals/managers/employers]...those who are left to compete in the manual labour market do appear to be disadvantaged relative to the British. The Black Caribbeans and Pakistanis on the other hand appear to be disadvantaged in comparison...in the salaried labour market but are not so distinctive in the manual labour market (Heath and McMahon 2000: 23).

These complex patterns cannot be explained simply in terms of discriminatory practices. While therefore proponents of the concept are right to alert us to the subtle ways in which organisations treat people differently on the basis of their race or ethnicity, we must not assume that discriminatory practices ineluctably lead to patterns of racial disadvantage or that patterns of racial disadvantage are necessarily the result of discriminatory practices.

Conclusion

For most of the post-war period, sociologists concerned with explicating the position of minority ethnic groups in the labour market have emphasised racial disadvantage. For many, the extent of racial disadvantage signified the emergence of a racially defined underclass. While the underclass debate in America has taken a somewhat different form to that in Britain, our analysis of the labour market position of minority ethnic groups in Britain sheds serious doubt on the thesis that minority ethnic groups are concentrated in an underclass. To acknowledge that all minority ethnic groups face racial discrimination and experi-ence racial disadvantage in the labour market is one thing. To argue that racial discrimination leads ineluctably to the forma-tion of a racially defined underclass is quite another. Although racial disadvantage persists, ethnic minorities utilise whatever resources they have to resist racial discrimination. The evidence which we have examined indicates in fact that their investment in education and self-employment often does pay off, so that, contrary to the predictions of the underclass thesis, 'there is...an overall trend of progress in the job levels and earnings of ethnic minorities and a narrowing of the differentials between the ethnic majority and the minorities' (Modood 1998: p 62). In short, our examination of the (changing) position of minority ethnic groups in the labour market provides little support for the notion of an ethnically distinguishable underclass.

While there has been in the last decade 'widespread recognition...that British racial and ethnic minorities differ in economic attainment' (Model 1999: 966), such appreciation of ethnic diversity needs to be allied to a sensitivity to the continuing salience of racial disadvantage. Writers who highlight the prevalence of institutional racism point to the subtle and sometimes unintentional ways organisations – through stubbornly persistent occupational cultures and routine practices – engage in discriminatory practices and thereby reproduce racial disadvantage. There is a danger, however, in seeing patterns of racial disadvantage as simply the outcomes of discriminatory practices and in the process understating the complexity of the processes involved. The position of minority ethnic groups in the labour market is characterised by both racial disadvantage and ethnic diversity.

4 Social exclusion and the geography of race and ethnicity

'Arguably the single dominant issue on the current political agenda in contemporary Europe is the notion of social exclusion' (Ratcliffe 2000: 169). The term originated in France and was first used by Socialist governments in the 1980s to refer to people not covered by systems of social welfare (Percy-Smith 2000). It has subsequently been taken up by the European Commission in the context of the European Union's goal of achieving social and economic cohesion, where 'unemployment is seen as the key social problem' and '"employability" policies, rather than "passive" income maintenance, are central to the emerging perspective on combating social exclusion' (Duffy 1998: 232–3). With the advent of the Labour Government in 1997, the concept of social exclusion has crossed the Channel and become a central thrust of government policy: an interdepartmental Social Exclusion Unit (SEU) has been established and, like its European counterparts, 'work' has been seen as 'central to the government's attack on social exclusion' (Harriet Harman, Secretary of State for Social Security, quoted in Duffy 1998: 230).

Although a relatively new concept originating outside the academy, social exclusion is now extremely pervasive in both contemporary policy and social scientific discourses. It is, however, notoriously difficult to pin down and is used, somewhat like the concept of the underclass, in a variety of ways by conservatives, liberals and radicals (Sinclair 2000). Levitas (1999) has recently helped to clarify matters by distinguishing three distinctive discourses of exclusion: the redistributionist egalitarian (RED); the moral underclass (MUD); and the social integrationist (SID).

RED has traditionally focused on relative poverty, which has been conceptualised as a situation where people lack the resources to participate in customary styles of life and therefore are effectively prevented from enjoying full citizenship rights. A central concern has been to identify the structural causes of poverty and put forward policy proposals which reduce inequalities. Embracing the concept of social exclusion has not meant abandoning this concern with poverty and inequality. The term has been taken up in the belief that social exclusion is a more effective way of conceptualising the multidimensional nature of poverty and sensitising us to the fact that it is 'an ongoing process rather than a timeless state' and 'something done by some people to other people' (Byrne 1999: 1–2). To combat social exclusion and promote social justice, a range of measures are needed including a 'strongly redistributive tax and benefit system designed to offset inevitable market inequalities' (P Robinson 1998: 126). The work of Wilson (1999), which we considered earlier, is embedded in this discourse.

MUD is radically different. The excluded are a deviant and dangerous stratum whose exclusion is self-inflicted. They comprise the undeserving poor who indulge in deplorable behaviour and threaten social cohesion. While RED tends to see the welfare state as a mechanism which helps to alleviate inequalities and promote social inclusion, MUD by contrast castigates welfare benefits for generating perverse incentives and allowing an underclass to emerge and grow. To combat social exclusion and promote social cohesion we should not seek to interfere with the workings of the market in a misguided attempt to further equality but rather should try to incorporate the excluded back into society. To this end welfare benefits need to be reduced, deplorable behaviour needs to be condemned and members of the underclass need to be cajoled into paid work. The work of Murray (1996), which we examined earlier, exemplifies this approach to social exclusion.

SID represents 'a third way' (Giddens 1998) and differs from both the Old Left RED and the New Right MUD. Here 'society is viewed as ideally a cohesive, integrated whole – essentially a functionalist framework, in which the key concern is a perceived dysfunction: the apparent exclusion of certain categories of individuals and the possibility of social disorder emanating from their exclusion' (Littlewood 1999: 13). Unemployment is seen as the root cause of social exclusion and emphasis is placed on the integrative function of paid work. To promote social cohesion and integration, 'joined up' policies are needed to ensure that individuals have both the incentives and skills to gain employment.

While all three discourses inform public debate, the dominant discourse within both the European Union and Britain is that of SID, which like MUD and in contrast to RED, entails 'marginalising or eliminating the issue of inequality from the political agenda' (Stewart 2000: 4). Social exclusion is seen in primarily dichotomous terms so that the central concern in the case of work is whether people are in or outside the labour force rather than with the quality of paid work, let alone unpaid work. Theoretically, this

> notion of social exclusion points to a shift in the conceptualisation of poverty from extreme class inequality and lack of resources [evident in RED]...to a broader insider–outsider problematique – that is a change of focus in the poverty and inequality discourse from a vertical to a horizontal perspective. This shift of focus can to some extent also be described as a shift from a Marxist and Weberian tradition of class and status analysis to a Durkheimian 'anomie-integration' discourse (Andersen 1999: 129).

In Britain, and for that matter the European Union, race and ethnic issues have tended not to be foregrounded in the government's social exclusion agenda or seen as a priority for the SEU (Craig 2001). However, in the wake of the Macpherson report, the government has become less colour blind and less culture blind. The SEU now explicitly recognises that 'people from minority ethnic communities are at a disproportionate risk of social exclusion' and that this stems from the fact 'they are disproportionately concentrated in deprived areas' and 'also suffer the consequences of racial discrimination' (Cabinet Office 2000: 7–8). It is in this context that the government has begun to complement policies designed to combat deprivation in general with policies targeted at minority ethnic groups in particular.

It clearly is politically important that race and ethnic issues are foregrounded within the social exclusion agenda, given the priority of this agenda for the government, since this provides a potentially powerful mechanism for furthering racial equality. The question still remains, however, as to whether it is analytically useful to talk of 'minority ethnic social exclusion' (Cabinet Office 2000: 8).

For the SEU, 'social exclusion is a shorthand label for what can happen when individuals or areas suffer from a combination of linked problems' (SEU 1997, quoted in Percy-Smith 2000: 4). So far as minority ethnic groups are concerned, the SEU argues that 'there is sufficient data to demonstrate that people from minority ethnic communities disproportionately experience various aspects of social exclusion' (Cabinet Office 2000: 17). Such data point to the following: 'in comparison to their representation in the population, people from minority ethnic communities are more likely than others to live in deprived areas, be poor...suffer ill-health and live in overcrowded and unpopular housing' (Cabinet Office 2000: 17).

In the light of this, we shall examine the position of minority ethnic groups in relation to each of the above issues of poverty, health, areas of settlement and housing and on that basis reach a judgement as to the analytical usefulness of the concept of social exclusion.

Ethnicity and poverty

There is no official poverty line in Britain. There is, none the less, widespread agreement that poverty remains a serious problem and has grown rapidly since the late 1970s (Hills 1995). Although 'the focus of British literature on poverty has largely remained colour-blind', with scant regard being paid to race and poverty (Amin 1992), researchers have increasingly acknowledged that minority ethnic groups are especially prone to poverty.

To estimate the extent of such poverty and the risks faced by different ethnic groups, we need to measure the household income of different ethnic groups. The most systematic study to do this so far is the fourth PSI survey. Comparison of overall household incomes, whether derived from earnings, social security benefits or other sources, does not point to disadvantage for all minority ethnic groups. Indians, African Asians and Chinese are slightly better placed than Whites – in terms of proportions in the top and bottom income bands and in terms of average income – while Caribbeans are somewhat and Pakistanis/ Bangladeshis markedly worse placed. Such a comparison, however, does not take into consideration the number of people the household income has to support or provide an estimate of the extent of poverty in different groups. To do this, net (after tax) income needs to be adjusted for household size and 'each household's equivalent income' represented 'as a proportion of the national average' (Modood *et al.* 1997: 159).

Adopting the common convention of defining 50 per cent of average income as a poverty line, Berthoud estimates that 28 per cent of the majority ethnic group are on this basis poor. Although this is a somewhat higher figure than official estimates and may therefore slightly exaggerate the extent of poverty overall, what is revealing is the comparison between ethnic groups. Table 4.1 indicates that, when household size is taken into account, all minority ethnic groups are more vulnerable to poverty than Whites. The most striking finding, however, is that as many as four-fifths of both Pakistani and Bangladeshi households are poor – a result of high rates of unemployment among men; low rates of economic activity among women; low earnings for those in jobs; and large families to be supported on low incomes.

The fact that minority ethnic groups have lower equivalent household incomes means that they are likely to have lower living standards. This is partially borne out by Berthoud's analysis of possession of consumer durables, financial problems such as arrears in the payment of housing costs, and general money worries. All minority groups, except the Chinese, tend to have fewer consumer durables in the home than Whites. The Pakistanis/Bangladeshis in particular are short of such items, and even more than expected on the basis of their incomes. When we turn to financial problems, however, we find that Asians are 'no worse off, and sometimes better off, than might be expected, given their incomes [while] Caribbeans [have] exceptionally high levels of rent arrears, and [are] much more likely to report money worries than any other group' (Modood *et al.* 1997: 181). This suggests that Caribbeans – as a result of high rates of unemployment of young men without qualifications and the large number of lone parent families – are poorer than a simple comparison of household incomes indicates (Berthoud 1999).

Table 4.1 Households below average income by ethnic group, 1994(%)

	White	Caribbean	Indian	African Asian	Pakistani	Bangladeshi	Chinese
Below half average income	28	41	45	39	82	84	34
Between half and one and a half times average income	49	47	43	46	17	15	44
Above one and a half times average income	23	12	12	15	1	2	22

Source: PSI survey, adapted from Modood et al. (1997).

The fact that all the minority ethnic groups have lower equivalent household incomes than Whites suggests that racial disadvantage is more severe than analysis of their position in the labour market indicates. Even so, it should be noted that they are not overwhelmingly poor and as a result unable to partici-pate in customary styles of life. A subsequent analysis based on the Department of Social Security's Family Resources Survey for the two years, 1994/95 and 1995/96, demonstrates this even more clearly. Here 16 per cent of Whites, 20 per cent of Caribbeans, 22 per cent of Indians, 28 per cent of Chinese, 31 per cent of Africans and 60 per cent of Pakistanis/Bangladeshis were found to be poor. It is only among the last two ethnic groups that poverty is rife (Berthoud 1998). Miles's rebuttal of the underclass thesis is equally applicable to the thesis that minority ethnic groups are *en bloc* socially excluded in this sense. 'The view that Asian and Caribbean people in Britain collectively constitute a "black" underclass, a collectivity homogeneous in its poverty and economic disadvantage relative to "white" people as a result of racism and systematic exclusionary practices, is... mistaken' (Miles 1989: 123). Despite this, it has to be acknow-ledged that two minority ethnic groups – the Pakistanis and the Bangladeshis – are overwhelmingly poor. Such poverty does indeed suggest that many members of these communities lack the resources to be able to participate in customary styles of life and in this (RED) sense are socially excluded.

Ethnicity, deprivation and health

The concept of social exclusion reminds us that poverty is not just a problem of inadequate income. According to one writer, 'deprivation in housing, health and education add significantly to the financial inequality of' ethnic minorities (Alcock 1997: 163). We shall be examining housing in the next section and education in the next chapter to ascertain how deprived minority groups are in these institutional arenas. Here we shall focus on health.

Until the recent PSI study, 'there [was] no adequate data base which record[ed] the health status of different ethnic groups' (Culley and Dyson 1993: 24). We had to rely instead on information – much of which relates to mortality rather than morbidity – which recorded people's country of birth. Such data pointed to significant differences between the health of ethnic minorities compared to the ethnic majority and between different minority groups. Thus both Asians and Caribbeans were represented as having a higher rate of mortality from diabetes and a lower rate of mortality from respiratory disease compared to Whites. And while Asians were seen as especially vulnerable to heart disease, Caribbeans were pictured as particularly susceptible to hypertension (Townsend *et al.* 1992). These suggestions are – despite some qualification – broadly confirmed by Nazroo's analysis of the PSI survey.

Minority groups were more likely to report a higher diagnosis of diabetes and were less likely to report symptoms of respiratory disease. When comparisons are made between ethnic groups in their risk of heart disease and hypertension, the expected differences are both confirmed and qualified. While South Asians did have higher rates of heart disease than other groups, this was wholly attributable to higher rates among Pakistanis and Bangladeshis, and while Caribbeans did have a higher rate of hypertension than other groups, this predominantly related to women rather than men.

'As far as general health is concerned, Pakistanis and Bangladeshis were particularly disadvantaged compared with whites, having reported a 50 per cent greater risk of fair or poor health. Caribbeans were also disadvantaged compared with whites, having been about 30 per cent more likely to have reported fair or poor health'. In contrast to much previous research, however, there was no evidence that minority groups as a whole had poorer general health than Whites: 'the differences between Indians, African Asians, Chinese and whites reported here were small and not statistically significant' (Modood *et al.* 1997: 237).

A common explanation for differences in health between minority ethnic groups and the majority ethnic group attributes them to disadvantage experienced in their country of birth. The PSI survey, however, challenges this view by showing that those who were born in Britain or migrated at an early age were more likely than those who migrated as adults or teenagers to have poor health. This leaves us with three broad explanations for differences in health: biological, cultural and materialist (Hunt 1995).

For those sympathetic to a biological explanation of ethnic differences in health, it is noteworthy that different groups are characterised by distinct inherited disorders. While, however, there are specific inherited disorders which affect some ethnic groups rather than others, such as sickle-cell anaemia among African Caribbeans, these disorders are rare and only make a small contribution to the overall pattern of health among ethnic groups.

For those sympathetic to a cultural explanation, more significant than genetic differences between groups are cultural differences and the resultant differences in health-damaging behaviours. All too often, however, assertions are made by proponents of a cultural explanation, which both draw upon stereotypes and lack supporting evidence (Ahmad 1993). Although the PSI survey was unable to examine the effect of dietary and other cultural differences, Nazroo argues that cultural factors are unlikely to be central to an explanation of ethnic differences in health. 'This is because the cultural…variations between the different "unhealthy" ethnic groups and between the different "healthy" ethnic groups are likely to be just as great as the variations across the "unhealthy" and "healthy" divide (Modood *et al.* 1997: 240).

For those sympathetic to a materialist explanation, it is socio-economic status which is primarily responsible for ethnic differences in health. Previous studies have confirmed that socio-economic status is an important predictor of health for the general population (Townsend *et al.* 1992) and, using the standard of living as an indicator of socio-economic status, the PSI study was able to show that much of the ethnic variations in health could also be attributed to socio-economic differences between groups. This applied to both general indicators of poor health and specific illnesses, including mental illnesses (Nazroo 1997). While the propensity of Caribbeans to have higher rates of hypertension (and mental illness) and Pakistanis/Bangladeshis to have higher rates of heart disease suggest that other factors (including the biological and cultural) play a role in determining the nature of illnesses, the poor socio-economic position of Caribbeans and even more so Pakistanis and Bangladeshis plays a central role in explaining their poor health.

Although differences in access to adequate health care only play a subsidiary role in accounting for ethnic variations in health, there is evidence that, despite the greater likelihood of ethnic minorities consulting a GP (general practitioner) 'the quality of that consultation is less adequate than that for the white majority' (Modood *et al.* 1997: 255). Language problems are not always addressed; the preference of some for doctors who have a similar ethnicity and gender as themselves is not always met; and sensitivity to differences in the way symptoms (especially of mental illnesses) are presented across cultures is not always evident (Nazroo 1997). This poorer care may explain why the greater likelihood of consulting a GP 'did not translate into greater use of in-patient hospital facilities by members of ethnic minority groups' (Modood *et al.* 1997: 257). All in all, the evidence indicates that deprivation in health does add significantly to the financial hardship of some minority ethnic groups. While this means that many individuals in these groups suffer from a combination of linked problems (in this case poverty and ill health) and in this sense are socially excluded, it should be noted, contrary to the claim by the SEU, that such a finding is not applicable to minority ethnic groups as a whole.

The geography of race and ethnicity

Immigrants from the New Commonwealth and Pakistan who arrived in Britain after the Second World War settled in areas where there was demand for their labour. This meant that, while they formed (and continue to form) only a small proportion of the total population, in certain regions, cities and wards visible concentrations developed as the early pioneers were joined by new migrants (R Ballard 1994).

The 1991 Census confirms the continuing concentration of minority ethnic groups. Over 70 per cent of the minority population 'is found in just two standard regions of Great Britain, the South East and the West Midlands which together contain 40 per cent of the total population'. And within these regions the minorities are 'highly concentrated in the largest urban centres' (Peach 1996: 10–11). This is evident in Table 4.2, which indicates that all minority ethnic groups are, albeit to varying degrees, at least twice as likely as the majority ethnic group to be concentrated in a limited number of metropolitan areas. What is more, as

Table 4.2 Relative concentration of ethnic groups in selected metropolitan areas, Great Britain, 1991

	Total	White	Black-Caribbean	Black African	Black Other	Indian	Pakistani	Bangladeshi	Chinese
Great Britain	54 888 844	51 873 794	499 964	212 401	178 401	840 255	476 555	162 835	156 939
Greater London	6 679 699	5 333 580	290 968	163 635	80 613	347 091	87 816	85 738	56 579
West Midlands metropolitan county	2 551 671	2 178 149	72 183	4 116	15 716	141 359	88 268	18 074	6 107
Greater Manchester metropolitan county	2 499 441	2 351 239	17 095	5 240	9 202	29 741	49 370	11 445	8 323
West Yorkshire metropolitan county	2 013 693	1 849 562	14 795	2 554	6 552	34 837	80 540	5 978	3 852
Percentage ethnic group in named metropolitan areas	25.04	22.58	79.01	82.66	62.83	65.82	64.21	74.45	47.70

Source: Census, adapted from Peach (1996).

the size of area decreases, concentration becomes even more evident, with the result that in some wards and enumeration districts ethnic minorities constitute the majority of the population.

We need to be careful, however, not to exaggerate the extent of concentration. The number of wards where ethnic minorities comprise a majority of the population is small and a high proportion of the minority population 'live in areas where they constitute a small proportion of the total population' (Peach and Rossiter 1996: 118).

Urban ghettos or ethnic enclaves?

Following Peach, we can define ghettos as residential districts in which one ethnic group comprises the overwhelming majority of the population and where the vast majority of the ethnic group is found. In the United States, ethnic enclaves can be found in many cities, with residential districts distinguished by the presence within them of sizeable numbers from a particular ethnic group. On the whole, however, studies of the geographical distribution of European immigrants earlier this century reveal that 'only a minority of most European ethnics lived in such areas and that they rarely formed a majority of the population in the areas that were identified with them as a group'. By contrast, 'Black areas were over 80 per cent Black and over 90 per cent of Blacks lived in such areas' (Peach and Rossiter 1996: 115). While in short it does not make sense in the United States to talk of European ghettos (as opposed to ethnic enclaves), it clearly is appropriate to talk of Black ghettos.

How comparable is the spatial segregation of minority groups in Britain to that of Black people in America? The most common measure of ethnic segregation is the index of dissimilarity (ID). This involves a comparison of the residential distribution of two groups and an estimate of the proportion of each group which would have to change its area of residence in order to match the distribution of the group with which it is compared. An ID of 100 indicates complete segregation (a figure reached by African Americans in some census tracts) and an ID of 0 indicates no segregation.

Comparison of the IDs of ethnic groups at the ward and enumeration district level reveals as expected higher levels of segregation for all minority ethnic groups as the size of area becomes smaller. More interestingly, it also demonstrates that the level of segregation of different groups varies. Thus at the enumeration district level in Greater London and Birmingham, compared to Whites, the ID of Black Caribbeans is in the 40s; the ID of the Indians is in the 50s; the ID of the Pakistanis is in the 60s; and the ID of the Bangladeshis is in the 70s. The IDs of the Chinese and Black Africans are more variable, being in the high 40s in Greater London and the mid-60s in Birmingham. Although the IDs at the enumeration district level in some other cities are higher, a similar pattern prevails, with 'levels of segregation of the Black groups... generally much lower than those of the South Asian groups' and with 'Bangladeshi levels of segregation... almost universally high' (Peach and Rossiter 1996: 133). In no cases do the IDs reach 100 and when we examine those wards in Greater London where an ethnic group comprises at least 30 per cent of the population, we discover (in marked contrast to census tracts in the United States where African Americans predominate) that Bangladeshi areas are barely 50 per cent Bangladeshi and only one-third of Bangladeshis live in such areas. Since Bangladeshis are more spatially concentrated than other minority groups, it is evident that, while there are some ethnic enclaves in Britain, 'ghettos on the American model do not exist' (Peach and Rossiter 1996: 133). The situation in Britain is not dissimilar to that prevalent in France and Germany. 'Despite notable concentrations in inner city arcs around the urban cores and in industrial areas' for the most part 'immigrants do not achieve the substantial areas of majority presence such as those formed by blacks in the United States' (Peach 1992: 132).

It is conceivable that ghettos are still in the process of formation. Census data do not support this supposition, however. While comparison of the geographical spread of minority ethnic groups in 1981 and 1991 points to 'a greater degree of metropolitan concentration for minorities in 1991 than 1981', it also reveals 'modest decentralisation within metropolitan areas of ethnic concentration' (Rees and Phillips 1996a: 49). An analysis of one-year change-of-address data provides further evidence of suburbanisation among some minority groups, especially movement from Inner to Outer London boroughs and from London to the South East (Campion 1996), while a comparison of immigrant and British-born members of three minority ethnic groups – Black Caribbeans, Indians and Pakistanis – shows that British-born heads of household, especially among Indians, are more likely than immigrant heads of household to live in areas where ethnic minorities are scarce (V Robinson 1996). Although 'overall, the pattern is of continuity and surprisingly little change' (Rees and Phillips 1996b: 266), 'longitudinal studies of segregation in British cities' suggest 'that South Asian [and in particular Indian] segregation has declined since the early 1970s' (V Robinson 1990b: 285) and Census data confirm 'a progressive decrease [also] in the levels of segregation at all available scales' in the case of Black Caribbeans (Peach 1996: 37). The one exception to such de-concentration relates to Pakistanis and Bangladeshis. 'The rapid growth of the latter two predominantly Muslim minorities over the 1981–91 decade has been...characterised by a consolidation of their pattern of inner-city residence' (Phillips, quoted in Barke and Fuller 2001: 113). Overall the evidence points to slightly declining levels of concentration of minority groups, 'although this is taking place at different rates between the various groups involved' (Barke and Fuller 2001: 116).

According to some writers, 'immigrants and ethnic minorities ...have become locked into zones of social exclusion, ghetto-like areas of poor housing' (MacMaster 2001: 219). While we have yet to examine the position of minority ethnic groups in the housing market, the evidence which we have examined so far challenges the notion that ghettos have emerged or are in the process of formation. If ghettoisation is deemed to be an essential precondition for minority ethnic social exclusion, serious doubts can therefore be raised with the thesis that minority ethnic groups overall experience social exclusion in this sense.

Racial constraint or ethnic choice?

To recognise that the residential concentration of minority groups in Britain does not amount to ghettoisation is one thing. To deny the continuing extensiveness of such concentration is quite another. We may not consider the latter problematic, however. For 'in itself, the existence and persistence of residential segregation need not necessarily be of concern' (S Smith 1989: 36). If ethnic minorities are constrained to live in certain areas it is a matter of concern; if ethnic minorities choose to live in certain areas it may not be a matter of concern.

Two broad explanations have been put forward to account for the residential segregation of ethnic minorities (Cater and Jones 1989). The first highlights the constraints faced by minority ethnic groups. Racial discrimination in both the labour and housing markets entails not merely concentration but concentration in poor urban areas. And the location of the minority population in such areas compounds their disadvantage by limiting further employment and housing opportunities (S Smith 1989). The second emphasises that members of a minority ethnic group often prefer to live together. As a result minority ethnic groups are not only segregated from the majority ethnic group but also from each other. Chain migration was responsible for the initial concentration in a particular area and the consolidation of this original settlement, coupled with movement to adjacent areas has allowed a range of ethnic organisations to flourish (V Robinson 1990b).

Since class only provides a partial explanation of ethnic segregation (Peach and Rossiter 1996: 130), theorists have tended to adopt one or other of the explanations outlined above to account for the residential concentration of ethnic minorities. There is evidence which supports both.

Minority ethnic groups do face racial discrimination, as we have already seen. Taken together they are more concentrated than is apparent when the focus is on each group, with the result that in Greater London as many as 'half of the combined minority ethnic groups live in wards where they form nearly half the population' (Peach and Rossiter 1996: 132). Analysis of the areas of minority concentration in London, the Midlands and Pennine cities reveals that ethnic minorities tend 'to be concentrated in poorer residential areas' (Ratcliffe 1996: 19), while across the country 'Fifty-six per cent live in the 44 most deprived local authorities' (Cabinet Office 2000: 17). Such findings are more consonant with an approach which points to constraints rather than choice.

At the same time, the PSI survey indicates that 'many ethnic minority individuals prefer...to live alongside other people from ethnic minorities, and in particular, alongside others from their own ethnic group'. While residential segregation is evident, 'only one in five Pakistanis and Bangladeshis [live] in wards where the majority of residents [are] from ethnic minorities, and only one in seven Caribbeans, Indians and African Asians [live] in such wards' (Modood *et al.* 1997: 221). What is more, segregation is not simply between the majority ethnic group and minority ethnic groups. Census data 'demonstrate high levels of segregation between the various minority ethnic populations' (Peach and Rossiter 1996: 129) and local studies in Blackburn (V Robinson 1986) and London (Peach 1984) point to segregation within groups: in the first case, between Hindus, Sikhs and Muslims among South Asians, and, in the second case, between different island groups among Caribbeans. Such findings do suggest that cultural preferences are significant and are difficult to reconcile with an approach which exclusively focuses on constraints.

In view of the fact that both explanations have supporting evidence, it is increasingly recognised that both racial discrimination and ethnic choice play a part in any explanation of the residential concentration of minority ethnic groups. The debate now therefore tends to revolve around their relative significance. It is extremely difficult, however, to disentangle the factors involved. For the vulnerability of ethnic minorities to racist attacks may reinforce a cultural preference to live apart (Virdee 1995), while segregation arguably may reinforce racial/ethnic stereotypes. All we can safely conclude is that both racial discrimination and ethnic choice are significant. To talk about minorities being locked into (i.e. forced into) zones of social exclusion, in this context, oversimplifies a highly complex process and entails denying the role of agency (Ratcliffe 1999). Yet again we need to acknowledge both racial disadvantage and ethnic diversity. And the same is true when we turn to the adjacent issue of housing and account for the position of ethnic minorities in the housing market.

Ethnicity and housing

While there is widespread agreement that the levels of residential segregation are much lower than that in the United States, some writers none the less maintain that the disadvantage faced by minority ethnic groups in the housing market compounds their disadvantage in the labour market, entailing in turn a high risk of social exclusion.

The current position of minority ethnic groups in the housing market

Both the Census and PSI survey point to persistent racial disadvantage in housing. They indicate, for example, that, relative to the majority ethnic group, all minority ethnic groups are less likely to own their homes outright or live in detached houses and are more likely to experience overcrowding. Indeed both studies almost certainly underestimate disadvantage in housing because the measures of housing quality used are limited and do not take into account factors such as the state of repair of the property. This is a significant deficiency because previous studies of home ownership have shown that (partly as a result of racial discrimination) minority ethnic groups tend to 'disproportionately own the oldest housing in the worst state of disrepair' while studies of allocations of council housing have shown that (again partly as a result of racial discrimination) they 'receive a disproportionate share of the least popular types of housing and least popular estates' (Karn 1997: 276).

As evident as racial disadvantage, however, is ethnic diversity. Take for example housing tenure. While owner-occupation is the most common form of housing tenure, it is much more prevalent among some groups than others. Indians, African Asians and Pakistanis are more likely than Whites to be home-owners while Caribbeans, Bangladeshis and Black Africans are more likely than other groups to be in some form of social housing as council or housing association tenants. Such tenure differences between groups are, as Census analyses by Ratcliffe (1997), Dorling (1997) and Phillips (1997) indicate, partially explicable in terms of group differences in socio-economic position, household type and geographical location. Even so, the high level of owner-occupation among low-income South Asians stands out as a remarkable feature (Karn 1997) and perhaps indicates a cultural preference for this form of housing tenure.

Although owner-occupation is often seen as the most desirable form of housing tenure, we must not assume that it invariably entails a higher quality of accommodation. There are significant differences in the quality of accommodation occupied by home-owners and in some cases the level of amenities is lower than that found among tenants of social housing. Thus, Phillips detected in her analysis of the Census a significant cleavage among home-owners between Whites, Chinese and Indians on the one hand and Pakistanis and Bangladeshis on the other hand. While the former are the most likely to live in detached or semi-detached houses with central heating, the latter are the least likely (Phillips 1997). And Lackey noted how the PSI survey confirmed the greater likelihood of Pakistani and Bangladeshi owner-occupiers not only being concentrated in terraced housing, with fewer basic amenities than other home-owners, but also being located in 'properties with significantly poorer amenities than those available to social tenants from the same ethnic groups' (Modood *et al.* 1997: 223).

When the overall housing position of ethnic groups is compared, differences are evident both between 'majority and minority and between the various ethnic communities' (Ratcliffe 1997: 144). While all minority ethnic groups experience some disadvantage, what is most striking is the markedly disadvantaged position of Pakistanis and Bangladeshis. They 'live in the most deprived housing conditions' with 'over a fifth...in properties which were assessed by the [1991] English House Condition Survey as the "worst" in the country' (Karn and Phillips 1998: 130). In addition, they experience high levels of overcrowding. This is apparent when group comparisons are made in terms of the amount of bedroom space available. For Pakistani and Bangladeshi households (primarily as a result of household size) stand out 'as having much less bedroom space than other ethnic groups' (Modood *et al.* 1997: 211).

The changing position of minority ethnic groups in the housing market

Members of minority ethnic groups who arrived in Britain in the 1950s and 1960s 'had little choice but to occupy the bottom end of the market, ending up in poor private rental properties or, in the case of Asians, purchasing cheap deteriorating inner city terraced housing' (Karn and Phillips 1998: 128). Since then there have been important advances in the housing conditions of minority groups. Drawing on earlier Census and PSI survey data, one analysis pointed to progress since 1961 (Field *et al.* 1981) and indicated how 'the housing conditions of ethnic minorities…improved dramatically…both absolutely and relative to that of whites' over a twenty year period (Field 1986: 29). Improvement was manifest both in the increased level of basic amenities and the decline in overcrowding, and stemmed predominantly from changes in tenure patterns: a shift away from private rented accommodation to renting from the council in the case of Caribbeans and to owner-occupation in the case of South Asians.

Substantial progress in ethnic minority housing also characterised the 1980s and has continued into the 1990s. Analysis of the 1991 Census indicates 'a shift towards the equalisation of tenure patterns between young White households and minority ethnic households with UK-born heads, at least if we control for social class and household structure' (Ratcliffe 1997: 145). And a comparison of the 1982 and 1994 PSI surveys confirms that group differences in housing tenure are converging, especially when households 'of similar type, income and area' are compared (Modood *et al.* 1997: 217). What is more, both Census and PSI survey data concur that the housing options of ethnic minorities have widened over time, that relative progress has been made by all minority groups in access to detached and semi-detached properties and that their level of overcrowding in all cases has decreased considerably.

While in short minority ethnic groups remain disadvantaged in some respects, all have made important advances, both absolutely and relative to Whites, with Indians having made the biggest strides. In the light of this, Ballard's conclusion that 'there is no evidence that' the Pakistani community 'live in the lowest quality of housing' (R Ballard 1996: 147) seems both reasonable and indeed applicable to all minority ethnic groups. For the housing position of Pakistanis is, along with that of Bangladeshis, the most disadvantaged.

While the housing position of minority ethnic groups has improved overall, we must not forget that some members have not shared in this improvement. All ethnic groups are characterised by class divisions and, as we saw earlier, since the mid-1970s a process of class polarisation has been occurring. Changes in the British housing system since 1980 have tended to accentuate these divisions and reinforce such polarisation, especially within minority ethnic groups, with the result that some members have experienced deterioration in their housing position. Two changes in particular have contributed to this: firstly, the decline of large-scale grant-funded improvement in inner cities; and secondly, alongside legislation giving council tenants the right to buy their properties, a fall in the construction of social rented housing and the transformation of such housing into an increasingly under-resourced residual tenure for the poor (Karn and Phillips 1998). In view of the over-representation of ethnic minorities in inner cities and, especially among Caribbeans and Bangladeshis, on council estates, these changes have had a negative impact on the housing situation of a significant number of the minority population. Overall, however, the evidence indicates that any deterioration in the housing situation of some members of the minority population is more than counterbalanced by improvement in that of others, so that overall ethnic minorities have made important advances. Such a finding is clearly contrary to the thesis that minority ethnic groups are becoming increasingly locked into ghetto-like areas of poor housing and in this sense are experiencing social exclusion.

Evaluating the minority ethnic social exclusion thesis

The concept of social exclusion has been increasingly been taken up by social scientists in the last decade and readily applied to the socio-economic position of minority ethnic groups. Many writers have found it a more conducive concept than that of the underclass to conceptualise racial disadvantage evident in different institutional spheres since it does not have the same negative connotations. Others have preferred the concept of social exclusion to that of institutional racism since it implicitly acknowledges that the complex structural mechanisms which give rise to racial disadvantage cannot be reduced to discriminatory practices.

There is no doubt, however, that the concept has a multiplicity of meanings. Among other meanings, three can be distinguished. Often it refers to a distinct *social position*, the simplest case being one where most people are visualised as part of mainstream society enjoying full citizenship rights while those who experience social exclusion are seen as outside it and thus incapable of exercising their citizenship rights. Sometimes it refers to *socio-economic processes* which entail that some people become detached from mainstream society and therefore unable to participate effectively in economic, social, political and cultural life. Occasionally it refers to *particular areas* where inhabitants are segregated from mainstream society and live in ghettos unable to participate in customary styles of life (Ratcliffe 1999). These and other meanings are not always distinguished but they clearly point to very different phenomena.

When the Social Exclusion Unit (SEU) indicates that 'people from minority ethnic communities are at a disproportionate risk of social exclusion' (Cabinet Office 2000: 7), it is conceptualising social exclusion as an outcome rather than a process. This relates to the first meaning distinguished above, with social exclusion defined in terms of a distinct disadvantaged social position. Where the SEU wavers is in sometimes seeing social exclusion in universalistic terms as a situation which entails disadvantage across the board and at other times in particularistic terms as a situation which entails disadvantage in a particular institutional arena. By contrast, MacMaster conflates the second and third meanings distinguished above when he writes about minorities becoming 'locked into zones of exclusion' (MacMaster 2001: 219). To point to minorities becoming locked into disadvantage implies that that there are structural mechanisms at work which externally constrain minorities, while reference to zones of exclusion and ghetto-like areas of poor housing clearly has a spatial referent. Taking these three meanings of social exclusion in turn, we are now in a position to evaluate the usefulness of the concept.

Our examination of the evidence on poverty, health, areas of settlement and housing is broadly consonant with that of the SEU: people from minority ethnic communities are generally more likely to be disadvantaged than Whites. It is not altogether clear, however, why such racial disadvantage should be construed as evidence of social exclusion. The label does not bring with it new insights and indeed entails downplaying ethnic diversity. While the SEU is at pains to point out that 'there is much variation within and between different ethnic groups in all of these areas' (Cabinet Office 2000: 17), reference to 'minority ethnic social exclusion' understates differences between minority groups and indeed the significantly greater disadvantage experienced by Pakistanis and Bangladeshis relative to other groups in many institutional areas. A similar problem is evident when 'ethnic minority communities' are identified as an example of a 'socially excluded group' and it is claimed that 'we can see considerable evidence of the economic exclusion of those from ethnic minority groups' (Burden and Hamm 2000: 184, 188). For this implies that 'all minorities, or at least all of certain minorities (as "collectives" or "groups") suffer "exclusion"' (Ratcliffe 2000: 170). The danger again here is that ethnic diversity is overlooked and the internal differentiation of minority groups ignored.

Our analysis of explanations for some degree of residential segregation indicated that they took two main forms, with one emphasising constraints and the other choices. Writers who conceptualise social exclusion as a process rather than an outcome favour a form of explanation which highlights constraints. 'External structural forces' tend to be 'emphasised as the sole, or dominant, material factors and, in the process, the efficacy of agency on the part of minorities is denied' (Ratcliffe 2000: 170). The danger here is that the achievements of members of minority ethnic groups in drawing on the cultural capital of their own communities to improve their situation are overlooked.

Our investigation into the geography of race and ethnicity raised serious doubts that ghettos on the American model are evident in Britain. The evidence in fact indicated that over time a gradual process of de-concentration is taking place, at least for most minority ethnic groups. In view of this, there does not seem to be much credence, at least in relation to the residential patterns of minority ethnic groups in Britain, in applying the concept of social exclusion to areas.

To add to this catalogue of reservations with the concept of minority ethnic social exclusion, reference finally should be made to its converse, integration. An emphasis on the integration of minority ethnic groups 'apparently does not admit of cultural recognition and respect' (Parekh 2000: 81). The danger here is that the need, highlighted by the Macpherson report, for organisations to ensure that their routine practices and occupational cultures are culturally sensitive will be neglected.

Beyond racial dualism

Our analysis in this and the previous chapter of the position of ethnic minorities in the labour and housing markets leads us to challenge the thesis that minority ethnic groups *en bloc* comprise either an underclass or a socially excluded stratum in the UK. While all face racial discrimination and as a result encounter some disadvantage in common, such disadvantage is not extensive enough to warrant talk of a racially defined underclass or ethnic minority social exclusion. It is true that members of minority ethnic groups are often more likely than members of the majority ethnic group to experience those forms of disadvantage taken to be indicative of an underclass or social exclusion, but most members are not in this position. What is more, the position of distinct minority ethnic groups is markedly diverse and all, albeit to varying degrees, have over time improved their position both absolutely and relative to Whites.

Of the minority groups, Pakistanis and, even more so, Bangladeshis are the most disadvantaged and segregated. They are the only groups where the *majority* of members experience any of the forms of disadvantage thought to be characteristic of an underclass or socially excluded stratum. They therefore approximate the closest to an underclass or a socially excluded stratum. The vast majority are poor; most live in households where adults receive no earnings from employment/self-employment; and, in the case of Bangladeshis, those in work are predominantly employed in non-skilled jobs. Even here, however, there is evidence of relative progress over time and, while they are generally over-represented in disadvantaged positions, deprivation is not invariably the plight of a majority of members. Among men, persistent unemployment is not the norm and most households do not live in deprived housing conditions.

Although our critique of the thesis that minority ethnic groups constitute an underclass or a socially excluded stratum does not depend on showing that they have made relative progress, we have none the less pointed to important advances. Our optimism is not shared by all commentators, however. One analysis, which draws on Census data to compare UK- and non UK-born 21–50-year-old members of ethnic groups in terms of attainment in education, occupation and life-style (as measured by housing and car ownership) pessimistically concludes that 'the UK-born resembled the non UK-born far more than they differed from them' (Blackburn *et al.* 1997: 262). Such a conclusion serves as a salutary reminder that we must not be complacent and that equity for the minority ethnic population demands overcoming persistent barriers. However an analysis which compares two 'generations' at a particular point in time is not as compelling as an analysis (such as that undertaken by the authors of the PSI survey), which compares two cohorts at different points in time. The first generation includes some who have been upwardly mobile since coming to Britain, while the second generation is disproportionately skewed towards the lower end of the 21–50-year-old age span and thus includes many who are too young to have reached occupational maturity. But even if Blackburn, Dale and Jarman are right to question whether the attainments of ethnic groups are converging to any significant degree, it does not follow that the underclass thesis or the social exclusion thesis is substantiated. For, as they recognise themselves:

> it is clear that conventional perceptions of immigrant ethnic minorities forming an "underclass" or otherwise sharing a common experience of deprivation is unsound. This is not to deny that ethnic minorities . . . suffer disadvantages: the evidence on life-styles and unemployment show this. However, their experiences are not homogeneous and they are not passive victims. [Indeed] in some groups the immigrants and the UK-born have achieved higher . . . occupational levels than the indigenous Whites (Blackburn *et al.* 1997: 263).

An alternative: bringing culture and agency back in

Once it is acknowledged that minority ethnic groups constitute neither an underclass nor a socially excluded stratum, the question arises as to why so many commentators continue to represent the position of minority groups in these ways.

Implicit in many accounts is a model of power which depicts society as divided into oppressors and oppressed. Drawing on a particular interpretation of American society – where arguably the major division is a racial one – British society is portrayed as divided ethnically into two main groups: White oppressors and Black oppressed.

What lends credence to this picture is evidence that ethnic minorities face racial discrimination. For this suggests that whatever differences there may be between minority ethnic groups are less relevant than their common treatment as non-White. To focus on cultural differences in this context is at best a diversion from the real problem – racism – and at worst a form of victim blaming. Indeed, members of different minority ethnic groups may respond in some instances by defining themselves as Black, to signify their belief that only through solidarity with others who also suffer racial discrimination can racism be combated and their situation improved. Once a picture of society as divided into White oppressors and Black oppressed has grown in this way, it is a short step to conclude that the oppressed in a racist society are forced to be at the bottom of the occupational and income scale and are increasingly locked into an underclass or zones of social exclusion.

What such an account forgets is that power is a social relation and that in the case of ethnic relations in Britain, the majority ethnic group is not completely dominant and the minority ethnic groups invariably resist domination. Neither the majority nor the minority populations in fact constitute homogeneous groups.

The former consist of diverse groups, whose members do not wholeheartedly subscribe to racist beliefs. Thus, while a significant minority continue to admit to racial prejudice, most now say that they do not mind mixed marriages and express support for legislation to combat racial discrimination (K Young 1992; McKie and Brook 1996; IPPR 1997; Alibhai-Brown 1999). Indeed a comparison of the attitudes of young people with adults in the same household conducted in 1994 suggests that the espousal of racist beliefs is declining since 'on balance, young people appear to be more liberal and much less prejudiced than adults' (Sachdev 1996: 69).

The minority population consists of (partially) distinct communities, whose members have little in common other than being subject to racial discrimination. Although they sometimes unite – under the umbrella of sharing a common Black identity – to resist racism, this is rare. Asians (unlike Caribbeans) do not usually identify themselves as Black and indeed are more likely than Whites to express disapproval of mixed marriages with Caribbeans (Modood *et al.* 1997; IPPR 1997). Generally ethnic minorities draw on the resources of their own communities to resist racial discrimination. And far from being irrelevant, cultural differences are central. For 'it is precisely through...their skilled and creative redeployment – both individually and collectively – of the alternative resources of their imported cultural traditions that Britain's new minorities are not only beginning to circumvent racial exclusionism, but to do so with ever increasing success' (R Ballard 1992: 487).

Recognition that there are significant cultural differences between ethnic groups is not of course, a new phenomenon. And indeed, within Sociology and the other social sciences, some writers have placed great stress on them. Many sociologists, however, have been reluctant to admit that cultural differences are critical. There are two reasons for this. Firstly, they argue that racial discrimination/racism, and not culture, is fundamental in determining the life chances of minority ethnic groups. Secondly, they believe that representations of minority cultures frequently amount to little more than stereotypes, which moreover portray minority groups in pathological terms and implicitly hold such groups responsible for their own disadvantage.

What has been termed the 'cultural turn in social theory' (S Hall 1997a) has encouraged a reconsideration of the significance of culture and, at the same time, a re-conceptualisation of culture itself. Cultures have often been depicted as discrete systems with clear boundaries separating one from another; represented as integrated wholes with members sharing fundamental beliefs and practices in common; and characterised by distinct traditions which are passed from generation to generation. Such a picture entails seeing members of ethnic groups as products with unambiguous identities. This conceptualisation of culture and identity has, however, been criticised as both deterministic and essentialist. Social constructionism, which we drew upon in Chapter 1, emphasises that societies are not insulated from each other, that all involve social divisions and, above all, that culture entails a process of production (Ranger *et al.* 1996). Such a re-conceptualisation of culture and identity implies that members of ethnic groups are agents and do not have fixed identities.

A plethora of studies exemplify this new approach, which we shall explore further in Chapter 6, and as a result point to people's multiple shifting identities in a world characterised by globalisation. The sociology of race and ethnicity has been at the forefront of this development, discovering 'new ethnicities' which are fluid and dynamic (S Hall 1996). Thus young Caribbean people may share a common neighbourhood identity with young White people whom they have grown up with, and yet in other contexts where racism is more evident, draw on a wider Black identity (Back 1996). Switching language codes from a shared London English (which itself manifests the influence of both Cockney and Creole) to Creole illustrates this transition (Hewitt 1990). Young Asian people also 'create not one unitary cultural identity, but rather multiple identities' as they traverse the 'cultural fields' of the temple, home, shopping centre, school and disco (K Hall 1995: 253). They are aware of moving between different worlds (Asian and British) and shifting identities accordingly, but in the process often produce new identities, utilising the mass media and popular culture to fuse different cultural traditions (Gillespie 1995).

This emphasis on people as cultural producers rather than cultural products enables us to acknowledge the significance of culture without falling into the trap of essentialism. We do need to bear in mind, however, two points. Firstly, individuals do not have the autonomy to create any identities they wish. Contrary to the view of some recent (post-modern) theorists, we cannot shop around a cultural supermarket and try on what ever we fancy. Racial discrimination/racism, for example, severely constrains the possibility of identity construction for members of minority ethnic groups. Secondly, a recognition that people have multiple shifting identities in a world where cultures overlap does not mean that we cannot distinguish 'several cultural communities with their overlapping but nonetheless distinct conceptions of the world, systems of meaning, values, forms of social organisation, histories, customs and practices' (Parekh 1997a: 166–7). Individuals are cultural products as well as cultural producers. Members of minority ethnic groups – socialised, albeit to varying degrees, into distinct cultural communities – have thus been able to draw on the cultural capital of their own communities to resist racial discrimination and racism. Clearly some minority groups have been more successful than others, but once we acknowledge that people are not merely victims but active agents, the coexistence of racial discrimination and ethnic minority progress becomes explicable. In this context 'to speak of "the Black experience" to signify all the richness of the Diaspora [communities who have left their homelands and become dispersed] is both to oversimplify the everyday processes of exclusion and to minimise the creativity of response' (Cross 1991: 311).

Acknowledgment of the complexity of social divisions has become commonplace in recent social theory, with writers increasingly recognising the interaction of class, gender and ethnicity' (Bradley 1996; A Pilkington and Sherratt 1993). We have focused primarily on the interaction of ethnicity and class, but we also need to note the interplay of ethnicity, class and gender. One of the few British studies to do this focuses on the fashion industry in the Midlands (although see also Westwood and Bhachu 1988). Here one response to unemployment was to start up a labour-intensive small business in which minority ethnic women constituted the bulk of the labour force. This option was taken up by some Asian entrepreneurs who used 'patriarchal attitudes and practices to discipline and control such a work force often combined with an assertion of "ethnic" loyalty and honour' (Phizacklea 1992: 109). In the process, such (male) entrepreneurs used gender divisions within their communities as a resource to improve their socio-economic position. Yet again what is evident is the refusal of ethnic minorities to be victims.

Conclusion

In the last decade, social exclusion has become part of the sociological lexicon and has steadily been applied to the experience of minority ethnic groups. The concept has, however, multiple meanings and is embedded in very different discourses. The dominant discourse in Britain and the European Union tends to visualise social exclusion in primarily dichotomous terms: people are either excluded from mainstream society or integrated into it. Integration through paid work rather than equality is the policy goal.

The Social Exclusion Unit, set up by the government in 1997, now explicitly argues that people from minority ethnic communities are at a disproportionate risk of social exclusion. This is evident, it is argued, from evidence which points among other things to the fact that people from minority communities are more likely than others to be poor, suffer ill-health, live in deprived areas and reside in overcrowded and unpopular housing. While our examination of the experience of minorities in these institutional areas broadly concurs with that of the SEU, it is not altogether clear why evidence of racial disadvantage should be relabelled as social exclusion. What is more, the danger in referring to minority ethnic social exclusion is that significant ethnic diversity is underplayed. While our analysis does point to racial disadvantage in relation to poverty, residential areas and housing (though not in relation to health), what is more evident than racial disadvantage is ethnic diversity. The most striking finding from our analysis is the particularly disadvantaged position of Pakistanis and Bangladeshis in the four areas examined. The SEU conceptualises social exclusion as an outcome rather than a process. Writers who prefer to see social exclusion as a process tend to emphasise how external structural forces impact on people. The danger here, however, is that the role of agency is overlooked and people are seen as victims.

Although many writers (though not all) who point to social exclusion are reluctant to talk of an underclass, there are some similarities between the structural version of the underclass thesis assessed in the previous chapter and a thesis which points to minority ethnic social exclusion. Both tend to underemphasise ethnic diversity and both tend to neglect the way minority ethnic groups draw on the cultural capital of their own communities to resist discrimination and improve their situation.

5 Ethnicity and education

The sociology of education has been preoccupied for much of the post-war period with one central issue. The issue is of course that of social inequality, with 'the major focus of traditional concern [being] with social class' (Halsey 1995: 162).

The thesis that industrial societies are moving towards meritocracy has provided the backdrop for much of the research. According to this thesis, the logic of industrialisation entails a transition from a situation where status is ascribed at birth to a situation where status is achieved through one's own efforts. Class origins become increasingly less influential in accounting for class destinations as educational qualifications become the key determinant of occupational placement. The thesis predicts that, with the expansion of educational opportunities, the path from origin to education (a) will decline. In addition it anticipates that employers' recruiting strategies will ensure that the path from origin to destination (b) also declines while the path from education to destination (c) increases (Heath et al. 1992).

Although research in Britain has indeed confirmed that there is a trend for link (b) to weaken and link (c) to strengthen (Halsey 1977), its primary concern has been with link (a). Here, a range of studies, using odds ratios to calculate the relative chances of children from different class origins attending selective secondary schools (Halsey et al. 1980), obtaining one or more passes at GCE (General Certificate of Education) Ordinary level (equivalent to GCSE (General Certificate of Secondary Education) grades A–C) (Heath and Clifford 1996) and entering higher education (Egerton and Halsey 1993), have demonstrated, contrary to the predictions of the meritocratic thesis, that no change was evident among different birth cohorts during the twentieth century. The upshot of this research programme is clear. Despite a significant expansion in educational opportunities, which has benefited all social classes, class relativities have remained remarkably constant.

Despite the continuing significance of class for educational attainment, increasingly within the sociology of education attention has turned to gender and ethnicity. These comprise 'giants in the path of aspirations towards equality' (Halsey 1995: 162). For sex discrimination still 'excludes women from the top jobs and highest earnings' (Hakim 1996: 186) and race discrimination results, as we have already seen, in minority ethnic groups failing to gain 'the same returns on their investments (in education) as do native-born Whites' (Cheng and Heath 1993: 152). Contrary to the expectations of the meritocratic thesis, ascribed status is still clearly significant when the link between education and destination is examined.

What about the link between origin and education? Here change rather than continuity is evident in relation to gender. And the change is in the direction predicted by the meritocratic thesis of a declining link between origin and education. For 'the central empirical trend is of general and relative improvement in the levels of female educational attainment' (Moore 1996). While the evidence points then to a 'pattern of unchanging relative social class disadvantage', it indicates 'decreasing disadvantage for women' (Egerton and Halsey 1993: 192). The issue we now need to address is the link between ethnic origin and education.

Ethnicity and underachievement: myth or reality?

Educational opportunities have expanded considerably. Nevertheless, as we saw in the previous section, many sociologists still wish to argue that groups still do not have equal chances of acquiring valued qualifications. The working class, for example, still do not have the same chances as the middle class. In this view, the most appropriate indicator of the degree of opportunity is a measure of the relative educational achievements of different groups. 'It is in this sense that we can speak of a group underachieving in relation to other groups within the population' (Gillborn 1990: 107). Hence it is that some commentators talk of working-class underachievement and, more recently, of the underachievement of boys. When it comes to ethnicity, what has struck most commentators is the comparatively lower educational attainment of Caribbean (or West Indian) children. The Committee of Inquiry into the Education of Children from Ethnic Minority Groups, which was itself set up, at least in part, in response to widespread concern about the educational performance of 'West Indian' pupils, took this line. The interim (Rampton) report outlined the results of the Department of Education and Science (DES) annual school leavers' survey in 6 local education authorities (LEAs) for 1978/9 and the final (Swann) report reported the findings of the same survey in 5 LEAs for 1981/2. After comparing the achievements of White, Asian and West Indian pupils, the interim report concluded that 'West Indian children *as a group* are underachieving in our education system' (Rampton 1981: 10), while the final report concluded that 'there is no doubt that West Indian children, as a group, and on average, are underachieving, both by comparison with their school fellows in the White majority, as well as in terms of their potential, notwithstanding that some are doing well' (Swann 1985: 81). The prominence given to this official inquiry meant the notion of West Indian underachievement received wide coverage and was widely disseminated.

The concept of underachievement has proved to be highly contentious, however. One critic has argued that it assumes that groups are equal in all 'relevant respects' (Flew 1986: 24) and that this condition is not fulfilled in the case of West Indians because of evidence that they are inherently less able. Flew is correct in indicating that the concept does presuppose that ability is randomly distributed between groups, but as we shall see in the next section this is not an unreasonable assumption. Another critic has argued that the concept of underachievement privileges one aim of education, namely the pursuit of educational qualifications, over others and that other aims are more desirable (Jeffcoate 1984). While we may sympathise with this position, educational qualifications are none the less critical to people's life chances with the tightening link between education and destination and, given racial discrimination, are of the utmost importance to minority ethnic groups. A third critic has argued that the concept of underachievement implicitly blames the group deemed to be underachieving and that the notion of West Indian underachievement is particularly dangerous because it is likely to reinforce the common stereotype of Black people as inherently less able (Troyna 1984).

He is right to warn us of possible connotations of the term but it is used here in a purely descriptive way to refer to demonstrable differences in relative achievement between groups and does not privilege any particular social explanation for such differences, although it does of course expressly rule out a genetic explanation.

More than a decade has passed since the official inquiry drew our attention to West Indian underachievement. Since then more reliable findings have emerged which move beyond the rather crude ethnic breakdown employed by Rampton/Swann and enable us to address simultaneously issues of class, gender and ethnic background (A Pilkington 1997c). The two most significant overviews of research on ethnic differences in levels of achievement have been published by the Office for Standards in Education (OFSTED) (Gillborn and Gipps 1996; Gillborn and Mirza 2000). These reviews draw on two main sources of data. The first derives from LEAs, while the second derives from the Youth Cohort Survey (YCS), which comprises a longitudinal nationally representative survey of young people and represents a massive improvement on previous data.

While it cannot be said that ethnic monitoring is undertaken in a consistent way by LEAs or is even a universal feature of LEA data gathering, it is none the less interesting to note 'that for each of the main ethnic groups...studied there is at least one LEA where *that* group is the highest attaining' (Gillborn and Mirza 2000: 9). While we cannot read too much into such local

Table 5.1 GCSE attainment by ethnicity, in state schools, England and Wales, 1988, 1995 and 1997

Ethnic group	Five or more higher grade passes (%)			Improvement (%)	
	1988	1995	1997	1995–97	1988–97
White	26	42	44	+ 2	+ 18
Black	17	21	28	+ 7	+ 11
Indian	23	44	49	+ 5	+ 26
Pakistani	20	22	28	+ 6	+ 8
Bangladeshi	13	23	32	+ 9	+ 19

Source: YCS, adapted from Gillborn and Mirza (2000).

variability (which is anyway quite limited), this finding does remind us that there is no 'necessary or pre-determined ethnic ordering' and that 'no ethnic group is inherently less capable of academic success' (Gillborn and Mirza 2000: 9, 11). We need to bear this in mind when looking at the more reliable national data on ethnic difference in educational achievement from the YCS (Drew 1995; Demack *et al.* 2000). Table 5.1 presents a comparison of changes in the attainment of five ethnic groups at GCSE level (grades A–C) between 1988 and 1997.

Averages mask 'considerable variation in performance within ethnic groups and...significant overlap between groups' (Gillborn 1990: 127), but the average differences evident in Table 5.1 are none the less significant. The most recent results from 1997 confirm the finding of the Rampton and Swann reports that Caribbean pupils are underachieving relative to White pupils but at the same time point to significant variability among Asian pupils, with Indians attaining better results than Whites but Pakistanis and Bangladeshis performing on a par with Black pupils. While the proportion of pupils attaining five or more higher-grade passes has increased in all ethnic groups since the introduction of the GCSE, and between 1995 and 1997 relative inequalities of attainment for minority groups declined, over a longer period from 1988 to 1997 the differences in attainment between Indians and White pupils, on the one hand, and Caribbean, Pakistani and Bangladeshi young people, on the other hand, widened.

> Indian pupils have made the greatest gains in the last decade: enough to overtake their white peers as a group...Bangladeshi pupils have improved significantly but the gap between themselves and white youngsters is much the same...African-Caribbean and Pakistani pupils have drawn least benefit from the rising levels of attainment: the gap between them and their white peers is now bigger than a decade ago (Gillborn and Mirza 2000: 14).

In many ways it is the performance of Caribbean pupils which continues to constitute the greatest cause for concern. For while 'the performance of Pakistani and Bangladeshi pupils in the early years of schooling remains depressed' but manifests improvement 'once they become proficient in English...Black Caribbean pupils make a sound start in primary schools but their performance shows a marked decline at secondary level' (OFSTED 1999: 7).

This is evident from baseline data supplied by some LEAs which 'suggests that the inequalities of attainment for African-Caribbean pupils become progressively greater as they move through the school system' with 'differences becoming more pronounced between the end of primary school and the end of secondary education' (Gillborn and Mirza 2000: 17).

The YCS enables us to analyse a nationally representative sample of young people not only by ethnicity but also by gender and social class. We saw earlier that among young people as a whole there is an association between class and (to a lesser extent) gender, on the one hand, and success in education, on the other hand. What is evident when Tables 5.2 and 5.3 are examined is that this familiar association holds within each of the ethnic groups identified. Girls attain better results than boys and, even more markedly in most groups, middle-class pupils attain better results than working-class pupils.

Table 5.2 compares the proportion of pupils from seven ethnic groups, after controlling for gender, attaining five or more higher-grade passes at GCSE. Ethnic inequalities persist when a comparison is made of pupils of the same sex but from different ethnic backgrounds, with a considerable gap evident between Chinese, Indian and White girls, on the one hand, and Pakistani, Bangladeshi and Black girls, on the other hand.

Table 5.2 GCSE attainment by ethnicity, controlling for gender, in state schools, 1995

| Ethnic group | 5+ Higher grade GCSE passes (%) | | |
	Male	Female	All
White	37	47	42
Black	15**	26	21
Indian	39	49	44
Pakistani	16	28	22
Bangladeshi	23**	24**	23
Chinese	63*	63*	63**
Other	37	45	41
All	36	46	41

* Subsample 30 or less.
** Subsample greater than 30 but less than 100.
Source: YCS, adapted from Demack *et al.* (2000).

Table 5.3 GCSE attainment by ethnicity, controlling for class, in state schools, 1995

Ethnic group	5+ Higher grade GCSE passes (%)		
	Non-manual	Manual (skilled & semi-skilled)	Unskilled/ unclassified
White	55	27	19
Black	30**	25**	12**
Indian	64	40	19**
Pakistani/Bangladeshi	41**	25	17
Other	63	41**	25
All	55	28	19

**Subsample greater than 30 but less than 100.
Source: YCS, adapted from Demack *et al.* (2000).

Table 5.3 compares the proportion of pupils from five ethnic groups, after controlling for social class, attaining five or more higher-grade passes at GCSE. While this table points to class differences within each ethnic group,

> social class differences do not override the influence of ethnic inequality: when comparing pupils with similar class backgrounds there are still marked inequalities of attainment between different ethnic groups. Indeed, in some respects the analysis reveals new inequalities: showing that Black pupils from relatively advantaged backgrounds are little better placed, as a group, than white peers from manual backgrounds

and, it should be added, are markedly worse placed than Indian peers from manual backgrounds (Gillborn and Mirza 2000: 21). When we compare pupils from different ethnic groups, after controlling for both gender and social class, the results demonstrate that in 1995, 'Indian pupils did best, followed by white, Pakistani/Bangladeshi and Black pupils respectively' (Gillborn and Mirza 2000: 26). Placing gender, class and ethnicity in a relative perspective, we discover that

> the ethnic differences were larger than the gender differences and the social class differences were the largest of all.... We have to remember [however] that those ethnic groups with the lowest educational attainment (Pakistanis, Bangladeshis and Blacks) are those with disproportionately

large numbers in the lowest social class groups, Their problems are [therefore] ones of both 'race' and social disadvantage (Demack *et al.* 2000: 137–8).

The data from the YCS that we have examined so far refers to pupils at a single point in time, notably at the end of compulsory schooling, whether that was in 1988, 1995 or 1997. Young people from minority ethnic groups are, however, much more likely than White pupils to stay on in post-compulsory education. Indeed Drew found 'that, once attainment was taken into account, ethnic origin was the single most important factor in determining the chances of staying on' (Drew 1995: 180). This finding is echoed by the analysis of the participation rates of 16–19-year-olds in full-time education in the 1991 Census, which revealed 'the almost uniformly higher participation rate of ethnic minority groups during the post-16 period in comparison with the White group', a phenomenon 'little altered when differences associated with gender and social class are taken into account' (Drew *et al.* 1997: 25). Likewise, investigation of the participation in full-time education of 16–24-year-olds in the 1994 PSI survey indicated that 'no ethnic minority group had a lower participation rate in post-16 education than white people' and 'that people from ethnic minorities in general are also staying on for longer periods' (Modood *et al.* 1997: 76). Among those who had already gained GCE O-level or higher qualification, 'about twice as many ethnic minority as white persons were likely to be continuing in education', with the higher participation rate in post-compulsory education of Asian men being particularly striking. This clearly represents a significant 'ethnic minority drive for qualifications'. For staying on longer allows pupils more opportunity 'to upgrade existing qualifications and obtain further qualifications of value in the labour market' (Modood *et al.* 1997: 82).

Evidence that the greater likelihood of members from minority ethnic groups staying on pays off emerges from an analysis over time of the experience of 16–19-year-old youngsters who reached the minimum school leaving age in the mid-1980s (Drew 1995). Although this study uses a rather crude ethnic breakdown (Afro-Caribbean; Asian; White) and is now somewhat dated, it does show how young people from minority ethnic groups are more likely than those from the majority ethnic group to improve their qualifications over time. By the age of 18, 'Afro-Caribbean' students had caught up a little on White students in terms of proportions obtaining four or more O-levels (or their equivalent). Their relatively lower achievements at 16, however, had ramifications leading them to be more likely to study vocational rather than academic courses from which at 18 they emerged as the best vocationally qualified group, a finding consistent with the PSI study, which confirms that Caribbeans have a higher proportion of vocational qualifications than other ethnic groups. Meanwhile Asian students, who at 16 had been slightly behind White students in terms of proportions obtaining four or more O-levels, by 18 had not only caught them up but overtaken them, emerging at this age as the best academically qualified group.

What is striking overall is that 'ethnic minorities manifest a radical diversity, indeed extreme contrasts, in their educational attainment levels' (Modood *et al.* 1997: 80). By no means can the minorities be seen to be in the same position. This becomes clearly evident when ethnic groups are compared in terms of their highest qualification. While this classification of qualifications is rather crude so that it shows, for example, the proportion whose highest qualification is any O-level or equivalent where the equivalents may be vocational rather than, as in the YCS, the proportion with five higher-grade passes at GCSE (five O-levels) (T Jones 1993), the results are none the less revealing. Among people of working age, the PSI survey indicates that 'the Chinese, African Asians and Indians are much the best qualified groups.... Among men, then come Whites, with Caribbeans and Pakistanis being less qualified, and Bangladeshis the least so' (Modood *et al.* 1997: 64–5). Among women, by contrast, Caribbeans are more likely to be qualified than Whites, with Pakistanis and especially Bangladeshis generally much less qualified. This picture reflects the different starting-points of different groups as well as their different experiences of education in Britain. To ascertain what progress, if any, has been made, we need to look at different generations.

Most of those who came to Britain as adults – the migrants – did not have qualifications. There were, however, significant group differences, with Caribbeans, Pakistanis and Bangladeshis being poorly qualified while more than a third of Indians, African Asians and Chinese had a higher qualification (A-level or equivalent or higher). 'In most groups, the second generation (25–44-year-olds who were born in Britain or came as children) had made significant progress' (Modood *et al.* 1997: 81). This was particularly evident in the case of Caribbeans but generally much less so in the case of Pakistanis and not evident at all in the case of Bangladeshis. Comparison of the qualifications held by this second generation leads Modood to amend 'the two-way division between ethnic groups of migrants with a new middling or mixed category' (Modood *et al.* 1997: 72). While, on the one hand, African Asians and the Chinese generally had better qualifications than Whites and, on the other hand, Pakistanis and especially Bangladeshis generally had markedly worse qualifications than Whites, Indians and Caribbeans were in an intermediate situation, generally somewhat less well qualified than Whites. This second generation distinguished is, however, something of a ragbag, which includes people not fully educated in Britain. More revealing is the comparison of 16–24-year-old men and women – the new generation – in Table 5.4.

The new generation distinguished here includes many still in education and therefore many who have not yet 'achieved their ultimate highest qualification'. This means 'that in comparing them with their elders one is not comparing like with like'. What is more, 'ethnic minority, especially South Asian, participation in post-compulsory full-time education is much higher than that of Whites; moreover, ethnic minority persons on average acquire some of their qualifications at a later age than Whites'. Although there is evidence that this latter factor is declining over time, 'the effect of these two factors is that... ethnic minority qualification levels, especially those of South Asians, are disproportionately understated' (Modood *et al.* 1997: 72–73). Despite this caveat, Table 5.4 indicates that the position of Indians, African Asians and Chinese is similar to that of Whites except at degree level where their position is generally distinctly better. By contrast, and despite some progress, the attainment of Pakistanis and especially Bangladeshis continues to be markedly worse on the whole than other ethnic groups.

Table 5.4 Highest qualification held by 16–24-year-old men and women, by ethnic group, 1994

Ethnic group	White	Caribbean	Indian	African Asian	Pakistani	Bangladeshi	Chinese
*None or below O-level**							
Men	22	31	27	22	44	42	[17]
Women	26	18	21	17	40	52	[10]
*O-level or equivalent**							
Men	33	31	27	27	22	38	[40]
Women	31	30	24	31	31	29	[49]
A-level or equivalent or higher (degrees in parentheses)							
Men	46 (6)	38 (5)	46 (12)	50 (9)	34 (4)	19 (2)	[44 (5)]
Women	43 (3)	53 (2)	54 (13)	51 (17)	31 (10)	19 (5)	[41 (6)]

* O-levels are equivalent to grades A–C GCSEs; GCSEs were introduced in 1988. Figures in square brackets denote small sample size.

Source: PSI survey 1994, adapted from Modood *et al.* (1997).

Caribbeans seem to be in an intermediate situation, with young men having faltered in their progress and now not in a dissimilar position to Pakistanis, while young women have made significant strides.

The overall situation of the different ethnic minorities manifests continuities with their different starting-points. This is borne out by the 'correlation between the levels of qualifications of those born outside the UK and the levels of qualifications of those born in the UK' (Mortimore *et al.* 1997: 14) and the maintenance of a contrast between the achievement of Indians, African Asians and Chinese, on the one hand, and that of Pakistanis, Bangladeshis and Caribbean men, on the other hand. 'There are at least two other striking processes', however. 'One is the strong educational drive found in the ethnic minorities' which has allowed many to make significant progress. The other 'is the special progress of women' (Modood *et al.* 1997: 75), a phenomenon not confined to ethnic minorities but one particularly evident there.

The emphasis of much of the research on ethnic differentials in educational achievement since the late 1970s has been on the underachievement of West Indians or Caribbeans. The 1985 committee of inquiry emphasised 'that West Indian children, as a group, and on average are underachieving' (Swann 1985: 81). The terminology has changed over time, with the 1996 OFSTED report preferring the term 'African Caribbean' and avoiding the term 'underachieving', but the same emphasis is apparent. 'Recent research tends to show African Caribbean pupils as relatively less successful than their "Asian" and white peers' (Gillborn and Gipps 1996: 29). Such a conclusion, however, warrants modification in the light of our analysis of more recent research, which involves nationally representative samples and involves disaggregating ethnic groups by gender and national origin. While there are some differences in the results of research that focuses on the performance of pupils in schools (Gillborn and Mirza 2000; Demack *et al.* 2000) and the results of studies that look at young people's highest qualifications (Karn 1997; Modood *et al.* 1997), together they suggest that it is Caribbean young men rather than young women who are underachieving and that the position of two Asian groups is at best not markedly better and may even be worse.

Explaining educational inequality

In view of the fact that most of the existing research has focused on West Indian or Caribbean underachievement, we shall perforce here focus on different explanations for the lower educational attainment of this group rather than that of Pakistanis or Bangladeshis. It should be noted, however, that the explanations, which we shall be exploring, have been used to account for social class differentials in educational attainment and, with modifications, are used also to explain Pakistani and Bangladeshi underachievement. It will be evident that the debate between competing explanations is deeply political. Parekh illustrates this well:

> For example, an explanation in terms of genetic inferiority, the structure of the family or lack of cultural depth, fastens the blame on the West Indian community; an explanation in terms of the West Indian child's low self-esteem, ethnocentric curriculum, racist textbooks and the ethos of the school lays the blame at the door of the school and the educational system; and one that stresses racism and economic inequalities puts the responsibility upon the white society. Not surprisingly, the group which suspects that it might be blamed and asked to change its ways tends to marshal whatever arguments it can against the threatening explanation, or to demand impossible standards of proof and conceptual rigour from it while not bothering to provide these for its own alternative explanation, or to impugn the intellectual judgement and honesty of its advocates (Parekh 1983: 114).

The IQ question

The fact 'that West Indian children tend to score lower than white children on tests of intelligence' (M Taylor 1981: 67) has suggested to some people that the differences in educational attainment are primarily attributable to differences in intelligence, and that these differences are in turn genetically determined. Although the notion that racial differences in ability are inherited was thoroughly discredited by the scientific community after the Second World War, it was given renewed respectability by Jensen in an article entitled, 'How much can we boost IQ and scholastic achievement?' (Jensen 1969), has been popularised in this country by Eysenck (1971) and has been given a renewed lease of life with the publication of *The Bell Curve* (Hernstein and Murray 1994).

It might be argued that to devote space to an examination of the alleged genetic inferiority of Caribbean children is to confer 'intellectual legitimacy and social respectability upon an absurd view' (Parekh 1992: 97). The view is still, however, propagated by some academics and popularised through the media and cannot be left unchallenged. Parekh argues that the Swann report had no alternative but analyse and expose the genetic explanation and, given the publication of *The Bell Curve* since, we are in the same position.

The central thesis of *The Bell Curve* is that the United States is becoming a meritocracy, with intelligence becoming the key determinant of status. The result is a system of 'cognitive classes', with those at the top tending to be the most intelligent members of society and those at the bottom tending to be the least intelligent members of society. Examining the links between origin, education and destination in Britain, we challenged the meritocratic thesis in the first section. For Hernstein and Murray, however, and those who sympathise with their position in Britain (Saunders 1996), the thesis cannot be so easily dismissed. IQ (intelligence quotient) measures intelligence and it is individual differences in IQ (itself seen as primarily inherited) which explain differences in the class positions which individuals achieve.

Although the issue of group differences in intelligence is irrelevant to their central argument, Hernstein and Murray do broach the issue. They point to the significant 15-point gap in the average IQ scores between Whites and Blacks and, drawing mostly on the work of Jensen, claim that there are good reasons for believing that the IQ differences are primarily genetic in origin. Although they are careful enough in the end to conclude that they are 'resolutely agnostic' (Hernstein and Murray 1994: 311) on the precise mix of environment and genes, the overall tenor of their argument is clear. The over-representation of Black people in the lower cognitive classes is explicable in terms of their lower IQ scores and there is nothing which can be or indeed should be done to try to change this situation. Rather than bemoaning the fact that Blacks are intellectually inferior to Whites, we should celebrate the fact that they possess different qualities: 'It is possible to look ahead to a world in which the glorious hodgepodge of inequalities of ethnic groups – genetic and environmental, permanent and temporary – can be not only accepted but celebrated' (Murray and Hernstein 1994, quoted in Malik 1996: 207).

The publication of *The Bell Curve* caused a huge furore, with the contention that there are inherent racial differences in intelligence being particularly explosive. Here we shall soberly list the arguments which cumulatively indicate that 'the evidence for the mental superiority of one or the other [race is] so flimsy, confused and full of intellectual dishonesty as to be scarcely worth considering' (S Jones 1996: 205).

1 It is questionable whether race is a biologically meaningful concept. Although we can of course distinguish people on the basis of skin colour, those classified as White or Black do not, as we saw in Chapter 1, constitute distinct populations. Intermarriage is common in Britain, for example, and geneticists have shown that there is vastly more genetic variation within so-called races as between them (S Jones 1996).

2 It is questionable whether IQ measures intelligence. Gardner for example challenges the notion that there is such a thing as general intelligence and claims instead that there are distinct kinds of intelligence. IQ tests only measure some of these intelligences and are as a result culturally biased (Gardner 1995).

3 Although studies in the United States indicate a gap of 15 points in the average IQ scores of Whites and Blacks 'there are signs that the gap between black and white is narrowing' (Kohn 1996: 104), a phenomenon acknowledged even by Hernstein and Murray. What is more, studies in Britain indicate that 'the overall difference...is considerably smaller' (Swann 1985: 129).

4 In Britain differences between the social and economic circumstances of White and Black families are primarily responsible for the IQ gap. Mackintosh and Mascie-Taylor, who were commissioned by the Swann report to look into the IQ question, concluded that 'the often quoted gap between West Indian and White IQ scores is sharply reduced when account is taken of socio-economic factors' (Swann 1985: 81).

5   A crucial difference in the environments between Blacks and
    Whites depends on whether individuals are classified as Black
    or White. This factor – racism – 'cannot be pinned down by
    controlling conventional environmental variables' (Kohn
    1996: 100). In a study which critically examines Hernstein
    and Murray's thesis, the authors argue that attention needs
    to be given not only to socio-economic deprivation but also
    the segregation and stigmatised identity of Black people in
    the United States. Once these three effects of racism are
    taken into account, the IQ gap becomes explicable (Fischer
    et al. 1996).

6   Hernstein and Murray argue that environmental factors can-
    not explain IQ differences because studies of identical twins
    reared apart in different environments from an early age
    show that the heritability of IQ is too high. There are two
    problems here. Firstly, estimates of heritability (the propor-
    tion of the variation of a trait that can be attributed to
    genetic variation) differ, with Jensen putting it as high as 80
    per cent but Jencks putting it much lower at 45 per cent.
    Secondly, estimates of heritability are based on tests adminis-
    tered to particular groups and cannot properly be generalised
    to other groups. Thus 'the heritability of height might be
    extremely high in both a poor Third World village and
    a wealthy First World suburb – taller parents would produce
    taller children in both places. The richer population might be
    taller than the poor, but this does not preclude the possibility
    that a better-nourished generation in the South might in the
    future grow as tall as its distant peers in the presently devel-
    oped world. The correlation between the heights of parents
    and children might remain just as strong, but the heights
    themselves might change' (Kohn 1996: 103–4).

7   The only evidence which could convincingly show that
    Black–White differences in IQ were genetic in origin 'would
    be the demonstration of a difference in IQ scores between
    randomly selected groups of black and white children brought
    up in strictly comparable conditions' (Swann 1985: 130).
    Only three studies 'have even attempted to approximate
    these ideal conditions (albeit not very successfully)' and in
    these studies what is striking is that 'such differences have
    been extremely small' (Swann 1985: 130).

8 There is considerable evidence that IQ scores, which heredi-
tarians assume are relatively stable, are in fact rising considerably. Flynn (1987), who has found this phenomenon in over
twenty countries, concludes that 'IQ tests "cannot bridge the
cultural distance that separates one generation from another".
And if the tests cannot bridge the gap between generations,
they may be incapable of bridging other cultural gaps, such as
those between ethnic groups' (Kohn 1996: 105).

In view of these arguments, the Swann report's somewhat
circumspect conclusion 'that IQ is not a significant factor in
underachievement' seems more than justified.

Economic deprivation, culture and the home

Economic and cultural factors at one stage were considered by
sociologists to be critical to an explanation of group differences
in achievement. They are still considered important by many.
Although the 1944 Education Act removed some financial barriers which had previously reduced access to secondary education
for the working class, 'material factors' continued to be responsible for class differences in staying on after compulsory schooling
(Halsey *et al.* 1980). As for the more recent 1988 Education
Reform Act, it has been argued that 'choice and the market provide a way for the middle classes to reassert their reproductive
advantages in education' (Ball 1993). This is partly because of
their more favourable economic situation which allows private
transport, childcare, and so on, to be affordable but also because
of their 'cultural capital' which enables more informed choices of
schools to be made. If we turn to ethnic differences in achievement, again economic and cultural factors are significant. Thus
the underachievement of Bangladeshis is explicable in terms of
both extreme economic deprivation, which exceeds that of other
ethnic groups, and cultural factors – being the most recent immigrant group from South Asia, they are the least familiar with the
English education system and understandably have less facility in
the English language. The same factors – economic deprivation
and lack of fluency in English – go some way also towards explaining the underachievement of Pakistanis (Modood *et al.* 1997).

The Swann report points out that ethnic minorities are 'particularly disadvantaged in social and economic terms'. This is evidenced for example in the higher rate of unemployment of all minority ethnic groups which stems at least in part from racial discrimination. 'This extra deprivation over and above that of disadvantaged Whites leads in many instances to an *extra* element of underachievement' (Swann 1985: 89). The report recognises that underachievement cannot be wholly accounted for in these terms because groups similarly subject to discrimination and disadvantage differ in their levels of achievement. Since the report was published, evidence has mounted, as we have already noted in the previous two chapters, to indicate that, although minority ethnic groups may all be subject to racial discrimination, Indians can no longer be considered to be as a group economically disadvantaged in the same way as Pakistanis, Bangladeshis and Caribbeans are. This goes some way to accounting for the educational achievement of Indian pupils. Nevertheless, the differences in achievement between Caribbeans and Asians overall, many of whom are equally disadvantaged, needs to be explained. And here many, including both the Rampton and Swann reports, have turned somewhat cautiously to a cultural explanation.

Here is the Rampton report:

> A disproportionate number of West Indian women are forced to go out to work because of their economic circumstances . . . The percentage of West Indian men employed on night shift is almost double that of white males and the incidence of one parent families is higher for West Indians than for Whites. West Indian parents may therefore face particular pressures affecting their children in the vital pre-school formative years . . . . While it is now generally accepted that young children need to form a stable and consistent relationship with only a limited number of adults we are faced with a situation where West Indian parents are stretched in ways which make steady, relaxed care of their children hard to achieve . . . . Many West Indian parents may not be aware of the pre-school facilities that are available and may not fully appreciate the contribution that they can make to the progress of their child before he enters school (Rampton 1981, quoted in Cashmore and Troyna 1990: 133).

Here is the Swann report, seeking to grapple with the differences in achievement between Caribbeans and Asians:

Asians, it has been put to us, are given to 'keeping their heads down' and adopting a 'low profile', thereby making it easier to succeed in a hostile environment. West Indians, by contrast, are given to 'protest' and 'a high profile', with the reverse effect. Given the very different histories of the two groups, it is not an improbable explanation . . . It has also been put to us that the explanation lies in the particularly tightly knit structure of the Asian community and the Asian family, more tightly knit than is either the case with whites or West Indians (Swann 1985: 86).

By contrast the 1996 and 2000 OFSTED reports make no reference to cultural factors at all. There are three reasons for this. Firstly, OFSTED's remit is narrower than that of the other two reports, being focused 'on issues that directly influence pupils' achievements, especially where they relate to education policy, schools and matters that teachers might wish to address as part of their work' (Gillborn and Gipps 1996: 7). Secondly, certain cultural factors, which previously had been thought to be important in accounting for Caribbean underachievement, have been found empirically to be insignificant. Milner, for example, who earlier had been very influential in pointing to a negative self-image among West Indian children because of the inability of their culture to insulate them from racism, recognises 'that black children are now quite clear about their racial identity and view it positively' (Milner 1983: 163). What is true of negative self-image is also true of language. The Caribbean dialect known as Creole or patois, once thought to play a role in underachievement, is now generally recognised to be of minimal significance in this regard (A Pilkington 1984). Thirdly, there has been widespread rejection of cultural explanations because they are taken to imply that Caribbean culture is deficient, effectively blame parents for the underachievement of their children and in the process absolve the education system of responsibility.

There clearly is a series of problems in pointing to cultural differences. The boundaries between ethnic groups are fuzzy; there is a great deal of variation within ethnic groups; and there is the danger of overstating differences. Rampton's picture of the West Indian family is also applicable to many White families, for example. The risk of ethnocentrism is high, with other cultures being inappropriately judged by the standards of one's own. Thus Creole or patois was once seen as bad English when it is in fact a dialect of English and linguistically no better or worse than any other dialect. Cultures can be de-contextualised as though they are freely chosen ways of life without acknowledgment being given to their historic roots and their location in a particular social and economic context. It is clearly much more difficult for Caribbean parents to translate their high aspirations for their children into concrete support when they are subject to racial discrimination and economic insecurity. And there is indeed the danger, in pointing to cultural factors, that the mainstream education system is absolved of responsibility, with policies of compensatory education being put forward to counteract perceived cultural deficits.

However, we cannot dismiss cultural explanations by labelling them cultural deficit models. There are cultural differences. Thus 'marriage is markedly less, and divorce and solo parenthood markedly more, prevalent among Afro-Caribbeans than among other ethnic groups' (Elliott 1996: 46). Cultures are not equally effective in the support which they are able to provide children. Both Caribbean and Asian cultures are more effective than that of the White working class in encouraging children to stay on after post-compulsory schooling. And there is little doubt, as Stuart Hall points out and as Swann reiterates, that Asian cultures are more 'cohesive and supportive' than others. In suggesting that Caribbean culture is less conducive to educational success than that of Asians, it is not implied that the parents are to be blamed for the underachievement of their children. Caribbeans historically suffered 'a more severe process of cultural fragmentation' than Asians and since then have found it difficult to fashion 'a cohesive and supportive' culture, especially given the material disadvantage and racism they continue to face (S Hall *et al.* 1978). To recognise that the culture of the home is a significant factor in underachievement does not indicate merely a policy of compensatory education. Measures to improve the social and economic circumstances of Caribbean families and measures to combat racism are crucial. And it is of course incumbent upon the education system to be more active.

Effective and ineffective schools

Sociologists have increasingly moved away from looking at the economic and cultural factors that influence educational achievement and have focused instead on the contribution which schools make. One strand of research – known as school effect-iveness research – seeks to compare schools in terms of their effectiveness in promoting educational progress. Such research recognises that the effectiveness of schools cannot be judged purely by the educational achievements of pupils because these are influenced by the prior achievements of pupils and back-ground factors such as social class. A statistical technique has been devised known as multi-level modelling which seeks to control for extra-school factors such as prior attainment and intake to measure the contribution of schools themselves to edu-cational progress. The intention is to reach a judgement as to which schools are more effective on average than others in pro-moting progress and whether schools are more effective with one category of pupils rather than another. Two studies have paid particular attention to ethnicity.

Smith and Tomlinson conducted a study between 1981 and 1986 on 3000 pupils in 18 urban multi-ethnic comprehensives from four LEAs, including different parts of the country – London, the Midlands and the North. Although White pupils on average scored better in the final examinations, followed by Asians and then Caribbeans, the ethnic minorities in fact made better progress. By controlling for the prior attainment and intake of the pupils, Smith and Tomlinson were able to demon-strate significant differences between schools in their average effectiveness. Although some evidence of differential effectiveness was noted, much more significant in their view was the overall effectiveness of schools. Some schools in other words were much better than others in producing good exam results with children from similar backgrounds and with similar previous attainments. Indeed they concluded that 'the differences in exam results attributable to ethnic groups are very much smaller than those attributable to the school level. In other words, what school a child goes to makes far more difference than which ethnic group he or she belongs to' (Smith and Tomlinson 1989: 281). This is an important study. For 'the average differences in school effects reported could be sufficiently large to account for the reported differences in the average exam performances of ethnic minority and white pupils' (Drew 1995: 30). We would need, however, further evidence, which Smith and Tomlinson do not provide, that ethnic minority pupils do disproportionately go to less effective schools. Although Smith and Tomlinson's findings are very suggestive, the schools examined were not nationally representative, with the researchers having deliberately made efforts to include both schools which were 'thought to be successful and others less so' (Smith and Tomlinson 1989: 32). It is noticeable that 'the expectations of what all the pupils in these urban schools could achieve was low' (Tomlinson 1990b: 346), so that it is questionable how effective even the effective schools are in the areas where ethnic minorities tend to receive their education.

The other study of note is that of Nuttall *et al.* (1989) which was much more extensive covering 30,000 pupils in 140 Inner London Education Authority (ILEA) secondary schools. They found that the progress of ethnic minority pupils was generally as good as, if not better than, White pupils. The one exception comprised Caribbean pupils, who made slightly less progress. They also discovered that some schools were on average more effective than others, but in addition noted differential effectiveness in relation to Caribbean and Pakistani pupils. Although this study is also suggestive in pointing to differences between schools, there are problems. Unlike Smith and Tomlinson's study, class is not controlled for and doubts have been expressed about the validity of the prior attainment scores which were partially based on teacher assessments.

School effectiveness research is still at an early stage. There is evidence that schools differ in their effectiveness. On the other hand it is questionable how useful the concept of overall effectiveness is. For there is also evidence 'that the variation between departmental effectiveness is often greater than the differences between schools' overall levels of effectiveness' (Gillborn and Gipps 1996: 42). In addition there is the question of differential effectiveness, with Nuttall *et al.*'s study indicating that not all pupils benefit equally from attending apparently 'effective' schools. The research shows that schools do make a difference but as yet we cannot tell how much and for whom.

Racism and multi-ethnic classrooms

A second strand of research on schools is not concerned so much with differences between schools as the features that schools share. In the view of some writers, schools are suffused with ethnocentric values. The curriculum reflects the outlook of one culture and as such is biased against children from minority ethnic groups, who find that their own cultures are either ignored or belittled.

In the view of some commentators, the bias against Caribbeans is particularly severe and takes a racist form. An early piece of research which involved 510 teachers from 25 schools around the country revealed 'a high degree of consensus of opinion concerning the academic and social behaviour' of Caribbean pupils, with more than two-thirds of teachers agreeing in effect that such pupils are less able and give rise to more disciplinary problems. Since the teachers exhibited a much greater willingness to accept unfavourable generalisations about pupils of Caribbean origin than those of Asian or European origin, it does indeed seem 'that there is large scale stereotyping of West Indian pupils' (Brittan 1976, quoted in A Pilkington 1984: 139). Although we do not have recent evidence from questionnaires on teachers' attitudes towards ethnic minority pupils, a series of qualitative studies in schools indicate that 'African Caribbean and Asian pupils can be subject to different expectations' (Gillborn and Gipps 1996: 54). One study of a boys' comprehensive in the early 1980s noted, 'There was a tendency for Asian male students to be seen by the teachers as technically of "high ability" and socially as conformist. Afro-Caribbean male students tended to be seen as having "low ability" and potential discipline problems' (Mac an Ghaill 1988: 64).

To acknowledge that some teachers hold stereotypical views does not necessarily mean that they treat pupils differently in practice. If we wish to explore this question we need to study multi-ethnic classrooms. The first study to gain widespread recognition – and referred to in the Swann report – studied 70 White teachers in primary and middle school classrooms. Using a modified version of the Flanders schedule to measure pupil–teacher talk, Green discovered that Caribbean boys were much more likely to be criticised than other pupils and that, in the case of ethnocentric teachers, Caribbean girls were also much more likely to be criticised. He concluded that 'boys and girls of different ethnic origins taught in the same multi-ethnic classroom by the same teacher are likely to receive widely different educational experiences' (Swann 1985: 53). Green's work does not, however, explore the processes which underlie teacher–pupil relationships. To do this we need to turn to ethnographic studies. We shall focus below on five in particular.

Wright conducted an ethnographic study of two multi-ethnic comprehensive schools between 1982 and 1984, focusing on the fourth and fifth years. She found the teachers to be critical of rather than encouraging towards Caribbean pupils. The result was that 'the classroom encounters observed for both schools showed the interaction between the teacher and the individual Afro-Caribbean student to be frequently characterised by confrontation and conflict' (Wright 1987: 110). 'Behavioural criteria rather than cognitive ones' influenced the teachers' assessment of Caribbean pupils with the result that they 'were likely to be placed in ability bands and examination sets well below their actual academic ability' as measured in one school by their performance in the third year examination (Wright 1987: 123). The response of Caribbean pupils to the labelling process was to resist, in the process confirming their teachers' expectations and entering into a self-fulfilling prophecy which in some cases resulted in suspension or expulsion.

Gillborn studied a coeducational 11–16 comprehensive in the mid-1980s. Despite the fact that the teachers seemed much more committed to the goal of equality of opportunity than those studied by Wright, they believed 'that Afro-Caribbean pupils represented a greater challenge to their authority than any other group in the school' (Gillborn 1990: 25). Believing 'the myth of an Afro-Caribbean challenge' they sought to nip it in the bud. The result was that 'Afro-Caribbean pupils experienced a disproportionate amount of punishment, and that they were sometimes exclusively criticised even when peers of other ethnic groups shared in the offence' (Gillborn 1990: 43). A high level of tension and indeed conflict was evident between White teachers and Caribbean pupils, who responded to their differential treatment in some cases by resistance, in other cases by accommodation.

Mac an Ghaill studied a boys' comprehensive and a sixth form college in the early 1980s. Again conflict was evident between White teachers and Black pupils. The boys' comprehensive was rigidly streamed, with behavioural criteria rather than cognitive ones again disadvantaging Caribbean pupils. One teacher justified this approach in the following terms:

> There are boys of relatively higher ability in the lower sets, especially among the West Indians. I've told you before Johnson and Brian were marvellous at Maths, especially problem-solving. But it's their, it's the West Indians' attitude and that must decide it in the end. You can't promote a boy who is known to be a troublemaker who's a dodger. It will look like a reward for bad behaviour (Mac an Ghaill 1988: 81–2).

The response of Caribbeans often took the form of resistance, with the formation of a distinct subculture, the Rasta Heads. Some Asians also resisted, but their subculture – the Warriors – adopted a lower profile. The response of the Caribbean and Asian students at the sixth form college was different again. The Black Sisters adopted a policy of 'resistance within accommodation', being, like other young Black women studied in two comprehensive schools in London (Mirza 1992), anti-school but pro-education.

Wright studied four inner-city primary schools in 1988–89. Here 'classroom observation indicated that teachers tended to treat Afro-Caribbean children (especially boys) in a more restrictive way than other pupil groups. For instance issuing orders rather than encouraging them to express their ideas. Asian children, on the other hand, received less individual attention; in other words they tended to be overlooked or underestimated by teachers' (Wright 1992: 27). What is of particular concern 'in addition to the frequency of critical and controlling statements which Afro-Caribbean pupils received was the observation that they were likely to be singled out for criticism even though several pupils of different groups were engaged in the same act of behaviour' (Wright 1992: 39). The following extract from a nursery group of four-year-olds illustrates this:

TEACHER:	Let's do one song before home time.
PETER	(*White boy*): Humpty Dumpty.
TEACHER:	No, I'm choosing today. Let's do something we have not done for a while. I know, we'll do the Autumn song. What about the autumn song we sing. Don't shout out, put your hand up nicely.

MANDY	(*shouting out*) Two little leaves on a tree.
TEACHER:	She's nearly right.
MARCUS:	(*Afro-Caribbean boy with his hand up*) I know.
TEACHER:	(*talking to the group*) Is she right when she says 'two little leaves on a tree'?
WHOLE GROUP:	No.
TEACHER:	What is it, Peter?
PETER:	Four.
TEACHER:	Nearly right.
MARCUS:	(*waving his hand for attention*). Five.
TEACHER:	Don't shout out, Marcus. Do you know, Susan (*White girl*)?
SUSAN:	Five.
TEACHER:	(*holding up one hand*) Good…because we have got how many fingers on this hand?
WHOLE GROUP:	Five.
TEACHER:	OK, let's only have one hand because we've only got five leaves. How many would we have if we had too many? Don't shout out, hands up.
MANDY:	(*shouting out*) One, two, three, four, five, six, seven, eight, nine, ten.
TEACHER:	Good, OK how many fingers have we got?
MARCUS:	Five.
TEACHER:	Don't shout out, Marcus, put your hand up. Deane, how many?
DEANE:	Five.
TEACHER:	That's right, we're going to use five today, what makes them dance about, these leaves?
PETER:	(*shouting out*) The wind.
TEACHER:	That's right. Ready here we go.

Teacher and children sing: 'Five little leaves so bright and gay, dancing about on a tree one day. The wind came blowing through the town, whoooo, whoooo, one little leaf came tumbling down'.

TEACHER:	How many have we got left?
DEANE:	(*shouting out*) One.
MARCUS:	(*raising his hand enthusiastically*). Four.
TEACHER:	(*to Marcus*) Shush. Let's count, one, two, three, four.
TEACHER:	How many, Deane?

DEANE:	Four.
TEACHER:	Good, right, let's do the next bit.

(*Teacher and children sing the next two verses*)

TEACHER:	How many have we got left, Peter?
PETER:	I don't know.
MANDY:	Two.
TEACHER:	I know that you know, Mandy.
MARCUS:	Two.
TEACHER:	(*stern voice*) I'm not asking you, I'm asking Peter, don't shout out. We'll help Peter, shall we? Look at my fingers, how many? One, two. How many, Peter?
PETER:	Two.
TEACHER:	Very good. Let's do the next bit.

(*Teacher and children sing the next verse; at the end of the verse:*)

SUSAN:	One.
TEACHER:	Good, let's all count, one. Let's do the last bit.

(*Teacher and children sing the last verse; at the end of the verse:*)

TEACHER:	How many have we got left?
ALL CHILDREN:	None.
TEACHER:	That's right there are no leaves left. Marcus, will you stop fidgeting and sit nicely?

The final study to be explored was one conducted between 1985 and 1987 in a multi-ethnic comprehensive. Unlike the other studies, the author 'found no evidence of differential treatment of students on ethnic or racial lines either in classrooms or in wider school processes' (Foster 1990: 179). Minority students, especially Caribbean girls, in fact achieved better results than White pupils, albeit in a school where the standards expected were low. The school differed from the others studied in being located in a community with a long history of cooperation between different ethnic groups. It was generously staffed and the staff had a high level of awareness of race, being engaged in the implementation of an anti-racist programme.

Although Foster recognised that the distinct features of the school he studied may have resulted in him reaching different conclusions than the other ethnographic studies, he has, together with Gomm and Hammersley, since attacked the credibility of these studies. A series of articles have culminated in a book attacking ethnographic and other studies which purport to show that school processes contribute to educational inequality. Their conclusions are worth quoting. On studies claiming to show that schools are discriminatory in their allocation of students to different levels of course, they conclude: 'Taken overall this body of research fails to establish that discrimination against working class and black students occurs on any scale in the allocation of students to courses or through the effects of this allocation' (Foster *et al.* 1996: 105). On studies claiming to show discriminatory treatment in the classroom they conclude:

> There are also some serious problems with the evidential base on which descriptive claims about differential treatment rely. Sometimes no evidence at all is presented.... And when evidence is provided it is often of a kind which cannot effectively support the sort of claim made: for instance one or two examples are offered to establish the different frequency of particular sorts of teacher action in relation to different categories of student. Moreover many of the interpretations made of data are questionable (Foster *et al.* 1996: 138).

Given such scepticism towards evidence which points to inequalities at school level and in the classroom, their overall conclusion comes as no surprise: 'There is no convincing evidence currently available for any substantial role on the part of schools in generating inequalities in educational outcomes between social classes, genders or ethnic groups' (Foster *et al.* 1996: 174).

How satisfactory is this critique when applied to ethnicity, where the central concern has been with the attainment of Caribbean pupils? We shall begin by examining the evidence on discrimination in allocation to different levels of course.

Here there is considerable evidence that Caribbean pupils are under-represented in top sets and over-represented in bottom sets. Even the 1992/3 report of HM Chief Inspector of Schools acknowledged that they, along with other minority ethnic pupils, were in general 'under represented in the top ability sets' (Tomlinson and Craft 1995: 6). There is also evidence that placement is often not based on ability alone and that this disadvantages Caribbean pupils. We have already pointed to the evidence from Wright and Mac an Ghaill, which indicates that behavioural criteria and not purely cognitive ones were used in the allocation of pupils to examination sets and streams and that this practice disadvantaged Caribbean pupils in particular. And there is other evidence pointing in the same direction. For example, a study of one local education authority shows that

> when there was a mismatch between the VR [verbal reasoning] band in which a pupil had been placed by teachers and that based on test performance, Caribbean pupils were more likely to be placed in the lower VR band . . . while ESWI [English, Scottish, Welsh and Irish] pupils were more likely to be placed in a higher VR band than their test scores would suggest (Kysel 1988: 88).

Foster indeed noted that behaviour rather than ability influenced allocation in his own ethnographic study. As he puts it:

> the behaviour of older Afro/Caribbean boys tended to be regarded less favourably. In a sense their youth cultural norms conformed less closely to the teachers' conceptions of the 'ideal' and as a result they seemed somewhat more likely to be allocated to lower status groups in the school's system of differentiation (Foster 1990: 81).

And in a revealing footnote to their damning critique of evidence of discrimination, Foster *et al.* also recognise themselves that 'it may be of significance that the departures from what would be expected on the basis of measured ability that have been found within and across studies, while small, tend to be always in the same direction. This indicates that more thorough investigation is justified' (Foster *et al.* 1996: 81). This also, it should be pointed out, indicates that indirect discrimination is probably occurring since allocation on behavioural criteria has been shown to result, however unintentionally, in disadvantaging Caribbean pupils.

As for the consequences of streaming, Wright, Gillborn and Mac an Ghaill do point to a tendency for the attitudes of different streams to polarise, with those in the bottom streams tending to engage in resistance, and at some points in their book Foster *et al.* also acknowledge 'the operation of a differentiation–polarisation effect' (Foster *et al.* 1996: 103).

Let us move on to look at the evidence on inequalities in the classroom. Foster *et al.*'s critique is valuable in alerting us to some potential pitfalls of ethnographic studies. Although they can provide a rich understanding of classroom processes, there is the danger of selective perception, with one's observations being interpreted through the prism of a pre-existing theory. Other interpretations are always possible. Take the extract above about Marcus. We are led to assume that Marcus is particularly subject to censure because he is Caribbean. Could there not be other reasons? Are other Caribbean pupils also particularly subject to censure? In this particular study, Wright does in fact provide evidence to suggest that White teachers in general discriminated against Caribbean boys in general (Woods 1992). And this is crucial. For it is only by using different sources of evidence which corroborate each other that ethnographic studies are convincing. The ethnographic studies we have looked at are of variable quality in this respect, but all use a variety of methods to triangulate their findings. All also point to a relatively high level of conflict between White teachers and Caribbean pupils. Where Foster differs from the others is in seeing teachers responding appropriately to the behaviour of Caribbean pupils and playing no real part in generating conflict (Foster 1992).

Foster (1993a) argues that teacher typifications are based on observations of students' behaviour and academic ability in the classroom. He may be substantially correct. However, observations are not innocent and may be influenced by prior typifications. Here is a student on teaching practice in a boys' comprehensive learning the ropes from school management:

> I was told that I had to look out for the West Indians and what to do. If they went mad, one just had to leave them alone to cool down. There was nothing we could do, and things like that if they swore at us in their own language we must report it. They had trouble from them in the past.

The student was subsequently appointed to the school. Here he is, a year later:

> The West Indians are tough. I tried not to let anyone influence me in how I treated them but they look at you with wild eyes if you tell them to sit down. They are looking, expecting trouble. They are more prejudiced than white people. The Asians are better, you tell them to do something an' then meek an'[mild] they go an' do it (Mac on Ghaill 1988: 64–5).

In addition to evidence that old hands may influence teacher typifications, there is also evidence from the studies by Gillborn and Wright and, more recently from OFSTED (Smithers 2001) that the same behaviour may be treated differently by teachers. This is particularly disturbing if it results in Caribbeans being particularly subject to censure early in their school career, as in the case of Marcus. For Smith and Tomlinson (1989) indicate that students who are subject to constant criticism tend to underachieve.

To point to evidence which suggests that Caribbean pupils are subject sometimes to differential treatment in the classroom does not mean, however, that Foster's ethnographic study and Foster *et al.*'s subsequent critique of research in this area should be summarily dismissed. There is substantial agreement that, at least in the latter stages of schooling, the behaviour of some Caribbean pupils is not only defined by teachers as deviant but in fact is deviant. Where Foster and his critics fundamentally disagree is over their explanation of 'bad behaviour'. For Foster, primacy is given to extra-school factors. 'There may be a general tendency for Afro-Caribbean students on average to be less well behaved in schools' (Foster 1991: 168) because of their adoption of a distinctive subculture consequent on a recognition on their part of poor post-school prospects and rejection of racism in the wider society. For the others, primacy is given to school processes, with some Caribbean pupils pictured as turning towards a distinctive subculture in order to resist their differential treatment in schools. The debate between Foster and his critics is reminiscent of the debate over the criminalisation of Black people. For some writers, the greater involvement of Caribbean young men in street crime is primarily responsible for their greater criminalisation; for others, racism in the criminal justice system is primarily responsible for their greater criminalisation. More recently, however, there have been attempts by some criminologists 'to move beyond the either/or of racist criminal justice v black criminality' (P Taylor *et al.* 1995: 486) to recognise that both 'reinforce and feed off one another in a vicious circle of amplification' (Reiner 1993: 14). By analogy, we might suggest that in schools both differential treatment and 'bad behaviour' may result in the development of a vicious cycle.

This suggestion has been taken up by some recent ethnographic studies which seek to show how societal definitions of both ethnicity and gender impact upon the schooling experiences of Black pupils and create a vicious cycle. Connolly provides one example from his study of a multi-ethnic primary school. Here

> the over disciplining of Black boys tends to construct an image of them among their peers, as being 'bad' and quintessentially masculine. This, in turn, provides the context where Black boys are more likely to be drawn into fights and to develop 'hardened' identities, which then means they are more likely to be noticed by teachers and disciplined for being aggressive. The cycle is thus complete (Connolly 1998a: 114).

While Connolly attributes primary responsibility for the generation of this cycle to teachers, Sewell, in a study of a boys' secondary school, challenges the notion 'that teacher racism alone' leads Caribbean boys 'to adopt a culture of resistance to schooling' (Sewell 1997: 170). While he acknowledges that teachers tend to accept what Gillborn (1990) labels 'the myth of an African Caribbean challenge' and see boys in particular as threatening their authority, he also emphasises the role of the black pupils' subculture which 'helps to feed the stereotype that African-Caribbean boys are more openly aggressive/rude than their "weak" white counterparts' (Sewell 1997: 104).

Both the teachers and pupils are envisaged as influenced by cultural representations of Black males acquired outside the classroom. The teachers tended to share the ethnocentric assumptions of the wider society and assume 'that African-Caribbean boys were instinctively against authority while Asian boys were the complete opposite' (Sewell 1997: 61). The result was that Caribbean boys received a disproportionate amount of control and criticism compared to other ethnic groups. At the same time the Black subculture in the school drew on a wider street culture and placed emphasis 'on a Black collectivist anti-school ideology, on pro-consumerism and phallocentrism' (Sewell 1997: 108). While this subculture enabled the boys to resist the racism of the wider society and maintain a positive Black identity, its adoption of a macho form of masculinity was not conducive to academic success. The equation, for some boys, of academic achievement with being gay or effeminate was evident here and constituted a significant barrier to those pupils seeking educational qualifications.

The focus of conflict between teachers and Black pupils often revolved around displays of ethnicity from the boys. Black hairstyles were a particular bone of contention. The school sought to ban Black boys from having patterns in their hair while no such prohibition was made in relation to White boys who wore ponytails. The result was that Black hairstyles became 'a key factor in the display of an African-Caribbean masculine subculture that became an alternative to schooling' (Sewell 1997: 166). In this way a vicious cycle can develop, in which what is perceived as a lack of respect from teachers is met by an aggressive response from pupils who in turn are punished for their behaviour.

Such a cycle can, as in this school, have devastating consequences resulting in 'black young people [being] proportionately more likely to be excluded than members of other ethnic groups' (Gillborn and Gipps 1996: 52). Permanent exclusions are the most extreme sanction schools have. The sanction is now not only being more widely used for disobedience of various kinds but is being used disproportionately with Black pupils, especially Caribbeans. Figure 2 summarises the evidence gathered during OFSTED inspections in 1993/4.

To acknowledge that the evidence for indirect discrimination at the level of the school and to acknowledge that the evidence for differential treatment at the level of the classroom are stronger than Foster *et al.* suggest does not mean that it is schools that are most central 'in generating inequalities in education outcomes between…ethnic groups' (Foster *et al.* 1996: 174). Foster *et al.* are correct in reminding us that we cannot generalise from particular schools and particular classrooms to all schools and all classrooms. Indeed it is questionable whether the rationale for ethnographic research is to generate generalisations at all (Connolly 1998b). And even if there are common school processes – as suggested by the similar picture conveyed by most ethnographic studies – we cannot reach an informed judgement about the 'causal efficacy' of school processes in the absence of a comparison with the contribution of extra-school factors. The research on school effectiveness, which does seek to control for factors such as prior attainment and social class, suggests that variations between schools do make a difference but that extra-school factors are generally much more significant in

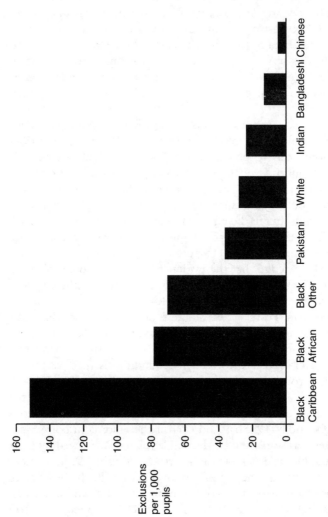

Source: Gillborn and Gipps (1996).

Figure 2 Exclusions from secondary school by ethnic origin, England (1993/4)

determining student progress (Drew and Demack 1998). Although this research is concerned with differences between schools rather than purportedly common discriminatory practices within schools and thus cannot be used to refute the suggestion that racism in schools is of critical importance in accounting for ethnic differences in achievement, it does suggest that we should be extremely circumspect before reaching a definitive judgement.

The need for caution is reinforced when we remember the complexity in patterns of ethnic educational achievement, which indicates that, while some minority ethnic groups are doing better than Whites, Caribbean boys are underachieving and that both Pakistani and Bangladeshi pupils are performing no better (Modood *et al.* 1997). The role of racism in accounting for this complex pattern is unclear. Are all minority ethnic groups subject to discriminatory treatment? If so, how do some groups and indeed some individuals successfully resist such treatment? Evidence of racism in schools may be stronger than Foster *et al.* suggest, but this does not mean that such racism is the major factor in accounting for ethnic differentials in educational achievement.

The debate, which we have been examining, about the contribution which school processes play in accounting for Caribbean underachievement is part of a wider debate about the purposes of educational research. Foster *et al.* adopt a 'methodological purist' stance, stressing that 'the purpose of research in this area should be to produce knowledge relevant to public debates, not to eradicate inequality' (Foster *et al.* 1996: 40). By contrast, Troyna and others adopt a partisan, or what Gillborn (1998) prefers to call a 'critical' position, seeing the purpose of research as that of documenting what is going on in order to challenge injustices (Troyna 1995). The methodological purists contend that researchers who adopt an avowedly anti-racist position too readily accept evidence pointing to indirect discrimination and differential treatment. The latter retort that at least they are explicit about their value commitments, whereas the methodological purists, by imposing extremely stringent criteria to evaluate studies pointing to indirect discrimination and differential treatment, are implicitly concerned to defend teachers.

Despite disagreement between those who adopt a methodological purist and a partisan stance, both in fact are opposed to 'falsifying data and suppressing "unhelpful" findings' (Gillborn 1998: 51) and both recognise the need for 'assessment of factual claims in terms of logical consistency and empirical adequacy' (Foster *et al*. 1996: 40). Where methodological purists and partisan researchers disagree is over whether the research on school processes meets these criteria. The former adopt extremely stringent criteria, argue that existing studies do not convince them 'beyond reasonable doubt' and on that basis conclude that 'it seems unfair and unwise to criticise current practices' (Foster 1993b: 551). By contrast, the latter show that it is always possible to challenge researchers' interpretations, argue that their ethnographic studies present convincing interpretations and on that basis conclude that it is incumbent on schools to re-examine their current practices. The political implications of the positions adopted by the two sides are clear. The first leans to a conservative privileging of current practices; the latter leads to a radical challenging of current practices. Somewhat ironically, given the explicit adherence of methodological purists to a scientific methodology, it is the partisan researchers who remain closer to a Popperian philosophy of social science. For at least they do put forward a theory to account for Caribbean underachievement. By contrast, the methodological purists content themselves with critiques 'mostly constructed in negative terms' (Gillborn 1995: 56) and do not at least in their joint book put forward any theory at all.

Towards a multifactorial explanation of educational inequality

When we explore divergent explanations for ethnic differentials in educational attainment (the primary focus of which here has been that of the underachievement of Caribbean children) we enter a politically highly charged terrain. Although sociologists are now less inclined to fall into the trap of the 'fallacy of the single factor' (Parekh 1983) and frequently acknowledge that a range of factors operating in a complex way are needed to explain Caribbean underachievement, there is still a tendency to prioritise some factors to the exclusion of others. In particular we have noted the inclination of some to dismiss cultural factors and of others to reject the role of school processes. Steering a path through these tortuous rapids, we can conclude that IQ is not a major factor but that there is evidence to suggest that a range of social factors are significant: economic deprivation, which itself stems at least in part from racial discrimination; cultural factors, which need to be carefully contextualised to avoid 'blaming the victim'; ineffective schools, which themselves are often located in disadvantaged areas; and (the often unintentional) racial discrimination in schools.

Ethnicity and educational policy

Central government policy on ethnicity and education has never been underpinned by a clearly formulated coherent philosophy. Nor has it generally involved specific policies aimed at ethnic minorities. For some, this is to be welcomed, with one writer considering that the 'racially inexplicit' policy characteristic of the UK in contrast to the 'racially explicit' policy characteristic of the United States was 'doing good by stealth' (Kirp 1979: 51). For others, the lack of explicit reference to 'race' and ethnicity in policy formulation constitutes spurious 'deracialisation', signalling a failure to tackle the central issue of racism (Troyna and Williams 1986). Despite differing evaluations of government policy, there is widespread agreement that the state has not attempted to take a lead in the area of ethnicity and education but has responded in an *ad hoc* manner. It is true that 'an enduring commitment to assimilation' (Grosvenor 1997: 50) has been evident throughout the post-war period, but this does not mean that we cannot distinguish different policy phases. Indeed it is not uncommon to identify three such phases – 'assimilation, integration and cultural pluralism' (Troyna and Carrington 1990: 20). What we must remember, however, is that these phases overlap each other; that they cannot easily be periodised; and that their influence on educational practice has been variable.

The initial response of the education system was presaged on the need for the 'successful assimilation of immigrant children' (DES 1965, quoted in Willey 1984). The major obstacle to achieving this was seen as the children's lack of proficiency in the English language. 'The emphasis was therefore on the teaching of English as a second language to immigrant children, often in specialist language or reception centres which also provided some basic pastoral support to counter "culture shock"' (Swann 1985: 192). Once this obstacle had been overcome, it was assumed that immigrant pupils would be absorbed within the overall school population. By 1965, however, the central government was concerned that 'as the proportion of immigrant children increases, the problems will become more difficult to solve, and the chances of assimilation more remote' (DES 1965, quoted in Willey 1984: 22). The response was to recommend to LEAs that they disperse immigrant pupils 'between different schools in an attempt to "spread the problem" and avoid any school becoming predominantly immigrant in character' (Swann 1985: 192). Such a recommendation was clearly designed to placate White parents and in the process identified immigrant pupils as the problem. A sentence italicised in the 1965 DES circular is revealing in this context:

> It will be helpful if the parents of non-immigrant children can see that practical measures have been taken to deal with the problems in the schools, and that the progress of their own children is not being restricted by the undue preoccupation of the teaching staff with the linguistic and other difficulties of immigrant children (DES 1965, quoted in Willey 1984: 22).

In order to implement the dispersal policy and discover the extent of language need, statistics were collected on 'immigrant children'. The latter were defined as both those who were themselves immigrant and those born in Britain to immigrant parents who had been in this country less than ten years. To enable local authorities to make special provision for immigrant children, the government provided under Section 11 of the 1966 Local Government Act some financial support. The definition of 'immigrant children' adopted by the government implied that the problems caused by increasing numbers of minority ethnic children in schools were temporary and would disappear after they had spent ten years in Britain.

The assimilationist phase lasted until the late 1960s. It clearly rested on a number of highly problematic assumptions: that minimal changes were needed to the education system; that the presence of immigrant pupils caused problems; that the problems faced by immigrant pupils stemmed primarily from lack of proficiency in English; and that assimilation, which placed the onus on ethnic minorities to change, was both achievable and desirable. Some of these assumptions began to be increasingly challenged during the 1960s. To many educationalists, the assumption that the 'problem' of ethnicity and education would evaporate once children had lived in Britain for ten years seemed overly optimistic. In particular, it was argued, attention should be paid to the cultural backgrounds of minority pupils and some recognition given to cultural diversity in schools.

The integrationist phase was born. Although this phase shared with the previous phase 'the common aim of absorbing ethnic minority communities within society with as little disruption to the life of the majority community as possible' (Swann 1985: 197), it did at least recognise that the needs of minority ethnic pupils could not simply be met by limited remedial provision. Two responses were particularly evident. The first involved some acknowledgement that ethnic minorities have special needs while the second stressed that other groups have similar needs. Multicultural education (MCE) exemplified the first, and the conceptualisation of the educational needs of minority ethnic pupils as part of a broader problem of inner city disadvantage, which has remained the central thrust of urban policy, the second. In the absence of any central lead, multicultural initiatives varied widely between LEAs and schools. In practice, MCE was rarely evident in all-White areas and even in multi-ethnic communities did not entail a reappraisal of the curriculum. Rather it was tacked on and 'preoccupied with exotic aspects of cultural differences' (Sarup 1991: 31), the concern often being to portray 'positive images' in order to compensate for an assumed cultural deficit. In a similar way, subsuming the needs of ethnic minorities within a wider category of the disadvantaged effectively identified them as a problem.

During the 1970s, recognition that integrationism constituted an inadequate response to the issue of ethnicity and education gradually filtered through, with the Select Committee on Race Relations and Immigration eventually recommending setting up an official 'inquiry into the causes of the underachievement of children of West Indian origin' (Swann 1985: 216). The creation in 1989 of an inquiry with the broader remit to report on the education of children from minority ethnic groups signalled the, albeit temporary, demise of integrationism.

Cultural pluralism emerged and with it a somewhat different vision. For a pluralist society is one 'which enables, expects and encourages members of all ethnic groups, both minority and majority, to participate fully in shaping the society as a whole within a framework of commonly accepted values, practices and procedures, whilst also allowing and, where necessary, assisting the ethnic minority communities in maintaining their distinct ethnic identities within this common framework' (Swann 1985: 5). Although there is still an assimilationist thrust evident and therefore some continuity with the two previous phases, more significant is the change of emphasis. The interim report (Rampton 1981) comprised the first official recognition of the significance of racism inside schools, while the final report (Swann 1985) advocated a form of multicultural education which incorporated an anti-racist element and was aimed at all pupils. At the same time some left-wing local authorities, woken from their slumbers by inner city disturbances, began to take the issue of racism seriously. Sceptical of the likelihood of the central government tackling racism, they pursued a number of anti-racist initiatives as part of a wider equal opportunities strategy (Solomos 1993). 'This culminated in the 1980s with the adoption of anti-racist or multicultural policies and practices in over three-quarters of British LEAs' (Grosvenor 1997: 92). Such initiatives were highly controversial, but along with the official reports helped to 'racialise' the issue of ethnicity and education in the sense that racism became an explicit object of public debate and policy formulation. Nor was the central government wholly inactive. Although reluctant to address the issue of racism, it did support a number of initiatives which signalled its belief in the importance of education for an ethnically diverse society. The upshot of all this was that the 1980s witnessed 'a growing awareness of the political, social and economic reasons for developing an education system relevant to an ethnically diverse society' (Tomlinson and Craft 1995: 3).

Unfortunately, internecine warfare ensued between advocates of multicultural and anti-racist education. For the former, 'the key issue facing schools is how to create tolerance for black minorities and their cultures in a white nation now characterised by cultural diversity.... The basic educational prescription is the sympathetic teaching of "other cultures" in order to dispel the ignorance which is seen to be at the root of prejudice and intolerance' (Rattansi 1992: 24–5). For the latter, the key issue is racism, which is not characterised merely as prejudice but instead is seen as embedded in structures and institutions. Combating racism 'requires a dismantling of institutionalised *practices* of racism...as well as a direct confrontation with racist ideologies, for example, in the school curriculum' (Rattansi 1992: 29). It is of course questionable how significant the 'bitter arguments between anti-racism and multiculturalism' were for teachers, but before the ink was dry on the Swann report's attempt 'to move beyond the multicultural/anti-racist impasse' (Gillborn 1990: 158), the whole enterprise was savaged by more powerful voices.

The New Right attacked what it saw as the politicisation of education, effectively identifying the central problem as anti-racism rather than racism. Much of the media joined in the attack, lampooning loony lefties for diluting and thereby undermining national culture. Often this involved significant misrepresentation. This was most marked in coverage of the Burnage inquiry (MacDonald 1989). The latter, which had been set up to investigate the background to the murder of an Asian student by a White peer, criticised the particular form of anti-racist education practised at Burnage. Although it was adamant about the reality of racism and the need for a more sensitive and subtle form of anti-racism, 'the national press tended to represent the report as "proof" that antiracism is a damaging extremist political creed' (Gillborn 1995: 81). In this context, it is not altogether surprising that a mere three and a half years after the Swann report, it was represented by a Minister of State at the DES as stemming from a different era:

In essence the Government has taken on board Swann's recommendation, but it feels that the way in which one deals with the whole of this problem is perhaps changing with time and one perhaps cannot go back to something which was thought through...and presented in a time and in an era which is very different from today (Angela Rumbold, quoted in Blair and Woods 1992: 36).

A new era had arrived!

The 1988 Education Reform Act (ERA) involved three major changes.

> The first of these was the introduction of a national curriculum for all state schools alongside a national system of assessment for pupils from 5–16 years.... The second major change concerned the introduction of a system of school management known as the Local Management of Schools.... The third major change involved the creation of a new tier of schooling comprising City Technology Colleges...and Grant-Maintained Schools (Chitty 1993: 15).

These changes deliberately eroded the power of local education authorities and embodied instead a concern for schooling to be both subject to market forces and under central control. League tables were introduced to expedite choice and a new inspection regime set up to maintain standards. The Act reflected two somewhat contrary principles. Moves to open up competition between schools indicated adherence to a neo-liberal market philosophy, while the introduction of a National Curriculum pointed to the espousal of conservative values centred on the preservation of a distinct national culture.

In many ways the 1988 Act and its successor, the 1993 Act represented something of a paradigm shift in the discourse surrounding educational policy. The concern with equality of opportunity, which had characterised much educational debate in the post-war period, was replaced by a concern with – to quote one Secretary of State for Education – 'choice, diversity and, above all, standards' (John Patten, quoted in Gillborn 1995: 32). Such a context has not been conducive to 'education towards racial equality' (Klein 1993).

Pessimism has been engendered by much of this legislation and the way it has been implemented. Take, for example, the introduction of the National Curriculum and the rationale given for it by the chief executive of the School Curriculum and Assessment Authority:

> A fundamental purpose of the school curriculum is to transmit an appreciation of and commitment to the best of the culture we have inherited.... That is why our statutory curriculum emphasises the centrality of British history, Britain's changing relations with the rest of the world, the English literary heritage and the study of Christianity, and why (some argue) it ought to follow the example of our European neighbours in

emphasising more than it currently does the roots of our civilisation in Greece and Rome' (Nicholas Tate, quoted in *Runnymede Bulletin*, no.292, 1996).

While Tate acknowledged the need for pupils to learn about 'other cultures', he emphasised that this was 'subsidiary'. Integrationism rather than cultural pluralism was back on the agenda. 'There [was], of course, the "multicultural dimension" in the National Curriculum. NCC [National Curriculum Council] non-statutory guidance [1991] assert[ed] that "multicultural education is the professional responsibility of all teachers in all schools". It sings Swann's song.... But inequality and injustice do not rate a mention. And no attempt has been made to link even the most anodyne of multicultural initiatives to assessed performance indicators of either pupils or schools' (Klein 1993: 195–6). Although in short MCE still had some official support, in practice it was seen as of peripheral significance.

Other changes were also greeted with dismay. Wider parental choice, it was argued, leads 'to an increased likelihood of racial and religious segregation in schools' (Tomlinson 1990a: 170), while the erosion of the power of LEAs means that 'the struggle for the promotion and infusion of anti-racist education must now take place at the meetings of every school governing body' (Troyna and Carrington 1990: 94). Concern was also expressed with the new funding arrangements for schools, with the 'reduced amount of monies now available' scarcely being conducive to 'progress in racial equality' (Blair and Arnot 1993: 267).

The advent of a Labour Government in 1997, committed to increased spending on 'education, education, education' has meant that, in contrast to the previous administration, equality of opportunity has been explicitly resurrected as a key objective. In his foreword to the White Paper, *Excellence in Schools*, which sets out the government's thinking behind subsequent reforms, the Secretary for Education and Employment described the government's key objectives as 'equality of opportunity and high standards for all' (David Blunkett 1997, quoted in Gillborn and Mirza 2000: 7).

The emphasis on the overriding importance of standards, however, and the consequent commitment to parental choice, the maintenance of diverse types of school, a revamped National

Curriculum, league tables and inspections represent significant continuities with the previous administration. For some commentators, the concern to raise standards has in practice taken precedence and the reliance on employing market mechanisms to this end has meant increased inequalities. The response of schools to a competitive environment generated by league tables, which rank schools in terms of the proportion of students gaining five or more higher grades at GCSE, has been to be more selective and to give extra support to those pupils identified as likely to meet this threshold. The result, it is argued, is 'a new IQism' (Gillborn and Youdell 2000: 210), which labels minority students as likely failures and justifies rationing provision to support those, often middle-class White students, marked for success. In this way national education policy entails increased inequalities. What is more, successful schools are eligible for more funding. The urban location and socio-economic position, however, of many parents from minority ethnic groups inhibit their ability to choose such schools for their children, thereby, it is argued, 'segregating most minority students in under-funded and under-staffed schools in urban areas' (Tomlinson 2000: 33).

While it is important to examine the unintended consequences of a market in education, the government's espousal of equality of opportunity cannot be dismissed as an empty form of words. The government has addressed equality issues primarily though its social exclusion agenda. This has meant for example, in the case of education, creating Education Action Zones. Such initiatives are attempts to combat social disadvantage and are not specifically targeted at minority ethnic groups, the assumption being that measures benefiting all disadvantaged groups will disproportionately benefit minority ethnic groups. Since the publication of the Macpherson report, however, the government has become rather less colour blind in addressing the issue of racial equality. An Ethnic Minority Achievement Grant (EMAG) was created in 1999 to replace the special funding previously available under Section 11 of the 1966 Local Government Act. Since LEAs have to bid for this funding, its advent, along with other initiatives, has encouraged LEAs and schools, whose arrangements for monitoring have been generally poor (OFSTED 1999), to adopt a more systematic approach to ethnic monitoring. At the same time, OFSTED, criticised for its failure in its inspections to report on racism in schools (Osler and Morrison 2000), has been given new guidance and training to enable it to tackle racial equality in schools more seriously. The government has even made some hesitant moves to give multiculturalism a greater emphasis in the curriculum. From 2002, all secondary school pupils will be obliged to study citizenship, and both this and personal and social education have a multicultural component. Curriculum 2000 has moved a little away from the previous colour-blind National Curriculum by making explicit, albeit piecemeal, references to race and cultural issues. It still remains the case, however, that multiculturalism is not included in the overarching statement of the curriculum's aims and values. To this extent multicultural education still remains somewhat peripheral and integrationism remains the order of the day.

The unwillingness of the government not to move further on multicultural education and develop more targeted initiatives to promote racial equality is not surprising, given the crisis of confidence which has occurred in the movement concerned with promoting racial equality. With notable exceptions (e.g. Troyna), there is widespread agreement that the dispute between the proponents of multicultural education (MCE) and anti-racist education (ARE) is now outmoded. Rather than seeing MCE and ARE as embodying contrary principles and therefore irreconcilable, we are instead enjoined to respect their relative merits and seek a synthesis of the two – 'anti-racist multicultural education' (Grinter 1985). This view is consistent with the discovery by some social theorists of a purportedly new phenomenon, cultural racism. The re-emergence of 'Islamophobia' has prompted Modood (1992a) to emphasise the importance of 'cultural racism' as well as 'colour racism' while analysis of cultural representations has led Gilroy to conclude that 'a form of cultural racism which has taken a necessary distance from crude ideas of biological inferiority now seeks to present an imaginary definition of the nation as a unified cultural community' (Gilroy 1992: 87).

While the emphasis on cultural racism confirms the need for a rapprochement between MCE and ARE, social theorists have more recently raised serious misgivings with the practice of both approaches. For not only do representations of the nation frequently assume that there are essential differences between cultures but so do MCE and ARE. The former tends to assume that the boundaries between ethnic groups are clear and that each ethnic group has a distinct culture which warrants respect. Such an approach, however, underestimates the degree to which globalisation dissolves boundaries. It implies 'some form of ethnic essentialism' (Rattansi 1992: 39) and thereby accepts the same assumption as cultural racism that groups are inherently different. It ignores intra-cultural differences and conflicts, and, in its refusal to judge other cultures, privileges the maintenance of existing cultural differences despite the self-contradiction involved in such a relativist position. ARE fares no better. For the tendency to assume that racism is the defining feature of the experience of minority ethnic groups entails a representation of ethnic minorities as essentially the same – part of the Black community. As such, it amounts to a form of 'cultural essentialism' (Rattansi 1992: 39), which ignores both inter- and intra-cultural differences. In the version of ARE criticised by the Burnage inquiry, a similar unwillingness to recognise difference characterises the representation of the majority ethnic group – White people – who are pictured as inherently racist. The concern of both MCE and ARE to counter ethnic stereotypes by presenting positive images has also been criticised. As Rattansi (1992: 34) points out, 'There is an unacknowledged disingenuity involved in replacing one lot of selective images with another set of partial representations'. Such criticisms from people concerned to promote racial equality exemplify a crisis of confidence in the MCE/ARE movement.

Our brief review of post-war policy responses to the education of minority ethnic pupils clearly does not point to steady progress to equality. Instead it points to a return to at best integrationist assumptions and a return to what has been called a 'spuriously deracialised' discourse. Initiatives designed to promote racial equality, such as MCE and ARE, are in retreat with the rise of what Tomlinson (1990a: 169) has called 'educational nationalism', a discourse which seeks to preserve British culture in the face of threats from 'alien' cultures and claims that ethnic minorities face no obstacles to assimilation. We should not overstate, however, the dominance of educational nationalism. For this discourse is by no means uncontested. MCE is still official policy. There are successful MCE (Tomlinson 1990a) and ARE

(Gillborn 1995) initiatives. A theoretical defence for a critical multiculturalism, which avoids essentialism, has been mounted (May 1999) and non-essentialist forms of education for racial equality have been devised (Ackroyd and Pilkington 1997). What is more, the Macpherson report has encouraged the government to acknowledge the seriousness of racism and develop action plans to combat it. This has encouraged it to become less colour blind and develop more targeted measures to promote racial equality. Whether these initiatives are able to counter the inegalitarian consequences which seem to flow from the maintenance of a market in education, we shall have to wait and see.

Conclusion

The sociology of education has been preoccupied for much of the post-war period with the question of social inequality. And within this field two theoretical frameworks have loomed large. Liberal theorists have put forward the meritocratic thesis, while radical theorists have advocated a reproductive framework. The former see education as a crucial determinant of life chances in modern societies as the link between education and destination strengthens and the link between origins and education weakens. The latter, by contrast, present a critical picture of education as a mechanism which maintains a strong link between origins and destinations. The stable link between class origin and education is consistent with a reproductive framework while the decreasing link between sex origin and education is consistent with the meritocratic thesis. What about the link between ethnic origins and education?

Our examination of the evidence suggests that, although there are significant average differences in achievement between pupils of Asian and Caribbean origin, there are also differences to be found within these two groups. When we disaggregate the Asian group we find that the underachievement of Pakistani and Bangladeshi pupils is masked by the success of Indian and other Asian pupils. When we do a similar exercise with the Caribbean group, we discover that it is boys especially who are underachieving. The performance of Indian, African Asian and Chinese pupils is more consistent with the meritocratic thesis while the performance of Pakistani/Bangladeshi pupils and Caribbean boys is more consistent with a reproductive framework.

When we turn to explanations for such underachievement, we enter a politically highly charged terrain, with advocates of competing explanatory frameworks often at loggerheads with each other. While sceptical of IQ being a major factor, it is argued that a range of social factors are significant: economic deprivation, which itself stems at least in part from racial discrimination; cultural factors, which need to be carefully contextualised to avoid 'blaming the victim'; ineffective schools, which themselves are often located in disadvantaged areas; and (the often unintentional) racial discrimination in schools.

Turning finally to education policy, we were unable to locate a clearly formulated coherent philosophy underpinning the state's pronouncements and practices in relation to ethnicity. Although assimilationist assumptions have tended to be dominant in the post-war period, there have been different policy phases: assimilationism, integrationism and cultural pluralism. For a brief period in the 1980s, cultural pluralism encouraged those concerned with 'education towards racial equality' to believe that progress was being made, but since then pessimism has become more prevalent as assimilationist and integrationist assumptions have renewed their sway.

6 Cultural representations and changing ethnic identities

There is, as Smith points out, 'nothing peculiarly modern about the problem of identity' (A Smith 1995: 129). Human beings have always differentiated themselves from others, named themselves and in the process distinguished between those who are deemed to be members of their community and those who are not. And throughout recorded history, collective identities, although often well established and apparently secure, have periodically been brought into question, signalling a crisis of identity. It is on these occasions that identity becomes an issue, 'when something assumed to be fixed, coherent and stable is displaced by the experience of doubt and uncertainty' (Mercer 1990: 43). The attention currently being paid to the question of collective identity suggests that we are living through such a period, when settled identities have been challenged and there is widespread unease about who we are.

Multiple identities

To provide an indication of what the question of collective identity involves, we shall begin by examining a specific case. In 1991 President Bush, keen to restore a conservative majority on the Supreme Court, nominated Clarence Thomas, a conservative black judge, to fill a vacancy which had arisen. Bush anticipated that White people who might have preferred a White judge would support the nomination because Thomas was lukewarm on equal opportunities legislation; and that Black people who tend to support such legislation would support the nomination because he was Black. During the Senate hearings on the appointment, Judge Thomas was accused of sexual harassment by a Black woman, Anita Hill, who had formerly been a junior

171

colleague of Thomas. The hearings caused a huge furore, with American people divided over the issue (Morrison 1993).

What is interesting for our purposes is the identities people adopted. As Hall points out:

> Some blacks supported Thomas on racial grounds; others opposed him on sexual grounds. Black women were divided, depending on whether their 'identities' as blacks or as women prevailed. Black men were also divided, depending on whether their sexism overrode their liberalism. White men were divided, depending not only on their politics, but on how they identified themselves with respect to racism and sexism. White Conservative women supported Thomas, not only on political grounds, but because of their opposition to feminism. White feminists, often liberal on race, opposed Thomas on sexual grounds. And because Judge Thomas is a member of the judicial elite and Anita Hill, at the time of the alleged incident, was a junior employee there were issues of social class position at work in these arguments too. (S Hall 1992a: 279–80).

People not only took up different positions according to the priority they attached to racism, sexism and liberalism. The arguments also went on inside the head of each individual. People found they were pulled in different directions by their competing identities, unsure whether their sympathies should be determined by their 'race', gender, class or political attitudes.

Clarence Thomas's nomination was eventually ratified. Our concern here, however, is not with Thomas's innocence or guilt but the multiple and competing identities involved. This example indicates that people do not have one fixed identity but a range of shifting identities, including ones based on ethnicity, gender and class. These identities cross-cut each other so that those who identify themselves as sharing a common position on one issue may be at loggerheads over another issue. The faith social theorists once had in one identity emerging as supreme has as a result lapsed. Marxists anticipated that class would constitute the central cleavage in modern society; feminists expected that gender would become central; and anti-racists stressed the primacy of ethnicity. Capital and labour, men and women, and White and Black were respectively envisaged as the major protagonists. By contrast what recent social theorists emphasise is the crudity of such binary oppositions and the need to recognise that individuals continue to have multiple and complex identities. The likelihood of class, gender or ethnicity emerging as a 'master identity' is rejected and instead we are enjoined to acknowledge difference and recognise, for example, differences between working-class Black women and working-class Black men.

It is conceivable that the Thomas–Hill case is exceptional. Let us therefore take two other cases which have been represented as dividing people simply along racial or ethnic lines and might constitute counter-examples to what has been argued so far. The first relates to the criminal trial in the United States of O J Simpson in which a famous middle-class Black man was accused of murdering his White wife and lover. The second relates to the publication in Britain of Salman Rushdie's novel, *The Satanic Verses*, and the uproar that it generated.

The extensive media coverage of the O J Simpson case was dominated by a narrative 'ruled by race' (T Morrison and Lacour 1997: xxvii), with the non-guilty verdict dividing Americans along racial lines. 'Yet to accept the racial reduction ("WHITES V. BLACKS," as . . . *Newsweek* had it) is to miss the fact that the black community itself is riven, and in ways invisible to most whites' (Gates 1996: 21). There was a recognition by some that Simpson's wealth enabled him to mount an expensive defence and there was outrage from many about the way he had abused his wife. The response of the Black community was not therefore uniformly favourable to the verdict but manifested instead both class and gender divisions. Although most ultimately agreed with the verdict, they were pulled in different directions by competing identities. And the same is true to a lesser extent of White people. Although most were shocked by the verdict, in terms of absolute numbers more Whites than Blacks concurred with the verdict.

The depiction in *The Satanic Verses* of the prophet Muhammad caused great offence to many Muslims in Britain. Protests against the book were initially peaceful but escalated with the book being publicly burnt in Bradford in 1989. Soon after this incident, the Iranian religious leader Ayatollah Khomeni published a *fatwah*, a death sentence on Rushdie. Although the Iranian government has since 1998 announced that it no longer supports killing Rushdie, the author still needs protection and has to live in hiding (Appignanesi and Maitland 1989). The Rushdie affair has, like the O J Simpson case, been subject to considerable media coverage with the dominant narrative in this case portraying Muslims as dangerous fundamentalists threatening liberal society and the issue portrayed as dividing people on ethnic lines (Parekh 1989). Matters are not, however, that simple. Most British Muslims belong to the Deobandi and Barelvi sects of Islam, which have little sympathy for the Shiite fundamentalism represented by Ayatollah Khomeni (Modood 1992b). While most were deeply hurt by Rushdie's depiction of their revered prophet and called for the book to be withdrawn, many opposed the *fatwah* and were unhappy with the more violent protests. Some Muslims even expressed support for Rushdie, with one women's group, Women against Fundamentalism, comprising individuals from different ethnic groups including Muslims, staging a counter-demonstration in support of Rushdie and against fundamentalism which it sees as oppressive to women (Yuval-Davis 1992). White people were also divided over the issue. Some Christian churches exhibited sympathy towards the hurt felt by many Muslims and argued that the protection afforded by the blasphemy laws to Christian beliefs should be extended to other faiths (Lewis 1994), while liberals were divided depending on the priority they gave to respecting cultural difference as opposed to free speech. Although the Rushdie affair did divide people partly along ethnic lines, it is evident that other identities were also involved.

Our examination of two cases, where seemingly people were divided simply on racial or ethnic lines, does not in short contradict our earlier contention. 'No one today is purely *one* thing. Labels like Indian, or woman, or Muslim, or American are no more than starting points' (Said 1993: 407). People do not in short have one fixed identity but multiple shifting identities. What all three cases suggest instead is that different identities will be salient in different contexts.

The social construction of identities

The claim that people do not have a fixed identity, but a range of shifting identities, indicates that cultural identities are socially constructed. We encountered social constructionism in Chapter 1 where we argued that both race and ethnicity are socially constructed. We can afford therefore to be brief here and explore a different example of identity formation, that of national identities.

National identities can be characterised by five features which together distinguish them from other collective identities: a shared belief that members 'belong together'; a perception that this association stems from a long history of living together which it is envisaged will continue into the future; a recognition that the community is 'active' and takes decisions; an acknowledgement that it is 'connected to a particular territory'; and the existence of a 'common public culture' which marks it off from other communities (Miller 1995a: 23–7). Although nations typically aspire to be politically self-determining, we cannot, however, equate nations with states: some states (including the United Kingdom) are multi-national and some people who share a common national identity (for example the Kurds) are scattered in a number of states.

Most people feel some attachment to a particular nation (and in some cases nations), with loyalty to the wider community being exhibited at times in a willingness to sacrifice personal gain to promote its interests. While national sentiment has historically sometimes degenerated into chauvinism, this is not inevitable. The pervasiveness of national identities in the modern world suggests in fact that they meet certain needs. They enable us, firstly, to see ourselves as part of some larger social whole and thus provide a framework for us 'to make sense of' our lives and, secondly, to foster 'bonds of mutual trust' which facilitate social solidarity and 'make successful democratic politics possible' (Miller 1995b: 153).

Although nations typically purport to have a long ancestry and trace their roots back to time immemorial, national identities cannot be seen in any way as primordial. While they may in some cases bear the imprint of a more ancient ethnic group (itself not a primordial phenomenon) which was dominant when the nation first took shape (A Smith 1995), the idea of a nation as a community which demands people's loyalty and aspires to exercise control over a particular territory is distinctly modern. For most of human history people have lived in small communities, seeing themselves as belonging to kinship groups and neighbourhood networks and in some cases a wider religious community. Nations only emerged as mass phenomena in the eighteenth and nineteenth centuries when a series of complex economic, political and cultural changes encouraged their formation and made it possible for national identities to be widely disseminated (Hutchinson and Smith 1994). The new media of communication, especially print, facilitated this process by standardising vernacular languages and enabling 'the mass of people within a particular state to understand each other through a common print language' (C Barker 1997: 189). This allowed people for the first time to feel part of what Anderson has called the 'imagined community' of the nation – 'imagined in the sense that 'the members of even the smallest nation will never know most of their fellow members, meet them, or even hear of them, yet in the minds of each lives the image of their communion' (Anderson 1983: 15).

Recognising that nations are modern inventions and comprise imagined communities entails an acknowledgement that national identities are socially constructed. This raises two further questions, however. How are national identities created? And how are they reproduced and transformed? Let us take the case of British identity.

The Act of Union in 1707 between England/Wales and Scotland, which created the British nation state, necessitated the construction of a British national identity. Protestantism played a central role in the initial formation of British identity in the eighteenth and early nineteenth centuries (as it had done earlier in the case of English identity), with Catholics being defined as the most significant Other. If we focus internally on British society itself, the most significant Other comprised the Irish, but we also need to focus externally and here the French at least initially comprised the most significant Other. As Colley puts it,

Great Britain was an invention forged above all by war. Time and time again, war with France brought Britons into confrontation with an obviously hostile Other and encouraged them to define themselves collectively against it. They defined themselves as Protestants struggling for survival against the world's foremost Catholic power. They defined themselves against the French as they imagined them to be, superstitious, militarist, decadent and unfree. And, increasingly as the wars went on, they defined themselves in contrast to the colonial peoples they conquered, peoples who were manifestly alien in terms of culture, religion and colour . . . Britishness was superimposed over an array of internal differences in response to contact with the Other, and above all in response to conflict with the Other (Colley 1992: 5–6).

While 'Britishness was, initially, primarily an elite identity, dominated by Englishness . . . it became a more secure mass national identity with the advent of industrialisation and mass literacy' (Guibernau and Goldblatt 2000: 133). Although we cannot of course regard the formation of British identity as typical, it is not exceptional for national identities to be formed in opposition to an Other or Others and for the permeation of such identities among different social classes to take a considerable time.

Of critical importance to the reproduction, and indeed transformation, of national identities is the process of representation, the way members of a culture use language and other symbolic systems to 'produce meanings through which we can make sense of our experience and who we are' (Woodward 1997: 14). National identities are reproduced through 'the *narrative of the nation,* as it is told and retold in national histories, literatures, the media and popular culture' (S Hall 1992a: 293). A variety of stories, images, symbols and rituals thereby produce meanings about the nation with which we are invited to identify. Such representations typically emphasise the continuity of the nation, which is portrayed as 'rooted in the remotest antiquity', and the ancient nature of its traditions. On inspection, however, 'traditions which appear or claim to be old are often quite recent in origin and sometimes invented' (Hobsbawm and Ranger 1983: 1). Thus the rituals and pageantry associated with the British monarchy originated in the late nineteenth century and 'until recently, the British royal family was overwhelmingly German in blood and often in preferred language as well' (Colley 1999: 27). However mythical the narrative may be, reminders of our shared nationhood are evident in the institutions which surround us and not least in the way *we* are daily addressed as members of the nation by the media. The result is that our national identities are deeply ingrained, a phenomenon which has been described as 'banal nationalism' (Billig 1995).

To recognise that representations of national identities do not merely reflect pre-existing identities but also help to construct them enables us to understand not only how identities are reproduced but also how they are transformed. To point to the social construction of identities is to point to their malleability and recognise that they are not fixed but change over time. For a long time the British felt confidence in their identity. Even when

Protestantism became a less central ingredient to their identity in the course of the nineteenth century, continuing economic success, pride in constitutional government and leadership of a large empire allowed the British to see themselves as belonging to a unique nation and as a civilising force in the wider world. In the course of the twentieth century, and especially after the Second World War, such confidence dissipated and with increasing urgency attention begun to be paid to the question of British identity. Economic decline, increasing criticism of its constitutional arrangements and the loss of empire have precipitated a crisis of identity. Membership of the European Union, the devolution of powers to Scotland and to a lesser extent Wales, and the 'very presence' of 'post-colonial peoples' in Britain serve to symbolise the changing nature of Britain and disrupt the narrative of the nation (Bhabba 1990: 218). In this context, new narratives are fashioned and, as we shall see below, alternative visions of the nation compete for our attention.

When we actually examine contemporary nations, we discover that, like the British, they are generally multi-ethnic. They have never in fact been culturally homogeneous or comprised unified cultural communities but 'are without exception ethnically hybrid – the product of conquests, absorptions of one people by another' (S Hall 1992b: 6), with the British, for example, the product of a series of such conquests – Celtic, Roman, Saxon, Viking and Norman – and various waves of immigration. While people who share a national identity necessarily also share to some extent a common public culture which distinguishes them from other communities, we should not assume that the latter is inevitably monolithic. The development of a British national identity from an elite to a mass phenomenon did not eradicate pre-existing ethnic identities and allegiances. It is possible therefore for people to have a common national identity and at the same time acknowledge differing identities of other kinds. The British, for example, continue to have an overarching identity which recognises the legitimacy of people having not only other national identities (English, Scottish, Welsh) but also ethnic identities. It has to be acknowledged, none the less, that 'national cultures are not simple repositories of shared symbols to which the entire population stands in identical relation. Rather they [need] to be approached as sites of contestation in which competition over definitions takes place' (Schlesinger 1991: 174). In multi-ethnic nations there is often a tension between the competing demands of unity and diversity: the need, on the one hand, for 'cohesion and a sense of common belonging' and the wish, on the other hand, of minority communities to 'preserve and transmit their ways of life' (Parekh 1998: 1). In practice it has often proved difficult to reconcile this tension. National cultures historically reflect the values of the dominant ethnic group who wish to uphold their vision of the nation. Since nations are imagined communities, other imaginings are of course possible and put forward, often by subordinate groups, in the light of social changes. The result, however, is that alternative and competing definitions of the nation vie for our attention. While therefore some seek 'to represent what is in fact the ethnic hotchpotch of modern nationality as the primordial unity of "one people"', see no need for changes in the national culture and demand complete assimilation from minorities (S Hall 1992b: 6), others put forward an alternative pluralist vision which entails public recognition of minority cultures and some modification of the national culture to reflect its multicultural character.

The emergence of a racialised regime of representation: us and them

We have seen above that collective 'identities are forged through the marking of difference' (Woodward 1997: 29). To point out what we are is at the same time to point out what we are not. To define ourselves is at the same time to maintain that we differ from others. Frequently the construction of identities expresses differences through binary oppositions: us and them, the Self and the Other. These oppositions are rarely neutral and often oversimplify matters. This is not accidental. The relation between Europeans, not least the British, and other peoples has until recently, and especially since the sixteenth century, been a highly unequal one. Economic, political and cultural domination therefore frequently entailed simplified representations, which relied on crude binary oppositions such as White/Black and Western/Oriental in which one pole of the binary was clearly the dominant one. Indeed it has been argued that imperialism's 'worst and most paradoxical gift was to allow people to believe that they were only, mainly, exclusively, white, or black, or Western, or Oriental' (Said 1993: 407–8).

European contact with populations elsewhere involved a process of representation and, with European expansion, a construction of the West's sense of itself through its sense of difference from others. The consequence was the emergence of a discourse which represented 'the world as divided according to a simple dichotomy – the West/the Rest' (S Hall 1992c: 280). While European images of non-Europeans, including Africans, were initially marked by some ambiguity, with a debate raging as late as the eighteenth century about the 'noble' or 'ignoble savage', this gradually changed so that by the nineteenth century 'any ambivalence was eradicated' (Ferguson 1998: 80). A simple division emerged which, in tandem with the increasingly popular idea of race, often took a racialised form. In a book which is concerned with representations generated within the western world about populations elsewhere, Miles provides two examples of this division. The first is based upon colour: 'In the act of defining Africans as "blacks" and "savages" and thereby excluding them from their world, Europeans in the eighteenth and nineteenth century were representing themselves as "white" and "civilised".' The second is based upon culture: 'European representations of the Islamic world extensively utilised images of barbarism and sexuality in the context of a Christian/heathen dichotomy.' (Miles 1989: 39–40).

While it is important to recognise that representations, which ground differences in colour and culture respectively, do not operate in an identical manner, it is equally important, however, not to overstate the opposition between a discourse which privileges biological markers like skin colour and a discourse which privileges cultural markers like religion. The former invariably points to cultural differences, while the latter often indirectly point to biological differences. Thus,

> 'Blackness' has functioned as a sign that people of African descent are closer to Nature, and *therefore* more likely to be lazy, indolent, lacking the higher intellectual faculties, driven by emotion and feeling rather than Reason, over-sexualised, with low self-control and prone to violence, etc. Correspondingly, those who are stigmatised . . . as 'culturally different' and therefore inferior, are often *also* characterised as physically different in significant ways (though perhaps not as visibly as blacks) (S Hall 2000: 223).

Within this discourse, the stubborn persistence of cultural differences across generations is seen to stem from the practice of inter-marriage within ethnic groups. A discourse which privileges cultural markers therefore often indirectly contains a biological referent. To use Hall's terms, 'biological racism and cultural differentialism, therefore, constitute not two different systems, but racism's two registers' (S Hall 2000: 223).

A good example of how this West/Rest discourse works can be seen in a book which focuses primarily on the Middle East – the territory occupied principally by Islamic peoples. What Said stresses is that European domination took not only political and economic forms, but also a cultural form. It involved the construction of a particular discourse, Orientalism, 'whose structure promoted the difference between the familiar (Europe, the West, "us") and the strange (the Orient, the East, "them")' (Said 1978: 44). Donald outlines very well how these differences between us – Europe, the West – and them – the Orient, the East – are developed in this discourse:

> First, chains of characteristics are attributed to these categories. Thus Westerners are depicted as civilized, logical, rational, virtuous, sceptical, empirical and dedicated. Orientals, on the other hand, are shown as gullible, cunning, prone to intrigue and flattery, lethargic, stupid, irrational and childlike. Second, these various attributes are taken to define that which is 'essentially Oriental', an essence that is then ascribed to 'nature'. The West has a *natural* affinity with self-government, the East a natural affinity with despotism. Finally, these representations are presented as fixed and unchanging identifications for the reader of Orientalist discourse: the West is us, and Orient is them (Donald 1992: 29–30).

A similar tendency to naturalise difference can also be found in popular representations of Black slaves in America. Although 'a fully fledged racialised ideology did not appear amongst the slave-holding classes (and their supporters in Europe) until slavery was seriously challenged by the Abolitionists in the nineteenth century', two main themes can be detected in earlier depictions of Black people: firstly, their 'innate laziness' and secondly, their 'innate primitivism'. Black people were essentially different from White people, in this view. For 'laziness, simple fidelity, mindless "cooning", trickery, childishness belonged to blacks *as a race, as a species*' (S Hall 1997b: 242–4).

While we can detect, alongside European expansion, the emergence of a discourse which represented the world as divided into the West and the Rest, for most British people, non-White people did not represent a significant Other until the period of 'high imperialism' in the late nineteenth century. During the eighteenth and early nineteenth centuries, Catholics represented the most significant Other for Britons, and the idea of race itself was used to make sense of social differences within and between European societies as much as differences between Europe and populations elsewhere (Miles 1993b). With imperialist expansion by European nations, 'racial difference became identified with the distinction between the West and the Rest' and the notion of White superiority became increasingly prevalent (Malik 1996: 226). This period witnessed a massive proliferation in popular representations of the empire through advertising and other media and an extensive dissemination of racialised representations of an external Other. 'Images of colonial conquest were stamped on soap boxes . . . biscuit tins, whisky bottles, tea tins and chocolate bars . . . . No pre-existing form of organised racism had ever before been able to reach so large and so differentiated a mass of the populace' (McClintock 1995, quoted in S Hall 1997b: 240).

Media representations of minority groups: continuity and change

Traces of these racial stereotypes can still be detected. For example, three nineteenth-century basic images of the Other – the slave figure, the native and clown or entertainer – 'are still to be observed, reworked in many of the modern and updated images' of contemporary popular culture. They represent the Other as primitive and are characterised by 'deep ambivalence', shifting between nostalgia for lost innocence and fear of the savagery 'lurking just below the surface' (S Hall 1995: 22). The question still arises, however, as to how common such racialised representation is. Black and Asian people have moved in the post-war period from the colonial periphery to the metropolitan centre. Are they still subject to what Stuart Hall (1997b) calls a 'racialised regime of representation'?

Continuities in representations of race

Most studies argue that minority groups still tend to be represented in a stereotypical way. Stereotyping constitutes a representational practice which 'reduces people to a few, simple, essential characteristics' which are deemed to be unchanging (S Hall 1997b: 257). To claim that stereotypes of Black and Asian people are prevalent in the media and popular culture implies therefore that complex differences are ignored and they are thereby defined as the Others. The gaze in this view is predominantly White, that 'of the dominant looking at the subordinate: how *they* are different from us rather than how *we* are different from them . . . where whiteness is taken as the profoundly unproblematic norm against which all "others" are measured' (Ross 1996: 4).

Much of the research on race/ethnicity and the media has focused on representations of minority ethnic groups. 'The collective findings of this research effort generally make for depressing reading. Under-representation and stereotypical characterisation within entertainment genres and negative portrayal within factuality and news forms, and a tendency to ignore structural inequalities and lived racism experienced by ethnic minorities in both, are recurring research findings' (Cottle 2000: 7–8). Examples abound. A recent analysis of popular film and television expresses dismay with 'the lack of diversity when encountering black [and Asian] images as well as the pejorative . . . connotations which such images provoke' (Ross 1996: 170). Other accounts also highlight the way minority ethnic groups tend to be depicted in terms of a restricted repertoire of representations. Thus, one study of British television points to the continuing presence of three stereotypical figures – 'the trouble maker, entertainer and dependant' (Barry 1988: 101), while another points out how 'in the main, soaps, sitcoms and drama still tend to depict black [and Asian] people in overly stereotypical forms' (Mercer 1989: 3).

A similar picture is evident in recent studies of the news, which generally support the findings of earlier studies that the dominant framework for the presentation of news on race and ethnicity is one which projects 'an image of Britain as a *white* society in which the coloured population is seen as some kind of aberration, a problem . . . rather than as "belonging" to society' (Hartmann and Husband 1974, quoted in Van Dijk 1991: 17–18). An analysis of the British press in the 1980s is not atypical in this respect in arguing that minority ethnic groups 'are portrayed as constituting a threat to white British society, first through their immigration to this country and then, when settled here, as posing a law and order problem' (Gordon and Rosenberg 1989: 3). A more systematic analysis, which employed both content and discourse analysis to examine coverage of race and ethnicity in the press in the second six months of 1985 and the first six months of 1989, concurs. Although the author acknowledges that coverage in the 1980s was 'less blatantly racist' than in previous decades, he emphasises 'that stereotypes and the definition of minorities as a "problem" or even as a "threat" [were] still prevalent' (Van Dijk 1991: 245). Coverage was confined to a limited number of topics, most notably crime, race relations and immigration, with 'events . . . seen as most problematic or threatening to the interests of the white majority tend[ing] to be most prominent' and subjects, such as racist attacks, of particular concern to minorities being virtually ignored (Van Dijk 1991: 117). The headlines and editorials, especially of the right-wing press, tended 'to emphasise the negative role of ethnic minorities in such topics' and, even when the topics were of direct concern to them, minority group members were much less likely to be quoted than majority group members (Van Dijk 1991: 245).

Although less attention has been paid to television news, most studies have identified the presence of a similar framework to that found in the press. A thematic examination of the language and visuals of a sequence of news reports on migration and race in February 1995 revealed the dominant theme to be that of 'migrants as the threatening "other" which has to be kept out' (GMG 1997a: 39). Alternative views were apparent but these were given less weight and overwhelmed by the dominant theme. 'The result was news which was sometimes xenophobic in tone, which reinforced *our* identity and *their* exclusion and, perhaps more importantly, provided a rationale for the apparent need for exclusion' (GMG 1997a: 46). This study focused on national news, but a similar picture has been presented of regional news. In a study which takes as its central concern urban conflict rather than race and ethnicity, the author indicates that television news generally fails to address the issue of racial disadvantage. Analysis of the coverage of the Handsworth riots of 1985 revealed the dominance of a conservative approach. The riots were presented overwhelmingly 'as a criminal outbreak of lawlessness requiring a tough law and order response' (Cottle 1993: 198).

Both press and television news are often characterised in these studies as racist. We need, however, to make a distinction here between what Stuart Hall (1995) calls 'overt' and 'inferential' racism. Overt racism is apparent when 'favourable coverage is given to [those] who are in the business of elaborating an openly racist argument' while inferential racism is evident when coverage is seemingly balanced but 'racist premises [are] inscribed . . . as a set of *unquestioned assumptions*'. Sometimes overt racism can be detected but more often what is at issue is inferential racism. Television news and current affairs programmes in particular are concerned to be balanced and yet debates are often 'predicated on the unstated and unrecognised assumption that the *blacks* [or other minorities] are the *source of the problem*' (S Hall 1995: 20). Thus debate over the effectiveness of Britain's border controls – on which participants may take different positions – rests on the implicit premise that most asylum seekers are bogus and need to be kept out (Van Dijk 2000).

The cumulative effect of stereotypical and negative representations of minority groups in the news and more generally in the media and popular culture, it is often argued, is 'to promote and consolidate a racist "commonsense" which serves to justify and help maintain racial inequality' (Gordon and Rosenberg 1989: 38). While representations of minority communities are subject to selective perception by audiences and their meanings open to diverse interpretations, the assumption is that individuals 'who do not have first-hand experiences of those communities will have no reason to challenge them' (Ross 1996: pxx). Few studies have investigated how audiences decode media texts in this area. There is none the less some support here for the claim that dominant representations play a significant role in influencing people's perceptions of minority groups and that dominant news frameworks in particular help to structure 'perception of the key issues in race relations' (A Pilkington 1986: 144). Thus the study of television news on migration and race, which we explored above, points out how 'the dominant themes of the news on migration produce[d] very strong resonances in public beliefs' (GMG 1997a: 46) and the study by Van Dijk on the press emphasises how individuals on the whole accepted 'the "terms" of the debate . . . as defined by the Press' (Van Dijk 1991: 243). While it is acknowledged that evidence of media influence on people's attitudes is much less clear-cut, there is a degree of consensus that the role of the media is a primarily negative one and that it generally reinforces rather than combats racist attitudes.

Given the purported continuing dominance of a racialised regime of representation, a number of writers argue that it is not surprising that the construction of British identity frequently excludes minority ethnic groups. While it is recognised that references to the alleged racial inferiority of particular groups are now relatively rare outside the confines of neo-fascist parties, it is argued that references to supposed essential differences between minority ethnic cultures and the national culture are common-place. As one author puts it,

> A form of cultural racism which has taken a necessary distance from crude ideas of biological inferiority now seeks to present an imaginary definition of the nation as a unified cultural community. It constructs and defends an image of national culture, homogeneous in its whiteness, yet precarious and perpetually vulnerable to attack from enemies within and without. (Gilroy 1992: 87).

It is conceivable that British national culture will one day embrace minority groups, but at the moment, it is argued, this seems a forlorn hope. For Caribbeans are frequently presented as belonging to a pathological culture and thus prone to criminal-ity, while Asians are often presented as a threat to the British way of life by virtue of the strength and cohesiveness of their cul-tures. For different reasons, both groups are therefore judged to be incompatible with authentic forms of Britishness.

Two illustrations will suffice to indicate what Gilroy has in mind. The first relates to a Conservative election poster in 1983 which 'set an image of a young black man, smartly dressed in a suit . . . above the caption "Labour says he's black. Tories say he's British"'. The poster not only suggests that being Black and British are mutually exclusive identities but also indicates that 'the price of admission to the colour-blind form of citizenship promised by the text' is for black people 'to forsake all that marks them out as culturally distinctive' (Gilroy 1987: 57–9). Our second example relates to an editorial in *The Sun* in May 1998 commenting on the story blazoned on its front page with the headline, 'THIS LITTLE PIGGY IS A RACIST'. Under the title, 'Pig headed', the *Sun* says 'WATCH out, bigots about. That's the sign that should go up in Leicester. Racial and religious intolerance are rearing their ugly heads. *Not among the whites – among the local Asian Muslims.* They complain that a collection of ceramic pigs in a house window is racially offensive.' Under a subheading, 'Culture', it goes on:

> *The unbending attitude of militant Muslims who think they have a right to impose their culture in a Christian country is frightening.* There has to be give and take if we are all to get on together. But it seems WE give and THEY take. This does nothing for racial harmony. It just makes Muslims look mean-minded – which the vast majority are not. This country is very easy-going and accepting of its new citizens. But pigs will fly before we put up with this kind of nonsense.

This editorial is clearly addressed to a White readership whose tolerance is envisaged as having been stretched too far. Although there is an acceptance that Asian Muslims can become British, the price of admission is manifest: they must become like us.

What is interesting about both these examples is that neither makes any explicit reference to race or hierarchy. And yet many commentators, including Gilroy, would characterise these as racist representations. In what sense can they be described as racist then?

A note on racism

Racism is a term of very recent origin. It emerged in response to two phenomena: firstly, a growing body of scientific evidence which challenged the nineteenth-century doctrine that people can be characterised, on the basis of physical markers, as belonging to a limited number of discrete groups, some of which are inherently superior to others; and secondly, the realisation that Nazism had used this doctrine to define Jews as an alien and inferior race and thus justify genocide (Miles 1989). The term, which from the outset carried extremely negative connotations, was coined to refer to the doctrine of race, a set of beliefs which at one time had been scientifically justified but were – from the vantage point of the 1940s – considered to be discredited and morally reprehensible. In the wake of the Holocaust, however, people have become reluctant to put forward such beliefs and make explicit references, at least in the public arena, to the racial inferiority of the Other. Two responses to this phenomenon are evident. For some sociologists (Banton 1985), declining belief in the doctrine of race indicates that racism is in decline, but for others (Rex 1970), it points to the need to revise our definition of racism. Revision has in turn taken broadly two different forms (Miles and Small 1999).

In one case, it has involved extending the meaning of the term in such a way as to include both beliefs and practices which lead to racial disadvantage and indeed even to cover racial disadvantage itself. Such an approach has been characterised as a form of 'conceptual inflation' (Miles 1989): the concept of racism loses any specificity and its value as an analytical tool diminishes as important distinctions such as that between beliefs which legitimate racial inequality, racially discriminatory practices and patterns of racial disadvantage are obscured.

In the other case, racism has continued to refer to beliefs rather than practices or outcomes. Revision has involved extending the meaning of racism in such a way as to include not only the doctrine of race but also other beliefs which legitimate racial inequality. While a discourse which makes explicit reference to race and hierarchy is less prevalent in the post-war period, in its stead has arisen another discourse 'whose dominant theme is not biological heredity but the insurmountability of cultural differences', a discourse 'which at first sight does not postulate the superiority of certain groups or peoples in relation to others but "only" the harmfulness of abolishing frontiers, the incompatibility of life-styles and traditions' (Balibar 1991: 21). This discourse performs a similar role to the earlier one in legitimating racial inequality and therefore can be characterised as a form of racism – cultural racism. While this discourse cannot be described as 'new' (M Barker 1981) since Muslims, as we saw earlier, for a long time have been subject to this discourse, and while it has not wholly displaced one which focuses on race and hierarchy (Mason 1995), its proliferation indicates that one can no longer assume that racism takes one form. Before, however, we can conclude that there are different racisms, including scientific and cultural racisms, it behoves us to identify the core characteristics of racism.

Here racism will be defined as a discourse which involves four features: identifying groups, which reproduce themselves over time, on the basis of physical markers; seeing essential differences between them; associating Others with negative characteristics; and visualising the dissolution of boundaries as undesirable. Scientific racism in this view focuses on race and hierarchy, while cultural racism focuses on essential cultural differences. We should not assume, however, that reference to essential cultural differences always entails cultural racism. While the poster above arguably does exemplify cultural racism, given its implicit negative evaluation of the culture of a group identified by a physical marker, a culture which is seen as essentially distinct from Britishness, the editorial above is arguably more appropriately seen as an example of 'ethnocentrism', since it identifies the Other 'primarily in cultural terms', notably religion rather than colour, before moving on to point to essential differences between this negatively evaluated group and the British (Rattansi 1992: 360). While it is often difficult in practice to distinguish between cultural racism and ethnocentrism, given – as we saw earlier – the tendency for the attribution of essential cultural differences to make indirect reference to accompanying biological differences, discourses clearly vary in the degree to which they manifest cultural racism and ethnocentrism, and their presence can, as Gilroy argues, entail a construction of Britishness which excludes minority ethnic groups.

Changes in representations of race

We should not overstate the extent of continuity in representations of minority ethnic groups. Although most analyses suggest that a racialised regime of representation remains dominant, albeit one marked by a shift from scientific racism to cultural racism, much of the literature relates to the 1970s and early

1980s and 'most surveys have relied on either very small timescales or on unsystematic data-collection' (Daniels 1998: 135). While there is some acknowledgement of '"improvements" in images of black [and Asian] images' in popular film and television during the 1980s (Ross 1996: 113) and some recognition that 'the headlines in 1989 [were] less prominently negative than those of 1985' (Van Dijk 1991: 70), such grudging admissions of change, however, downplay the growth in both the volume and range of representations of minority ethnic groups.

In Britain, 'the public service ideal . . . has allowed black programming to develop, whether on Channel 4 or on BBC2' (Daniels 1996: 184) and 'the emergence of the new Black British cinema' has enabled, through films such as *My Beautiful Launderette*, 'a wider, more extended and hybrid national "community" [to be] imagined' (Higson 1998: 357). In some cases, programmes and films developed primarily for minority audiences have become popular also with White audiences. The Black sit-com *Desmond's* and the Asian comedy *Goodness Gracious Me* fit into this category. Although integrated casting is still exceptional in popular film and television, it is increasingly evident that Black and Asian actors in both mainstream cinema and television 'are now playing "ordinary" characters . . . and the new way of presenting black [and Asian] people . . . effectively says to the audience that black [and Asian] people are just like white people' (Abercrombie 1996: 70–1). This is apparent in popular programmes such as *The Bill* and *EastEnders* in Britain and *The Cosby Show* in America. It is still admittedly rare for Black or Asian actors to receive star billing but even this has become more common. This has sometimes resulted in 'reversing the stereotypes', with Black macho heroes exhibiting a complete lack of deference to Whites as in the so-called 'blaxploitation' films like *Shaft*, and sometimes in the production of 'positive images' of minority communities as in the representation of the Black middle-class family, the Huxtables, in *The Cosby Show* (S Hall 1997b: 270–2). While writers continue to disagree about the efficacy of strategies that involve either reversing negative stereotypes or producing positive images in countering a racialised regime of representation, there is little doubt that both 'expand the *range* of racial representations and the *complexity* of what it means to "be black [or Asian]"' (S Hall 1997b: 272).

Changing representational practices are also evident in advertising. 'Colonial images and crudely nationalistic emblems are relatively rare in the current period' (Solomos and Back, 1996: 186) and 'the under-representation of non-whites in advertising' is no longer evident (GMG 1997b: 24). Instead some multinational corporations now both acknowledge and celebrate difference. A classic example of this is the 'United Colours of Benneton' advertising series in which the message of human unity is predicated upon an acceptance of racial and cultural difference. While this campaign and others have been criticised for reinforcing stereotypical differences and representing Others as exotic, shifts towards a positive valuation of difference 'can unsettle the valence of racism within popular culture' (Solomos and Back 1996: 194). Even more unsettling, however, are the attempts by some artists to challenge our traditional ways of looking through the development of new forms of representation. An example is the presentation by Toscani, the photographer responsible for the Benneton campaign, of a series of well-known people with transformed racial characteristics. The picture of the 'Black Queen' for example reveals and in the process challenges our taken for granted assumptions about the necessary Whiteness of British identity (Alibhai-Brown 2000a).

The primary focus of research on representations of race and ethnicity in the media and popular culture has involved interpreting the meaning of texts. While it is increasingly recognised that texts do not have one fixed meaning and are indeed open to diverse readings, there has been relatively little attention paid to the way audiences use the media and popular culture. Studies which do examine audiences, however, challenge the notion that the role of the media and popular culture is overwhelmingly negative. One writer points to the emergence in Britain among young people of Black expressive cultures which adapt and transform musical forms transmitted by transnational communication networks 'to circulate a new sense of what it is to be British'. These forms often entail a fusion of Black, White and Asian popular music and, although seemingly trivial, 'point to the opening up of a self-consciously post-colonial space in which the affirmation of difference points forward to a more pluralistic conception of nationality' (Gilroy 1993: 61–2). Another study based on an ethnographic investigation between 1988 and 1991 of young Punjabi Asians in Southall also indicates how the media and popular culture can be used to construct identity, in this case a British Asian identity. The presence in the home of media which represent different cultures – including Hindi films and the sacred texts of Hinduism on the one hand and Western soaps and local news on the other hand – tend to engender among young people 'a developed consciousness of difference and a cosmopolitan stance' (Gillespie 1995: 206). While many parents use Hindi films 'to foster cultural and religious traditions', young people often use them 'to deconstruct "traditional culture"', with some boys rejecting them because they reinforce a degrading image of India and some girls finding them a source of support for their faith in romantic love. Despite parents' disapproval of Western soaps for undermining traditional values, young people are drawn to such programmes even when, as in the case of *Neighbours,* they concern mainly White middle-class suburban Australians. Perceiving there to be parallels in the role gossip plays in their own community and *Neighbours* as a mechanism of social control, young Punjabis see the soap opera as 'a complex metaphor for their own social world' (Gillespie 1995: 207) and use the programme as a focal point of discussion on trips to McDonald's in Hounslow where they sip CocaCola and buy into the dream, promulgated by multinational corporations, of a world of consumerist freedom where ethnic and other differences cease to matter.

Examination of the way audiences use media and popular culture reinforces our earlier analysis of changes in representations. We need to be extremely circumspect about accepting the contention that a racialised regime of representation continues to be dominant and the role of the media and popular culture is still primarily negative. A recent study of the news across radio, television and the press over a six-month period from November 1996 to May 1997 confirms the significance of changing representational practices. The content analysis revealed that about 'three quarters of news items' that dealt with 'race' issues 'conveyed a broadly anti-racist message' (Law 1997: 44). That is to say the dominant framework for news concerning race and ethnicity is now one which is concerned to 'expose and criticise racist attitudes, statements, actions and policies . . . address the concerns of immigrant and minority ethnic groups and show their contribution to British society, and . . . embrace an inclusive view of multi-cultural Britain' (Law 1997: 18).

Significant progress in the way the news media handled race issues was evident. No explicit racist messages in cartoons could be found and stories denouncing anti-racism had largely disappeared. Instead of coverage denying the existence of racism – which Van Dijk (1993) has claimed is typical of elite discourse in the media and elsewhere – extensive coverage was given to instances of racism. In contrast to previous research, immigration was generally treated in a sympathetic way and the press silence on racist attacks was no longer evident. There was little evidence of the 'new' racism being endorsed and both multiculturalism and Islam were on the whole more likely to be valued than vilified. To conclude this catalogue of progress, the study found that access of minority voices had improved along with the use of terminology in naming groups. While the dearth of research on the production of news makes it difficult to account for the shift in coverage between the 1980s and 1990s, attention needs to be given to 'the changing contexts of production' (Cottle 2000: 15–23) including 'changing cultural, political and government discourse over race issues, changes in minority ethnic employment profiles in some news organizations, increasing recognition of anti-racism and multiculturalism in regulatory environments, and competitive rivalry in news production' (Law 2002: 159–60).

We must not exaggerate, however, the extent of progress. While deliberate bias against minorities was found to be rare, about a 'quarter of news items still conveyed a negative message about minority groups' with the old framework depicting minority groups as a social problem at times all too evident especially in the tabloid newspapers (Law 1997: 44). What is more, when account is taken of both news items with a broadly anti-racist message and those conveying a negative message about minority ethnic groups, 'the diversity of roles played in British news was narrow and limited as they were presented primarily as either victims of racism and discrimination, perpetrators of crime or problematised immigrants' (Law 2002: 76). Indeed, the author of this study of race in the news – while continuing to point to 'a significant change in news coverage of race issues since the 1980s in the UK' – now conceptualises the shift as 'moving from overt hostility to anti-racism towards the presentation of an "anti-racist show"' (Law 2002: 76, 159). The choice of the term, 'show' qualifies the significance of changes in coverage by suggesting that the prevalence of an anti-racist framework is 'mere display' and masks the dominance of a discourse where Whiteness is the norm against which others are seen, the marginal role of members of minority ethnic groups within news organisations, and 'a collective failure to provide appropriate quality news services for black and minority ethnic communities and consumers' (Law 2002: 159). To recognise continuing racial inequalities within news organisations and limitations in the current coverage of race news does not mean, however, that the advent of an anti-racist framework is not significant and that this is 'mere display'.

What can we conclude overall about representations of race and ethnicity? A racialised regime of representation was dominant in the nineteenth century and can still be detected. It is no longer hegemonic, however, but coexists with representations which challenge the old stereotypes. The result is that 'representations of black people . . . are frequently ambiguous and ambivalent. Such ambiguities are the site of *cultural struggles* over meaning rather than the fixing of definitive meanings for audiences' (C Barker 1999: 169). This means that different definitions of the nation compete for our attention. While some do, as Gilroy argues, exemplify cultural racism (or ethnocentrism) and present an exclusive picture of Britishness, others can be characterised as anti-racist and present an inclusive picture of Britishness. What we shall discover below is how this issue of national identity has become increasingly hotly contested with increasing globalisation.

Globalisation, representation and identity formation

There is widespread recognition that we are living through a period of rapid social change. For some theorists, such change signals the arrival of a new phase of modernity – late modernity or high modernity. Recent transformations indicate in this view an acceleration of changes unleashed by modernity. For other theorists, the dramatic nature of recent social changes signifies the emergence of a new type of society – post-modernity. Recent transformations are, in this view, so fundamental that we are witnessing the birth of a society which can no longer be described as modern but is in some sense post-modern. This debate need not detain us here. For our concern is with globalisation and there is widespread consensus between theorists who conceptualise our condition as either one of late modernity or post-modernity that a central feature of the changes which characterise the contemporary world can be captured through this concept of globalisation.

Society is often visualised as a social system with distinct boundaries separating it from other social systems. In the process, modern society – which sociologists have tended to take as their central subject matter – is effectively equated with the nation state. Such an equation reflects the nineteenth-century origins of sociology when 'nation-states became supreme because they won at war, were economically successful and, subsequently, achieved a significant degree of legitimacy in the eyes of their populations and other states' (Held 1992: 103).

There are two problems with picturing society in this way. Firstly, human behaviour has never been explicable purely in terms of the place where an individual lives. One writer, for example, has distinguished four sources of power (economic, ideological, political and military) and argued that these have always generated 'overlapping, intersecting networks of power relations' which have often extended across sizeable geographical areas (Mann 1993: 9). The influence of major religions, patterns of trade and indeed war and conquest testify to this. Secondly, since the onset of modernity, the world has increasingly shrunk as the interconnectedness between seemingly separate societies has grown. Indeed we have already noted above how European expansion entailed not only economic and political domination but also cultural domination, resulting in a new discourse whereby the West defined itself in relation to the Rest. The sheer impossibility of understanding societies in isolation is evident if we examine what for a long time was seen as the typically English habit of enjoying a sweet cup of tea. The tea came from India and the sugar from the Caribbean (S Hall 1991).

While globalisation, in the sense of the interconnectedness of societies, has been a feature of modernity since the sixteenth century, a number of social theorists have suggested that in the last two decades we have entered a qualitatively new phase of globalisation. One of its main features has been described as 'time–space compression', in recognition of the fact that our lives are increasingly and remarkably quickly influenced by distant events. A key condition of globalisation has been the development of information and communications technology. Two examples will suffice. The computerisation of financial markets enables vast amounts of capital to be transferred each day from one side of the world to the other, with sometimes devastating effects on national economies, while the advent of satellite communications makes it possible for there to be instantaneous communication across the globe and for national boundaries to be crossed with impunity. The result is that events occurring miles away can now have an almost immediate impact on us. David Harvey characterises this new phenomenon well: 'As space appears to shrink to a "global" village of telecommunications and a "spaceship earth" of economic and ecological interdependencies – to use just two familiar and everyday images – and as time horizons shorten to the point where the present is all there is, so we have to learn to cope with an overwhelming sense of compression of our spatial and temporal worlds' (Harvey 1989: 240).

While there is widespread agreement that globalisation is a central feature of the era in which we are living, the same level of agreement cannot be found in answer to the question as to what has brought it about and what it will lead to. All that we can safely conclude at the moment is that globalisation 'is essentially dialectical in nature and unevenly experienced across time and space' (McGrew 1992: 74).

Globalisation is a dialectical process in the sense that it does not bring about 'a generalised set of changes acting in a uniform direction, but consists of mutually opposed tendencies' (Giddens 1990: 64). Let us take two examples. Firstly, the tendency towards cultural homogenisation as opposed to cultural differentiation. Globalisation does entail a shift towards some cultural homogenisation, but at the same time it results in cultural differentiation. Across the world people now drink CocaCola at McDonald's, wear Levi jeans and Nike trainers and watch Hollywood films. The persistence of local differences inhibits, however, complete standardisation, and indeed a fascination with difference encourages the growth of ethnic markets so that ethnically distinctive food, dress and music are also now available around the world. Secondly, there is the tendency towards centralisation as opposed to decentralisation. Globalisation does make it more possible for organisations to develop which transcend national boundaries. Examples include transnational corporations, organisations which seek to exploit markets on a world scale but which may themselves permit organisational decentralisation, and the European Union, an organisation which seeks through some pooling of sovereignty to enable nation states which individually are incapable of resisting global forces to recover jointly some control. At the same time globalisation generates a powerful decentralising dynamic as communities feeling that the 'world' has become 'too large to be controlled . . . aim at shrinking it back to their size and reach' (Castells 1997: 66). Examples include the 'resurgence of various forms of nationalism and calls for a return to the pure (if mythic) certainties of the "old traditions"' (Morley and Robins 1995: 8). The resurgence of nationalism in Eastern Europe in the wake of the disintegration of the Soviet Union and its European satellites, and the advent of religious fundamentalism, including both Islamic and American Christian forms, represent cases in point.

The effects of globalisation are not only complex but there is also an unevenness with which globalisation has been experienced across space and time. Although it has gathered increased momentum in the last two decades, its consequences are not uniform across the globe. While we cannot equate globalisation with Westernisation, 'it is still the images, artifacts and identities of Western modernity, produced by the cultural industries of "Western" societies (including Japan) which dominate the global networks' (S Hall 1992a: 305).

Globalisation tends to undermine the power of tradition and custom on our lives by making us aware of alternative ways of living. Increasing reflexivity in turn has significant implications for our collective identities. While identity formation is a dynamic process and identities are constantly being redefined, not only can common (albeit selective) memories generate a sense of continuity over time but the maintenance of clear spatial boundaries between us and them can also facilitate a sense of cohesion. In this way collective identities can solidify and, at least for a time, become established. While modernity itself tends to make 'identity distinctly problematic', given 'the sheer scope and complexity of recognisable identities' which arise in its wake (Calhoun 1994: 10, 20), globalisation markedly accelerates this process. Globalisation tends to destabilise established identities as alternative representations compete for our attention 'in a world of dissolving boundaries and disrupted continuities' (Morley and Robins 1995: 122). The result is that we can no longer take our identity for granted but are obliged to choose who we are, albeit within social constraints. Some identities may disappear as people assimilate in response to a trend towards cultural homogenisation, but this is only one possibility. The trend towards global homogenisation is strongly resisted and can lead 'to a strengthening of local identities' and indeed 'the production of new identities' (S Hall 1992a: 308).

The strengthening of local identities can be seen in the reaction of groups who feel threatened by the presence of other cultures. Examples abound of people who seek to return to their cultural roots and rediscover the purity of a lost cultural identity. We have already pointed to two cases above: the resurgence of ethnic nationalism and the rise of religious fundamentalism. The production of new identities can be found especially among 'people who have been dispersed forever from their homelands' (S Hall 1992a: 310). As members of the new diasporas created by post-colonial migrations, they have to learn to live in more than one culture. Rejecting the search for cultural purity, they may opt to fuse different cultural traditions and create new hybrid identities. Both these responses to globalisation – the strengthening of local identities and the production of new identities – can be detected in Britain. We shall explore in turn in the next two sections the reaction, firstly, of members of the majority ethnic group and, secondly, of members of minority ethnic groups to this perceived crisis of identity.

Globalisation and the construction of British identity

In Britain a period of economic and political decline has coincided with what are seen by some as threats from above and below. From above, increasing integration into the European

Union is felt by some members of the dominant ethnic group to threaten national sovereignty; and from below, the formation of ethnic minority 'enclaves' within the nation state is felt by some members of the dominant ethnic group to be a threat to the British way of life. One response has been 'a particularly defensive, closed and exclusive definition of "Englishness" being advanced as a way of warding off or refusing to live with difference' (S Hall 1992b: 6). There has been a marked increase in this response, with the rise in the number of 'Little Englanders', people in Britain who see themselves as more English than British and who are likely to hold racist and xenophobic views (Curtice and Heath 2000). A good example of a Little England response is the speech given by a Conservative MP in 1989 in the wake of calls to allow British passport holders from Hong Kong the right to settle in Britain:

> The fact that the Hong Kong Chinese are very hardworking and hold British passports does not make them British. If millions of Chinese come to the UK, they would not integrate and become yellow Englishmen. They would create another China, another Hong Kong in England, just as former immigrants have created another Pakistan in Bradford. This possibility should make us consider what has already happened to this green and pleasant land – first as a result of waves of coloured immigrants and then by the pernicious doctrine of multi-culturalism . . . Every year that goes by the English are battered into submission in their own country and more strident are the demands of ethnic nationalism. The British people were never consulted as to whether they would change from being a homogeneous society to a multi-racial society. If they had been, I am sure that a resounding majority would have voted to keep Britain an English-speaking white country. (John Townend, quoted by Miles 1990: 148).

This speech exemplifies cultural racism. Groups are distinguished on the basis of physical markers; they are envisaged as having essentially different cultures; and the presence of these Others is deemed as undermining the integrity of 'our' British/English culture. 'Englishness [or for that matter Britishness] does not, however, have to be constructed invariably in racialised terms' (Brah 1996: 175). We should not assume, therefore, that this response to globalisation is typical. John Townend is somewhat of a maverick and while an exclusive definition of Britishness is still promulgated in some quarters, it is significant that the reaction in 1997 to a more senior Conservative politician's (Lord

Tebbitt's) 'warning that multiculturalism was a "divisive force" for society as a whole' was generally critical, and much more so than in previous decades to earlier speeches critical of multiculturalism, with 'support . . . received within mainstream politics [being] fairly limited' (Solomos 1998: 205). In a society in which chicken tikka massala has now overtaken both fish and chips and roast beef and Yorkshire pudding as the nation's most popular dish, it is more difficult to maintain a culturally isolationist stance.

An alternative response to globalisation insists that we must learn to live with difference. One example comes from an interview with Gordon Brown, the Chancellor of the Exchequer, on the eve of elections to the Scottish Parliament. After pointing out that he sees himself as Scottish, British and European and can 'accommodate all of these', he says, 'I see Britain as being the first country in the world that can be a multicultural, multi-ethnic and multinational state . . . . We have a chance to forge a unique pluralist democracy where diversity becomes a source of strength' (Brown quoted in Richards 1999: 18). Such a definition of Britishness does not hanker after cultural purity but consciously seeks to redefine national identity in a way which both acknowledges and celebrates difference. This example of an attempt to produce a new British identity is by no means atypical, but it coexists with other less inclusive definitions.

While globalisation has put the issue of national identity on the agenda, no clear settlement of this issue is in sight. We are witnessing instead very different responses by members of the majority ethnic group to globalisation, with some, concerned to strengthen local identities, hankering for 'the comforts of Tradition', while others, conscious of the need to produce new identities, emphasising instead 'the imperative to forge a new self-interpretation based upon the responsibilities of cultural Translation' (Morley and Robins 1995: 122).

Globalisation and minority ethnic identities

In moving from the majority group to minority ethnic groups, we are turning our attention to people who are obliged to move between cultures. According to some writers, the diasporic experience of being at least partially 'a stranger in a strange land is typical of the human condition' in the global age (Cohen 1997: 133). For globalisation tends to destabilise all identities and in the process relativise previously taken-for-granted identities. In this context, it is more difficult for people to 'hold onto the illusion of one fixed and unchanging identity' and the experience 'of identity as inherently in flux' therefore becomes a common one (McGuigan 1996: 141). Be that as it may, there is little doubt that identity formation among minority groups has to some extent a distinctive dynamic, partly because members typically move between different cultures and partly because they face racism.

Ethnic identities among the first generation

What is apparent when we examine minority identities is both their diversity and their changing nature. At the risk of some simplification, we shall begin by contrasting the situation of first generation Caribbeans and South Asians. In both cases, an initial pioneering phase of migration was followed by a process of 'chain migration where friends and relatives were encouraged and helped by pioneer migrants to follow them' and ethnic colonies developed (Anwar 1998: 2).

The Caribbeans arrived in the 'mother country' conscious of differences in shades of Black and island identities among themselves. They found, however, that these and other differences counted for nothing as far as the indigenous population was concerned. They were all 'coloured'. Despite in many ways being culturally not very distinctive from their White neighbours, they faced discrimination because of their colour. Such rejection ruled out for most of them the possibility of assimilation into British society. Their high expectations were dashed and they therefore turned to each other and created a space for themselves in particular areas where they could feel at home. In other words, they created a colony within White society where, despite 'having lost their extended family and community networks in the migratory process' (Modood *et al.* 1994: 30), a plethora of distinctive Black life-styles were able to flourish (Pryce 1986). Subject to racism, they became steadily aware of their common Caribbean identity and developed a 'conscious-ness of themselves as a black enclave within British society' (James 1993: 251).

The South Asians migrated to Britain generally believing, like many Caribbeans, that one day they would be returning home. The early migrants were generally single men whose primary objective 'was to raise the family's standing in the local social hierarchy' through sending home remittances to supplement their family's capital resources (R Ballard 1994: 11). They there-fore worked long hours to maximise earnings and tolerated crowding together into all-male households to minimise expen-diture. As their stay lengthened, however, so 'they began to reconstruct a familiar social order around themselves, complete with all its associated cultural norms' (R Ballard 1994: 15).

Although often critical of English mores, confidence in the possibility of creating a civilised life in Britain grew. Extended families were reunited, properties were bought and religious institutions were re-established. The construction of ethnic colonies based on specific castes, sects and kinship groups in turn 'had a major effect on the behaviour of settlers who found themselves under growing pressure to conform . . . to the ideal norms of their own particular group' (R Ballard 1994: 18). Socialised to believe that the interests of one's community should always take precedence over those of individual members, the need to maintain a sense of izzat or personal honour was re-emphasised. While the networks of reciprocity were for the first generation primarily based on loyalties to specific castes, sects and kinship groups, and members of minority groups were conscious of other manifest differences between themselves, they often saw religion as central to their ethnic identity. Despite sharing with Caribbeans a common experience of racial discrim-ination, they therefore tended generally not to define themselves as sharing a common Black identity (Modood *et al.* 1997).

While both the Caribbean and Asian communities have main-tained over time a strong sense of ethnic identity, we should not assume that ethnic identification necessarily implies participation in a plethora of distinctive cultural practices (Baumann 1996). Although the experience of being rejected by White society prompted some second-generation Caribbeans to express their 'ethnic distinctiveness through the black churches, Patois-Creole

and use of hair and dress' and in this way become more culturally distinctive than their parents, the PSI survey identified few
items which pointed to any real cultural distinctiveness among
British-born Caribbeans (Modood *et al.* 1997: 336). First generation Asians were much more likely than first generation
Caribbeans to participate in a range of distinctive cultural practices but even here the PSI survey discovered that over time
there has been 'a relatively linear process of declining cultural
distinctiveness' (Modood *et al.* 1997: 336). This is evident from
an examination of religious observance, the use of Asian languages, arranged marriages and the wearing of Asian clothes,
where there is a marked contrast between South Asians born in
Britain and their parents. We should not exaggerate the extent of
change, however. South Asians (and indeed Caribbeans) are still
much more likely than Whites to acknowledge the importance of
religion to their lives; an overwhelming majority are able to use
a community language; in most cases the arranged marriage
system has been adapted rather than abandoned; and at least on
special occasions women in particular are likely to wear Asian
clothes. What is more, there is an important division between
South Asians, with Pakistanis and Bangladeshis being much
more reluctant to abandon distinctive cultural practices than
African Asians and Indians.

Ethnic identities among young people

There is a tendency among some popular commentators, as Gilroy
(1987) argues, to portray the cultural heritage of Caribbeans and
Asians as posing particular difficulties for minority ethnic youth.
According to this account, 'Black youth culture contains an inflam-
mable rebellious element' while the 'problem for Asian youth
[is that they] inhabit a very different world at school from that of
home' (Brake 1985: 143, 139). Caribbean youth are thus presented as implacably antagonistic towards the wider society and
prone to hostile outbursts, while Asian youth are pictured as more
quiescent but caught between two cultures.

What lends credence to this picture of Caribbean youth is that
they take pride in their Blackness, are more vociferous than their
parents in their opposition to racism and were prominent in some

high-profile inner city disorders in the 1980s. We should not assume, however, that this means that they are alienated from the wider society and feel intense hostility towards it. The assertion of a Black identity does not imply a rejection of Britishness but a demand for respect towards a valued identity. Most in fact not only see themselves as Black but also recognise that in many ways they are British. While there is some hesitancy in calling themselves British because they recognise that their colour is an 'obstacle to their being accepted as British', most 'identify with and actively participate in . . . British society [and] see themselves as mainly culturally British' (Modood *et al.* 1994: 108). In only one respect do their attitudes diverge significantly from their White peers and that relates to their distrust of the police (Modood *et al.* 1997). Their participation in inner city disorders represented the culmination of a historically antagonistic relationship between the police and Black youth, but it is noteworthy that subsequent disorders have involved predominantly White youth and, most recently, Asian youth. In the light of evidence pointing to racial discrimination by the police, what is more remarkable than the participation of Black youth in the disorders of the 1980s is their remarkable patience since then.

Caribbeans constitute 'an exemplary case of a cultural diaspora' (Cohen 1997: 144). As part of this diaspora, Caribbean youth in Britain have drawn upon cultures developed by Black populations elsewhere in the world to 'redefine what it means to be black, adapting it to distinctively British experiences and meanings' (Gilroy 1987: 154). The main inspiration in the 1970s was the Caribbean, with reggae being a key medium for transmitting Rastafarian ideas, but since then 'African-American styles [have] become more visible' with 'the influence of rap and hip-hop culture [being] crucial' (Osgerby 1998: 127). In some cases, attempts to redefine what it means to be Black have led to an essentialist conception of Blackness, according to which Black people are construed as having one fixed identity which entails that they are essentially different from White people. Some Caribbean youth who, faced by racism, drew on Rastafarianism to identify with their African roots arguably took this line. In other cases, attempts to redefine Blackness have led not to 'a strengthening of local identities' but to 'the production of new identities' (S Hall 1992a). The political use of the term

'Black' in the 1970s to provide a new focus of identification for both Caribbean and Asian communities constitutes a good example. While in no way denying cultural differences between these communities, some Caribbeans and Asians redefined Blackness to signify their common subjection to racism.

According to some theorists, the production of new identities often involves fusing different cultural traditions and creating hybrid cultures. Hybridity is not necessarily progressive, however. While, for example, White subcultures such as that of the mods and skinheads 'drew inspiration from the perceived "coolness" [and popular music] of their black peers', that did not stop them being racist (Osgerby 1998: 123). Nor is hybridity exceptional. Indeed all 'cultures evolve historically through unreflecting borrowings . . . and appropriations' (Werbner 1997: 4–5). When theorists such as Stuart Hall (1992a) extol hybridity, what they have in mind are deliberate attempts to draw on different cultures in order to challenge conventional boundaries. Used in this way, hybridity is not the norm and can indeed be progressive. Back provides an example from his ethnographic study conducted between 1985 and 1989 of two neighbourhoods in South London. In one of these neighbourhoods, the dominance of a discourse which recognised the legitimacy of different ethnic groups living together enabled 'a negotiated form of identity and ethnicity [to be] generated' by Black and White young people (Back 1996: 241). In this situation the notion that Englishness and Blackness are mutually exclusive identities could not be sustained, and conventional boundaries were crossed. We need to be careful, however, not to overstate the way new identities of this kind impact on wider cultural norms or transform people's lives, since inequalities between groups frequently remain impervious to such changes (Anthias 2001).

According to Hall and Gilroy, Caribbean youth are at the forefront in producing hybrid identities. Jungle music constitutes a good example of what they have in mind. 'A peculiarly British musical genre, jungle was also a bearer of strong links with specifically black cultural traditions, a cultural hybrid generated as black youngsters negotiated and translated their way through the different cultural contexts created by post-colonial migration' (Osgerby 1998: 203). What is more, the musical ethos of jungle was transcultural, entailing an aesthetic which challenged the notion that people belong to cultures which are essentially different. Evidence that inter-ethnic friendships are becoming more common and that Caribbeans increasingly have White partners (with the result that, for people born in Britain, half of Caribbean men and one-third of Caribbean women now have a White partner) suggests 'that this process of mixing, of hybridisation, will increasingly be the norm where rapid change and globalisation have made all identities unstable' (Modood *et al.* 1997: 338). The idea of hybridity is likely to have a particular appeal to the increasing number of people of mixed ethnic background as 'illustrated by the golfer Tiger Woods, who, rather than be thought of as the first black man to win the US Masters golf tournament, preferred to describe himself as a "Cablinasian"' to signify his Caucasian, Black, Indian and Asian roots (Gabriel 1998: 2).

In switching our attention from Caribbean youth to South Asian youth, it seems that ethnic boundaries – at least with Whites and Caribbeans – are more clearly demarcated. Inter-ethnic friendships are less common, mixed marriages are rarer, and culturally distinctive practices are more prevalent. For some commentators, this creates a problem for Asian youth who are caught between two cultures, the culture of the home and the culture of the school, with their contrasting conceptions of the relationship of the individual and community. This position is clearly articulated by Ghuman: 'Young people of Asian origin ... face special problems of adjustment during adolescence because of the conflict of values and social mores between home and the wider society' with the result that they 'are likely to face an "identity crisis" because of the very different expectations of the family and the school' (Ghuman 1999: 11). While White people (and indeed Caribbeans) tend to view marriage as a contract between two individuals, South Asians tend to view it as an arrangement between families. In view of this it is not surprising to learn of South Asian adolescents expressing a preference for the Western model of marriage based on individual choice and of conflicts between them and their parents.

We must be careful not to caricature the situation, however. While it is true that the attitudes of young South Asians (especially African Asians and Indians) towards arranged marriages and indeed 'mixed' marriages increasingly differ from those of

their parents, 'there is no evidence to support the implied assertion that conflict levels are higher among Asian families than
among white families' (Brah 1996: 80). Indeed, a study focusing
on Sikhs found 'very little evidence of overt intergenerational
conflict' at all (Drury 1991: 398). While conflicts do occur (as
they do in all families), 'outright confrontation is much rarer . . .
than processes of debate, accommodation and adaptation'
(Gillespie 1995: 108). When it comes to the crunch, confrontations are avoided by parents modifying the traditional arranged
marriage system to incorporate elements of consultation and
negotiation, and by children accepting the authority of their
parents (Anwar 1998). In some cases such conformity by the
children may be reluctantly given. At the end of the day, however, growing up in an Asian family encourages individuals to
feel loyalty to their community and the experience of being
rejected by British society helps to reinforce this feeling. In the
light of this, it is not surprising that one study of young Asians
came to the conclusion that most 'valued their kin and culture
more than the freedoms which are supposed to be so desirable'
(Stopes-Roe and Cochrane 1990: 52).

Although young Asians are more likely than their parents to
be constantly moving between a variety of social worlds which
are often grounded on different cultural conventions, we should
not assume that they are faced with an either/or situation,
whereby they have to choose between two radically distinct
cultures. The majority learn 'to be bi-cultural and bilingual'
(Ghuman 1999: 81) and are adept in being able 'to switch codes
as appropriate' (R Ballard 1994: 31). What is more, and despite
some variability between different Asian groups, they often also
seek to create their own synthesis of Asian and British values and
'are prone to using hyphenated identities for self-description'
(Ghuman 1999: 81). Most are proud of their ethnic identity
(which is often conceptualised in religious terms) but also recognise that they are in many ways British. In the light of this, it is
noteworthy that young Asians tend to be more individualistic
and ethnically assertive than their parents. While a growing indi-
vidualism indicates an acceptance of some British values, increasing ethnic assertiveness points to a fierce rejection of other
British values and a demand for public recognition of a valued
ethnic identity.

Aware that they are often not accepted as British, some Asians respond by 'strengthening local identities' and asserting their essential difference from other ethnic groups. This may involve a retreat 'to the familiar certainties of the past' where 'the meaning of life is deemed to be permanently and incorrigibly revealed in a sacred text, body of rituals, or a pool of inherited and inviolable traditions' (Parekh 1989: 141). This response has been particularly evident among some Muslims, who have felt insulted by the attacks on their religion with the publication of Salman Rushdie's *The Satanic Verses*.

As prevalent, however, is 'the production of new identities'. Gillespie (1995) found that young Punjabis in Southall drew upon both the culture of their own ethnic community and popular culture to construct a British Asian identity, while a study of Muslim girls pointed to the way a commitment to Islam provides an opportunity 'to choose which elements from other cultures (British or Asian) they can utilise. By taking a more conscious approach to Islam, Muslim women [were] able to analyse British and Asian culture to see which elements [were] compatible with the Islamic code. Thus inconsistencies with Asian culture, such as dowry giving and the arranged marriage system, and with British culture, such as gambling and drinking, [could] be eliminated from their various lifestyles' (Butler 1995: 21). While it is important not to overstate the freedom of Asian youth to construct their own identity, given both the existence of racism in the wider society and the pressure, especially on girls (Beishon *et al.* 1998), to conform to the behavioural norms of their own ethnic community, the production of new identities by young Asians is by no means exceptional.

Although much more attention has been given to the role of Caribbean youth in producing new hybrid identities, hybridity is also evident among some Asian youth. The emergence of bhangra in the 1980s is a case in point. Fusing traditional Punjabi and Bengali music with hip-hop and house, it 'signalled the development of . . . a distinctively British Asian youth culture' (Back 1996: 220). Apache Indian epitomises this above all with his music, which not only fuses 'ragga *plus* bhangra *plus* England *plus* Kingston *plus* Birmingham' but also challenges taken-for-granted boundaries between groups, appealing to ethnically diverse audiences (Back 1996: 227). While it cannot be said that hybrid identities are a characteristic feature of Asian youth and were not evident in a study, for example, of young Chinese people (Parker 1994), such new ethnicities are becoming more prevalent.

Globalisation tends to destabilise established identities and this is certainly no less true of minority groups than the majority group. Members of minority ethnic groups necessarily move between different social worlds, which rest on different cultural assumptions, and are aware that they are subject to racism. They cannot take their identity for granted and are obliged to be reflexive. Although a variety of responses to globalisation can be detected, they tend, like those of the majority ethnic group, towards one of two kinds. The first kind of response involves strengthening traditional identities and seeks to retreat to the familiar certainties of the past. The second kind of response recognises that this is not possible and seeks to draw on different cultures to construct new identities.

Conclusion

The question of identity has received extensive attention recently from social theorists. It is now widely recognised that we do not have one fixed identity but a range of shifting identities and that these are socially constructed. Of critical importance to this process of social construction is representation. Taking national identities as an example, we find that competing representations often vie for our attention and construct the nation differently. In the British case, some exemplify cultural racism (or ethnocentrism) and exclude minority ethnic groups, while others are explicitly multicultural and thus more inclusive.

Historically, Asian and Black people were represented as the Other essentially different from Us, with a racialised regime of representation being dominant. Despite the persistence of stereotypical images of Asian and Black people in contemporary media and popular culture, recent studies point to significant changes in representational practices. A racialised regime of representation now therefore coexists with representations which challenge the old stereotypes. This means that racialised representations of the nation are by no means any longer hegemonic.

It has become increasingly evident that the question of identity needs to be explored in a global context. Globalisation has proved unsettling to established identities and has generated among both the majority and minority groups different responses. One response has been to strengthen local identities by searching for cultural purity and retreating to the familiar certainties of the past. Cultural racism and religious fundamentalism constitute examples. The other response has been to produce new identities by drawing on different cultural traditions, fully cognisant of the need to live with difference. Examples include representing the nation in an ethnically inclusive way and the creation of hyphenated identities such as Black-British/British-Asian.

7 The politics of race and citizenship

The state did not anticipate the scale of post-war immigration from the New Commonwealth and Pakistan and certainly did not plan to help the newcomers settle in Britain. Rather, individuals from the Caribbean and the Indian subcontinent took up the opportunity, as British subjects, to come to Britain to take jobs at a time when the country was experiencing a labour shortage. The measures taken by governments initially tended to be *ad hoc*, comprising responses to immediate problems. Eventually, however, a policy accepted by both the main political parties emerged.

The state's policy on race and ethnicity

This policy had two aspects: controls over immigration on the one hand and measures designed to combat racial disadvantage and aid integration on the other hand. These two sides of state intervention are neatly encapsulated in the oft-repeated phrase of a former Labour Minister: 'Integration without control is impossible but control without integration is indefensible' (Roy Hattersley, 1965, quoted in Solomos 1989: 115). While the Conservative Party was the first to advocate immigration control (which the Labour Party later came to support), the latter was the first to put forward measures to redress racial disadvantage (which the Conservatives then accepted).

We must not exaggerate the extent of consensus, however. From the start this bipartisan policy was fragile. While some consensus was evident between the frontbenches, intra-party divisions meant that it did not have strong roots in the backbenches. What is more at times the policy reached breaking point. Nevertheless, and despite evident twists and turns, throughout the post-war period the major political parties have generally sought to depoliticise a potentially divisive issue by maintaining since 1965 restrictive immigration controls with measures to promote integration. For the sake of clarity of exposition, we shall take the two prongs of policy in turn.

Post-war immigration policy

A period of laisser faire? 1948–1961

The opportunity, which the British Nationality Act of 1948 reaffirmed for citizens of the British Commonwealth to enter Britain, seek work and settle here with their families, lasted throughout the 1950s. The right of Caribbeans and Asians to migrate to Britain was indeed publicly defended by politicians in both the main political parties. While Conservative spokesmen pointed out that citizens of the Commonwealth were 'British subjects', Labour spokesmen emphasised that they were 'our comrades' (Rex and Tomlinson 1979).

We should not assume, however, that the 1948 Act was designed to encourage immigration to solve Britain's labour shortage after the war. It did not create new rights to immigrate but confirmed the situation that prevailed before 1948. What prompted the government to pass legislation to define 'an "imperial" notion of citizenship' (Geddes 1996: 11) was the fact that some countries, such as Canada, after gaining independence were developing their own citizenship laws. Anxious to prevent countries leaving the Commonwealth, the government reasserted 'its faith in the unity of Empire, by recognising all citizens of territories that made up the Empire/Commonwealth – Britain, the colonies and self-governing member states of the commonwealth – as British subjects' (I Spencer 1997: 54). Within this broad category of British subjects, the Act created 'Citizenship of the United Kingdom and Colonies' for those who were not citizens of an independent Commonwealth country. This decision 'was a political manoeuvre designed to ward off potential calls for colonial independence' (Paul 1997: 23). In short, the Act sought to maintain Britain's international position, and neither party 'thought there was any serious likelihood of large numbers of its Asian and black colonial subjects taking up their right to live and work in the United Kingdom' (I Spencer 1997: 55).

The period from 1948 to the early 1960s is often characterised as one of laisser faire, with both parties keen to distance themselves from the vociferous minority on the back-benches who objected to the arrival of Black and Asian immigrants. The release of government papers reveals, however, that both the Labour and Conservative governments during this period privately shared the concerns of the anti-immigration lobby. 'The set of the official mind was always opposed to the permanent settlement in Britain of Asian and black communities' (I Spencer 1997: 19). While the arrival of Continental and Irish aliens was acceptable because 'they passed an unwritten test of racial acceptability' (Paul 1997: xiii), fears were expressed 'that "coloured" immigrants in large numbers could not be assimilated' (I Spencer 1997: 154). Given these concerns, the administrative measures used in the inter-war period 'to exclude and control Jewish and black migrants' (Solomos 1993: 52) were maintained in the post-war period for British subjects of colour. Indeed both the Labour Government of 1950–51 and the Conservative Government of 1951–55 contemplated legislative controls. These plans were temporarily suspended because 'there was a widespread recognition within ruling circles that while any controls on immigration had to be racial in form, the government could not be seen as openly espousing discriminatory controls' (Malik 1996: 21). A strong case needed to be mounted, given the lack of clearly articulated public anxiety, the country's labour shortage and the significance attached to the Commonwealth (Carter *et al.* 1993).

The case was strengthened in 1958 when the resentment felt by some White residents towards their new neighbours spilled over into 'white riots' (E Pilkington 1988) and in Nottingham and Notting Hill White youths openly attacked Blacks. The riots prompted politicians to take one of two positions. According to the first view, the riots exemplified racism. Disadvantaged Whites had vented their frustrations on a group of people whom they considered inferior. For there to be racial harmony, governments needed to devise policies to combat racism and to eradicate the disadvantages faced by both Whites and Blacks. According to the second view, the riots indicated that traditional British tolerance towards immigrants had been stretched beyond reasonable limits. The presence of a large number of Black and culturally distinct immigrants had provoked resentment. To allay people's anxieties and thus promote racial harmony, governments needed to restrict the number of Black and Asian immigrants and encourage those already here to assimilate.

The 1962 Commonwealth Immigrants Act

Although the subject of race relations rarely arose during the 1959 election, the re-elected Conservative Government faced mounting demands for immigration control. No longer as willing to envisage the Commonwealth as critical to the country's international position and with immigrant flows rising as individuals sought to beat the ban, the government eventually succumbed to the pressure and passed the Commonwealth Immigrants Act of 1962. Under the Act, citizens of the British Commonwealth had to acquire an employment voucher to come to Britain unless they held passports issued in Britain or through a British High Commission abroad. Three types of voucher were distinguished: Category A for those with a specific job; Category B for those with skills in short supply; and Category C for other applicants.

Although the 1962 Act was purportedly concerned with immigration control, the immigrant groups who were the most numerous virtually every year – the Irish and Commonwealth immigrants of European origin – 'barely merited a mention at the higher levels of government' (I Spencer 1997: 153). The concern was with Asian and Black immigration and the Act was therefore '*de facto* a measure aimed at immigrants from the newer, non-white Commonwealth' (Saggar 1992: 105).

Although the Act was vigorously opposed by the Labour Party, the election of the Conservative candidate, Peter Griffiths, at Smethwick in the 1964 general election, prompted the party to change its mind. The Conservative candidate's victory on what most commentators consider to have been an extremely racist platform had been gained against the national trend. The lessons were not lost on the Labour Government. Far from repealing the 1962 Act, it tightened it up by abolishing Category C vouchers (on which Asians and Blacks were most reliant) and reducing the overall number of vouchers for Commonwealth immigrants in 1965.

The 1968 Commonwealth Immigrants Act

Two events in 1968 confirmed that the second view depicted above (namely that traditional British tolerance towards immigrants stretched beyond reasonable limits) had won the day. They were the passing of legislation designed to reduce the number of East African Asians entering Britain and what one writer has called 'the rise of Enoch Powell' (Foot 1969). Let us take each in turn.

The 1962 Act did not cover East African Asians who had opted, on the independence of Kenya and other African countries, to hold British passports. When, however, increasing numbers took up their right to migrate to Britain during 1967, as a result of the Kenyan government's 'Africanisation' policy, panic set in. The Commonwealth Immigrants Act of 1968 was rushed through Parliament and became law within a week. Under the Act, people who held British passports did not have the right to enter and settle in Britain unless they had a 'close connection' with the country, for example a parent or grandparent born in Britain. The Act was clearly racially discriminatory in nature. For its effects were to allow White people of British origin who had settled abroad to enter Britain but to prevent East African Asians from doing so until they were lucky enough to be granted one of the limited number of vouchers issued each year. Although the Home Secretary announced to Parliament, 'I repudiate emphatically the suggestion that [the Bill] is racialist in origin or in conception or in the manner in which it is being carried out' (Jim Callaghan, 1968, quoted in Lattimer, 1999: 28), Cabinet papers, which have now been released, tell a different story. Thus in a memo sent to colleagues six weeks later, the Home Secretary wrote:

> It is sometimes argued that we can take a less serious view of the scale of immigration and settlement in this country because it could be, and currently is, more than offset by total emigration. This view overlooks the important point that emigration is largely by white persons from nearly every corner of the United Kingdom, while immigration and settlement are largely by coloured persons into a relatively small number of concentrated areas. The exchange thus aggravates rather than alleviates the problem (Jim Callaghan, 1968, quoted in Lattimer 1999: 29).

The intervention of Enoch Powell

If 1968 witnessed a piece of legislation which was effectively racist, it also saw a leading politician apparently lend respectability to racism. Senior politicians were no strangers to racialised discourse, but Powell's intervention allowed the previous private discourse to become public and as a result politicised an issue which the frontbenchers had sought to depoliticise (Malik 1996). In graphic language, Powell advocated halting Asian and Black immigration and indeed explored ways to repatriate those already here. Unless such measures were taken, he argued, the future was fearful. In his most famous speech, he concluded: 'As I look ahead I am filled with foreboding. Like the Roman I seem to see "the River Tiber foaming with much blood"' (Enoch Powell, 1968, quoted in Solomos 1993: 67). Although this speech was denounced by many politicians and caused him to be sacked from the Shadow Cabinet, Powell received phenomenal support from the public. In the light of this, few politicians were tempted any longer to take a more liberal line on immigration. Indeed, some have argued that the last minute swing to the Conservatives in the 1970 election was attributable at least in part to Powell who persuaded 'voters who had originally intended to vote for Labour to switch to the Conservatives because of their tougher stance on the immigration issue' (S Taylor 1992: 151).

The 1971 Immigration Act

With the advent of a Conservative Government in 1970, a new Immigration Act was passed, which codified the previous legislation and tightened the controls on Asian and Black immigration even further. 'The Act was of considerable symbolic significance' (I Spencer 1997: 143). For it signalled the demise of the historic distinction between the rights of 'British subjects' and 'aliens' and indicated that Britain now saw its future within Europe rather than the Commonwealth. Indeed, by a remarkable coincidence, the Immigration Act became law on the same day that Britain entered the European Economic Community.

Under the 1971 Immigration Act, Commonwealth citizens needed permission to enter Britain unless they fell into one of three categories: they were 'patrials' and thus had a 'close connection' with the country; they were close relations of those who had emigrated to Britain under previous legislation; or they were part of the quota of East African Asians accepted each year. If they did not fit into one of these categories, they needed to be in possession of a work permit which replaced the employment voucher and henceforth had to be renewed annually. The work permit did not carry with it the right of permanent settlement and 'introduced for those non-patrial Commonwealth citizens who came to Britain to work a status which was closely akin to that enjoyed by guest workers in the Federal Republic of Germany and other European states' (I Spencer 1997: 144). In effect, the Act reinforced the racially discriminatory nature of the previous immigration legislation.

In view of the paucity of 'patrials' in the New as opposed to the Old and predominantly White Commonwealth, virtually the only Asian and Black immigrants allowed in since the Act have been close dependants of those already here. This outcome was intended, as secret Cabinet minutes – recently released – indicate. The main motive behind the Act, as the Cabinet secretary made clear at the time, was 'to avoid the risk of renewed "swamping" by immigrants from the new Commonwealth'. Such immigrants were seen as a problem because, to quote the Home Secretary, 'the vast majority would want to settle permanently and by reason of this factor and of the fact that they come generally from a different cultural background, the task of assimilation – as experience so bitterly shows – is all but impossible' (Reginald Maudling, 1971, quoted in Travis 2002). By effectively bringing primary immigration from the Indian subcontinent, the Caribbean and Africa to a halt, the government expected that the 1971 Act would bring the immigration issue to an end. This hope was soon dashed, however.

The rise of the National Front

In 1972 President Amin expelled all British Asians from Uganda. Aware that these British passport holders would otherwise be stateless the British government reluctantly admitted 27,000 refugees. This manifestation of liberalism did not last long, however. Indeed the emergence of a 'new political phenomenon' in the shape of a political movement for whom racism was a central plank, persuaded most politicians against any further liberalisation (S Taylor 1992).

The new political phenomenon was the growth in support for an extreme right-wing movement, the National Front. The movement had been formed in 1967 from other extreme right-wing movements and inherited from its predecessors both its personnel and ideology. Indeed continuities have been detected between the National Front and two previous fascist movements, Mosley's British Union of Fascists and Leese's Imperial Fascist League. Not only were leading members of the National Front connected with these movements, but they also retained, as a central element in their ideology, the belief that Jews were conspiring to overthrow the natural order, in which the White race was dominant, so that they could rule the world themselves. In seeking popular support, leaders of the National Front played down this ideological strand and emphasised instead the need for Asian and Black immigrants to be repatriated. Such scapegoating of Asians and Blacks brought the party little success until the government decided to admit the Ugandan Asians in 1972. Capitalising on the issue, National Front candidates in the local elections in 1973 gained some electoral support, with over 10 per cent of the vote in a number of cities.

More important, however, than its electoral support – which peaked in 1976–77, when a new panic arose about the numbers of Asians from Malawi being admitted to the country – was the publicity which the party received through its demonstrations and election campaigns (A Pilkington 1986). Like other British fascist organisations before and since, the National Front had limited appeal outside a few localities and was indeed vigorously challenged by anti-racist organisations such as the Anti-Nazi League.

The visibility, however, and apparent popularity of a party which openly expressed racist views encouraged the main political parties to maintain a very restrictive immigration policy and ensured the durability of the immigration issue. Indeed, following a change of leadership, the Conservative Party indicated that it did not feel as bound as its predecessors to abide by the hitherto bipartisan policy to avoid party competition over the issue. In an extremely revealing interview in 1978 before she became Prime Minister, Margaret Thatcher made reference to the National Front. After pointing out that some White people felt 'swamped by people with a different culture', she spoke of the fears 'driving some people to the National Front', a party considered to be at least 'talking about some of the problems' (Margaret Thatcher, 1978, quoted in A Pilkington 1984: 149). Although the immigration issue had dropped down the agenda by the time of the 1979 election, there is little doubt that the Conservative Party's advocacy of further immigration restriction was an electoral asset and contributed to the debacle of the National Front in the general election. For there was an above average swing to the Conservatives in those areas where the National Front had previously polled well.

Immigration and the 1981 British Nationality Act

The advent of the first Thatcher Government, committed to further restriction of immigration, entailed two main policy changes. The first sought to control secondary immigration while the second sought to bring citizenship law in line with the changes effected by the immigration legislation of 1962, 1968 and 1971.

With primary immigration from the New Commonwealth and Pakistan already effectively halted, the only way further Black and Asian immigration could be restricted was by controlling secondary immigration. To this end new immigration rules were introduced in 1980. These restricted the rights of dependants, fiances and spouses of British citizens to settle in this country. The rules were generally much tighter than those they replaced and included the establishment of 'the primary purpose rule', which prohibited the entry of fiances and spouses unless they could demonstrate that the primary purpose of their marriage was not to settle in Britain.

The 1948 British Nationality Act had established citizenship of the United Kingdom and the Colonies for those who did not have citizenship of an independent Commonwealth country. This form of citizenship 'had been gradually rendered obsolete by decolonisation, the change in Britain's position in the world and the growing political distance between Britain and many of its ex-colonies' (I Spencer 1997: 148). The 1981 British Nationality Act therefore replaced it with three new ones: British citizenship, British Dependent Territories citizenship and British Overseas citizenship. Only those who were British citizens, mainly 'patrials', had the right to settle in this country. Those granted British Dependent Territories citizenship, mainly people in Britain's remaining colonies such as the residents of Hong Kong and the Falkland Islands, had the right to settle in the dependency in question while those given British Overseas citizenship, the remainder, did not have the right to settle in any country at all.

Much of the criticism of the Act centred on the last form of citizenship. For some of the people in this category – East African Asians – had previously had the right to settle in Britain under the quota system set up in 1968 while others – mainly Asian – did not have any other nationality. The unwillingness of the government to give British citizenship to those without any other 'contrasts markedly with the solicitude shown to certain people – mainly white' (Bonner 1983, quoted in A Pilkington 1984: 149) and points to racial discrimination.

This is borne out by the subsequent responses to the plight of the Falkland Islanders and the Hong Kong Chinese. The government responded to the Argentinian invasion of the Falkland Islands by promptly sending a task force to liberate the islanders who, despite having not been granted British citizenship in 1981, were deemed to be 'British in stock and tradition' (Margaret Thatcher, 1982, quoted in Paul 1997: 185). After the war their status was changed in recognition of their true Britishness and they were granted British citizenship under a special Nationality Act in 1982. By contrast the government exhibited extreme reluctance to adopt a comparable strategy in relation to the Hong Kong Chinese before the handling back of the colony to China in 1997. Afraid, however, that a significant exodus might destabilise the economy, the government eventually relented and granted British citizenship under another special Nationality Act in 1990 to 50,000 of the colony's key personnel. This concession was designed to reassure the elite of the colony and encourage them to stay. The status of the vast majority of Hong Kong Chinese, however, was not changed. For, unlike the Falkland Islanders, they were not deemed truly British. 'By establishing tiers of citizenship and limiting the right of abode' in this way 'the Conservative administration reconstructed British nationality to suit its conceptions of which Britons in law were true Britons at heart' (Paul 1997: 184).

According to some writers, 'the 1981 Nationality Act effectively closed the immigration door and thus killed the salience of the issue' (Saggar 1992: 135) so that by the 1983 general election, 'immigration . . . [had] dropped off the bottom of the political agenda' (Crewe 1983, quoted in Saggar 1992: 128). Such a judgement, however, now seems premature. For while 'labour recruitment and spontaneous labour migration' may have become less significant, 'other types of migration, such as family reunion and refugee and asylum-seeker movement' have grown in importance and ensured the continuing salience of the immigration issue both in Britain and elsewhere (Castles and Miller 1998: 102).

Tightening immigration control and the 1988 Immigration Act

The re-election of the Thatcher Government in 1983 witnessed no slackening in immigration controls. Although the government did not resurrect the repatriation option, as some (for example, Miles and Phizacklea 1984) feared, it instituted two further controls at the point of departure in order to prevent the illegal settlement of visitors and asylum seekers. The first involved a new requirement that visitors from New Commonwealth countries should have a visa before they entered Britain. The second made it an offence for airlines and shipping companies to carry passengers without proper documentation.

While the immigration issue again did not play a significant role in the 1987 general election, the Conservatives did make a manifesto commitment 'to tighten the existing law to ensure that control over settlement becomes even more effective' (S Taylor 1992: 160). Thus, and despite the fact that under international conventions people have transnational rights to family reunion and asylum, the third Thatcher Government sought to restrict secondary immigration and make it more difficult for people to claim asylum.

The 1988 Immigration Act focused on secondary immigration and entailed the withdrawal of the rights of spouses and dependants to enter Britain. British citizens no longer had the automatic right to be joined by their spouses and dependants. 'The right now became conditional on showing that [those] seeking entry to the UK would be provided with adequate accommodation and financial support, and thus would not seek resort to public funds' (Layton-Henry 1992: 207). The 1992 Asylum Bill focused on an issue which has grown in significance since the late 1980s, following the end of the Cold War and the civil war in former Yugoslavia: namely, the growing number of asylum seekers. Before the Bill became law, however, a general election was called by John Major, the new Conservative leader.

The 1993 Asylum and Immigration Appeals Act

Despite the Labour Party's opposition to the Asylum Bill, immigration was again not a key issue in the campaign until the last few days, when Sir Nicholas Fairbairn, a Conservative MP, resurrected the issue. He raised the spectre of Britain under a Labour government being 'swamped with immigrants of every race and, on any excuse, of asylum or bogus marriage or just plain deception' (Nicholas Fairbairn, 1992, quoted in S Taylor 1992: 161). Although the leadership distanced themselves from this speech, other Conservative politicians, including the Home Secretary, echoed its sentiments along with the Conservative press. Indeed it has been suggested that the last minute swing to the Conservatives and consequently their fourth successive election victory in 1992 was due, at least in part, to the party's playing the 'race card'.

The incoming Major Government continued the policy of tightening immigration, focusing particularly on attempts to curtail the rapid increase in asylum seekers. The Asylum and Immigration Appeals Bill, which had been held up by the 1992 general election, was resurrected and became law in

1993. In the context of an already significant rise in the proportion of asylum claims refused, the Act curtailed the rights of asylum seekers by, among other measures, withdrawing entitlement to housing and effectively restricting rights of representation and appeal. In addition 'the government used the occasion of the Asylum [Act] to abolish rights of appeal against an IO's [immigration officer's] decision in the case of visitors and students' (Cohen 1994: 96).

The 1996 Asylum and Immigration Act

In an attempt to deter asylum applications even further, new regulations were introduced in 1996 allowing only those claiming asylum at their point of entry to the country eligibility for welfare benefits. When the appeal court overruled these regulations on the ground that this would entail 'a life so destitute that . . . no civilised nation can tolerate it' (Morris 1998: 250), emergency legislation was rushed through Parliament to circumvent the appeal court's decision. Since the vast majority of asylum seekers apply for asylum after entry to the country, the 1996 Asylum and Immigration Act meant that most asylum seekers were no longer entitled to benefits. In view of the fact that they also cannot apply for a work permit for six months and the process of obtaining one normally takes at least another six months, most asylum seekers typically 'have no source of income available to them' for more than a year (Bloch 1997: 117). In addition to these restrictions on the rights of asylum seekers, the Act also introduced penalties for employers who employed illegal immigrants, a measure which has unfortunately led 'to discriminatory checks and the rejection of applicants from resident ethnic minorities' (S Spencer 1998: 78).

The 1999 Asylum and Immigration Act

The advent of a Labour Government in 1997 has not entailed a significant relaxation in immigration controls. While initiatives such as the abolition of the primary purpose rule have indicated a renewed willingness to listen to the concerns of minority communities, and while recognition of the need to attract immigrants in areas of substantial labour shortage has prompted Ministers to acknowledge the importance of immigration to a thriving economy, more evident than these changes in immigration policy for the 1997–2001 government were the continuities.

The primary concern of the government was with asylum seekers. The number of people seeking asylum doubled from 1997 (when there were 35,000 new asylum seekers) to 2000 (when there were 75,000 new asylum seekers), with the backlog of cases still to be determined in 2000 being 60,000. Against the backcloth of hostile media coverage, which pointed to an inexorable rise in the number of asylum seekers, depicted a substantial proportion of them as bogus and visualised those gaining entry to the country as creating serious problems (Rowe 2000; Van Dijk 2000), the government passed an Asylum and Immigration Act in 1999. This Act introduced vouchers worth 70 per cent of income support rates, which could only be spent by asylum seekers in designated places; devised plans to disperse asylum seekers around the country so that the cost of supporting them was spread more evenly; and established detention centres to house those whose appeals had been refused. While these measures were advertised as firm but fair, the UN (United Nations) Committee for the Elimination of Racial Discrimination in 2000 pointed to the continuing plight of asylum seekers in Britain and their increasing vulnerability to racist attacks and harassment. A wealth of evidence in fact confirms that 'of all the communities in the UK, asylum-seekers are the most obviously and damagingly socially excluded' (Parekh 2000: 215) and that the consequences of the 1999 Act, like previous Acts, were 'neither humane nor efficient' (*Independent on Sunday* 2001).

The production in 2002 of a White Paper, detailing the re-elected government's proposed measures for dealing with asylum seekers, economic migrants and new citizens, has been heralded as a fresh approach which entails a 'coherent strategy' on nationality, immigration and asylum policy. Entitled *Secure Borders, Safe Haven – Integration with Diversity in Modern Britain* (Home Office 2002), it proposes that new applicants for citizenship need to demonstrate a knowledge of English and citizenship, and need to make a formal statement of allegiance to Britain; that a Highly Skilled Migrant Programme is introduced to encourage economic migrants whose skills are in demand to work in Britain; and that a system of induction, accommodation, reporting and removal centres is set up to manage the entire asylum process. Implicitly acknowledging the failure of the 1999 Act, the White Paper envisages the phasing out of the stigmatising voucher system and modifying the dispersal system to ensure that people who speak the same language are able to live alongside each other. We shall have to wait and see whether, and how, these proposed measures are implemented before we can judge whether they are more effective than previous immigration, asylum and nationality legislation in creating in a global age 'secure borders' and a 'safe haven'.

Immigration and the European Union

Since 1973 Britain has been a member of the European Community (EC) and, as such, been committed to the establishment of a common market. The 1986 Single European Act furthered this objective by pledging to establish by 1992 a single European market for the free movement of people, goods, services and capital. A recognition of the economic benefits of free movement has been accompanied, however, by a belief 'that removal of internal frontiers' necessitates 'tighter controls of external borders' (Geddes 1996: 107). Initially European governments sought to harmonise their immigration policies through informal inter-governmental cooperation but, with the creation of the European Union (EU) as a result of the 1991 Maastricht Treaty, the situation has become increasingly formalised. The EU, which came into force in 1993, 'has three "pillars": the EC itself for social and economic policy; the Western European Union for cooperation on defence and foreign policy; and committees of ministers and officials to deal with police and judicial cooperation and immigration from outside the Union' (Dummett 1998: 205).

While some progress has been made towards the free movement of people within the EU, it has been restricted to EU citizens, that is, citizens of the member states of the EU, and has been accompanied by increasing efforts to control immigration from outside the EU, a process dubbed by some as 'a multi-lateral movement towards the creation of a Fortress Europe' (Mitchell and Russell 1994: 145). The exclusion of third-country nationals, who are legally resident in a member state, from the right to free movement legitimised Britain's unwillingness to follow most other member states in 1995 and abandon border controls, while the inability of some member states of the EU to clamp down on immigration from non-EU countries has not encouraged second thoughts since. What is more, even the right of EU citizens to residence within Britain has become 'largely conditional upon not being a charge on the state i.e. having no recourse to public funds' with the introduction in 1994 of 'a "habitual residence" test, denying means-tested benefits to those who had not already established residence' (Morris 1998: 248 – 9).

A racialised immigration policy?

British immigration policy has continued to be restrictive. The clampdown on 'undeserving asylum seekers' and the mainten-ance of controls on residents of the EU, however, does not entail seeing the 'alien menace' purely in terms of skin colour. 'Colour is now less relevant' than it was 'from the 1950s to the 1980s' (Cohen 1994: 68). Having said this, there is evidence that British immigration policy in particular and EU immigra-tion policy in general 'rebound disproportionately on non-white populations from impoverished third world countries' (Morris 1998: 249) and can contribute in Britain 'to a political atmos-phere surrounding the welfare state in which the legitimate claims of welfare need [among minority groups] may be seen as suspect' (Ginsburg 1992: 161) and 'inappropriate checks [are] made on lawful Black and Asian residents' (S Spencer 1998: 78).

For most of the post-war period, the primary concern of immigration policy has been with restricting Asian and Black entry into Britain. Initially this involved 'a set of administrative arrangements and practices' but over time 'a rigorous and complex set of rules and laws' emerged in order 'to bring to an end Asian and Black entry into Britain for the purposes of settlement' (I Spencer 1997: 149). These changes in immigra-tion and nationality law since 1945 'perfectly mirror . . . the change in Britain's international position' from 'head of a vast

Empire' to (albeit reluctant) integration within 'a European Community' (I Spencer 1997: 150). For European citizens have replaced citizens of the Commonwealth in having rights to enter and settle in Britain.

While the concern of governments throughout the post-war period to limit the entry of Asian and Black immigrants challenges the widely held theory that an otherwise liberal state was obliged by public opinion to turn to immigration controls, there is little doubt that politicians have frequently been reminded of the existence of strong opposition to Asian and Black immigration and therefore been persuaded to adopt increasingly restrictive controls. In the aftermath of the election in Smethwick, against a national swing to Labour, of a Conservative candidate on a racist platform, a leading member of the Labour Cabinet, Richard Crossman, pointed to the dangers electorally of appearing too liberal on immigration and commented that the Labour Party thereafter 'felt (it) had to out-trump the Tories by doing what they would have done and so transforming their policy into a bipartisan policy' (Richard Crossman, 1975, quoted in A Pilkington 1984: 150).

One problem with adopting this strategy is that 'the political objective of strict immigration control conflicts with the reality of . . . continuing migration flows and with the constraints on the ability of the state to enforce further controls' (Miles 1993a: 206). The consequent inability of the state to deliver its promises of 'secure borders' fuels fears in the electorate about immigration and such fears in turn encourage political parties to propose tougher immigration controls. The result is that measures designed to placate racist attitudes can end up reinforcing them. It is interesting in this context to note the claim of the leader of the far-right British National Party, Nick Griffin: 'The asylum seeker issue has been great for us. We have had phenomenal growth in membership. It's been quite fun to watch government ministers and the Tories play the race card in far cruder terms than we would ever use, but pretend not to. The issue legitimises us' (Nick Griffin, 2000, quoted in Mynott 2000: 17).

While the major political parties have generally avoided competing for votes over the immigration issue and a bipartisan policy has indeed been pursued, there is little doubt that the Conservatives continue to be perceived as tougher and therefore gain electoral advantage in raising the issue. The temptation has not always been resisted, as Powell's intervention in the late 1960s and Thatcher's in the late 1970s testify. Indeed the existence of an electoral strategy which entails exploiting the immigration issue was confirmed by Lansley, head of the Conservative Party Research Department, who admitted in 1995, 'Immigration, an issue we raised successfully in 1992 . . . played particularly well in the tabloids and has more potential to hurt' (Andrew Lansley, 1995, quoted in S Spencer 1998: 80). Although the Major Government did not, to its credit, seek to exploit the immigration issue in the 1997 general election, the Labour Party remains, as it has done since the early 1960s, somewhat defensive over the issue. Aware of 'the clear electoral support for tough immigration controls', it sees 'no political alternative . . . than to continue its support for stringent immigration controls, even though these are inevitably open to attack as in some respects racist' (Layton-Henry 1992: 177). Significant liberalisation does not look imminent.

Integration policy and race relations legislation

If immigration legislation and administration have tended to be racist, being presaged on the assumption that an increase in the number of Asian and Black immigrants is inherently undesirable, the same is not true of the other prong of government policy in relation to race and ethnicity. Measures designed to combat racial disadvantage reflect the adherence of governments to liberal principles. Policies have taken both 'racially explicit' and 'racially inexplicit' forms (Kirp 1979). The first explicitly target minority ethnic groups and aim directly to benefit them, while the second make no reference to minority ethnic groups but aim to benefit them indirectly. An example of the first is the legislation on 'race relations', while an example of the second is the urban programme. Here we shall be primarily concerned with 'racially explicit' policies.

The 1965 and 1968 Race Relations Acts

The government has attempted to combat racial discrimination through a series of Race Relations Acts. The first in 1965 prohibited incitement to racial hatred and outlawed racial discrimination in places of public resort such as hotels and restaurants. A Race Relations Board was set up under the Act to receive complaints of discrimination and, if necessary, act as a conciliator. The significance of the Act was twofold. For the first time Parliament 'introduce[d] legal redress against racial discrimination' (Saggar 1992: 79); and in tandem with the tightening of immigration controls, it cemented a bipartisan policy. The Conservative Party agreed not to oppose the legislation to outlaw discrimination, while the Labour Government not only ceased to oppose immigration controls but also, as we saw earlier, made them tougher. As a junior minister at the time said in defence of the policy, 'Integration without control is impossible but control without integration is indefensible' (Roy Hattersley, 1965, quoted in Solomos 1989: 115).

The period between 1965 and 1968 has been characterised by some commentators as 'the liberal hour'. With the immigration issue seemingly dealt with, attention now was focused on the issue of integration. Roy Jenkins, within months of becoming Home Secretary, declared a new vision of the multiracial society he wished to strive towards. He sought integration rather than assimilation and this, he announced, was not to be seen 'as a flattening process of assimilation but rather as equal opportunity, accompanied by cultural diversity, in an atmosphere of mutual tolerance' (Roy Jenkins, 1966, quoted in Saggar 1992: 83). Given the limited scope of the 1965 Race Relations Act, he mounted a campaign to extend anti-discrimination law into new areas.

This campaign was successful and eventually a second Race Relations Act was passed in 1968, outlawing racial discrimination in employment, housing and commercial services. The scope of the first Act was extended in two ways. Firstly, anti-discrimination law was applied to new fields which were central for the life chances of minority ethnic groups. Secondly, the Race Relations Board (RRB) was given some, albeit limited, powers. If the RRB was unable to conciliate the two sides in a dispute, it was now empowered to take the case to court. The Act also set up a new body, the Community Relations Commission (CRC) to promote 'harmonious community relations'.

Despite the fact that the Act represented the culmination of a long campaign to extend anti-discrimination law, even before it passed through Parliament, 'the general optimism that had underscored the "liberal hour" had all but evaporated' (Saggar 1992: 84). For both the Kenyan Asian crisis and the intervention of Powell entailed the return of the immigration issue to centre stage. The liberal hour had passed.

Evaluations of this period differ. Some applaud the achievement of the government in laying the foundations for the development of equal opportunities (Banton 1985). Others, however, take a much more cynical line and insist that both prongs of policy – racial integration and immigration control – need to be taken into account before making a judgement. When this is done, the achievement of the government seems less impressive. Referring to the rationale for government policy, quoted above, two writers mount a trenchant critique of the liberal hour: 'Hattersley's clever syllogism was really arguing that in order to eliminate racism within Britain, it is necessary to practise it at the point of entry into Britain. But the Labour government's commitment to "limitation" was rather stronger than its commitment to "integration"' (Miles and Phizacklea 1984: 57).

The 1976 Race Relations Act

The 1970s witnessed, until Thatcher's intervention, continuing frontbench support for the bipartisan policy of strict immigration controls and anti-discrimination legislation. The Conservative Government tightened the controls, as we have seen, in 1971 and the Labour Government passed a new Race Relations Act in 1976. The Act was one of several in the mid-1970s designed to promote equality of opportunity. The 1975 Sex Discrimination Act paved the way and helped to generate the impetus in the following year for both the Race Relations Act and the Fair Employment (Northern Ireland) Act (which outlawed discrimination on the grounds of religious belief or political opinion in the province). By this time evidence had mounted to indicate that, despite a decline in overt racial discrimination, considerable covert discrimination still persisted. This prompted the government to pass a third Race Relations Act in 1976.

This Act was strongly influenced by anti-discrimination law in the United States. As such, it diverged from the previous Acts in three main ways. Firstly, the definition of racial discrimination was extended to include indirect forms and thus encompass organisational practices which had a disproportionately adverse effect on a particular group, even when there was no intention to discriminate. Secondly, the Commission for Racial Equality (CRE), which replaced both the RRB and the CRC, was empowered to carry out its own investigations of organisations to find out whether they were discriminating. If discrimination was discovered it could require the organisation to change its practices and check that this had been done. Thirdly, individuals who believed that they had been discriminated against were permitted to take their complaints directly to the courts or industrial tribunals rather than channel them through an intermediary organisation such as the old RRB or the new CRE.

The 1976 Race Relations Act and Equal Opportunities

We can distinguish two broad perspectives on equal opportunities – liberal and radical. The first is concerned to promote fair or like treatment and to this end seeks to devise '*fair procedures*' so that everybody, regardless of race, receives the same treatment and 'justice is seen to be done' (Noon and Blyton 1997: 177). The emphasis in this approach is upon sanctions against any form of racially discriminatory behaviour. The second 'represents a more radical approach since it suggests that policy makers should be concerned with the *outcome*, rather than the *process*, and should therefore be seeking to ensure a *fair distribution of rewards*' (Noon and Blyton 1997: 182). To treat everybody the same is, in this view, to ignore pertinent differences between people and does little to eradicate disadvantage which stems from discrimination in the past and current institutional practices which result in indirect discrimination. To ensure fair outcomes – such as an ethnically balanced workforce – what are needed are not merely sanctions against racial discrimination but measures which entail positive discrimination, that is, preferential treatment of disadvantaged groups.

The liberal perspective primarily informed the 1976 Race Relations Act. The emphasis was on like treatment, with the law enabling sanctions to be deployed against those found to be guilty of racial discrimination. Positive discrimination was not permitted and the 'overall thrust was individualist' with the legal process demanding proof that 'individual members of racial groups . . . [had] suffered discrimination' before racial discrimination could be established and sanctions deployed (Parekh 1996: 18). The Act did, none the less, move beyond like treatment in two respects. Firstly, the recognition that discrimination took indirect forms entailed an acknowledgement that practices which treated people in the same way could disproportionately and adversely affect some groups more than others. Secondly, organisations were encouraged under the Act to counter the effects of past discrimination and redress the under-representation of minority groups by developing positive action programmes. The rationale for such programmes, which included targeted advertising campaigns and training courses, was 'to encourage the previously disadvantaged to the starting gate for jobs, promotion and other opportunities' (Blakemore and Drake 1996: 12). Once at the starting gate, however, and in contrast to the situation which prevailed in the United States from the mid-1960s to (at least) the late 1980s and has developed in Northern Ireland since 1989 (Noon and Blyton 1997), no preferential treatment was permitted and legally enforceable quotas for disadvantaged groups were expressly disallowed.

Evaluating the effectiveness of the 1976 Race Relations Act

The 1976 Race Relations Act is still 'probably the most comprehensive in Europe' (Bindman 1996, quoted in Goulbourne 1998a: 103). Indeed, when it was passed, hopes were expressed that it would significantly reduce the level of racial discrimination. Subsequent experience of the way the legislation has been implemented, however, indicates that such optimism was misplaced. Several factors have contributed to making the Act less effective than originally envisaged.

Firstly, the legislation itself and its subsequent interpretation by the judiciary exempt much state activity 'from the ambit of the Act' (Lester 1998: 25). The scope of the Act is therefore limited.

Secondly, little attention has been given in practice to indirect discrimination. The result is that 'the vast majority of cases heard by tribunals [have been] concerned only with direct discrimination' (McCrudden *et al.* 1991: 271).

Thirdly, 'the results of formal investigations by the CRE have been rather disappointing' (Blakemore and Drake 1996: 126). In the absence of the possibility of 'class actions' on the American model, whereby claims can be put forward in court simultaneously on behalf of a large number of complainants, each of whom may receive damages, the role of formal investigations is extremely important and strategically more effective than supporting individual complainants. Unfortunately inadequate resources, initial lack of competence and limitations placed upon the CRE by the judiciary – which ruled in 1984 that investigations could only be mounted when evidence already existed of discrimination – have inhibited successful pursuit of this strategy (Bindman 2000).

Fourthly, the possibility for individuals to have a direct right of access to legal redress has in practice 'been largely weakened by the unavailability of legal aid in industrial tribunal cases' (Lester 1998: 26), the lack of expertise of tribunals in cases which involve complaints of racial discrimination and (in the cases upheld) the small amounts awarded in compensation. In view of this, it is scarcely surprising to discover that 'the prospect of successful litigation against those who discriminate is much greater and the economic consequences for those successfully sued are vastly greater' in the United States (Bindman 1981, quoted in A Pilkington 1984: 151).

Fifthly, the government has been reluctant to use its powers to enforce compliance with the Act (Law 1996). The government is in a powerful position, both as an employer and through its contracts with firms in the private sector, to promote an effective equal opportunities policy. In contrast to the United States and indeed Northern Ireland, a low priority, however, has tended to be given to this. Indeed under current legislation, local authorities and many other public authorities are expressly prevented from pursuing a strategy of contract compliance.

Frustrated by the workings of the Act, the CRE has on a number of occasions reviewed the Act and put forward a series of proposals to strengthen the legislation. On the first occasion, in 1985, the CRE did not even receive a formal response, while on the second occasion in 1991 – though a response was forthcoming – the government refused to implement any of its recommendations (MacEwen 1994). This reluctance to widen the scope of the law and increase the powers of the CRE is perfectly understandable, given the dominance during the 1980s and much of the 1990s of a government which extolled the virtues of the market. While Conservative administrations continued to espouse an ideal of equal opportunity, they insisted that nothing should interfere with the workings of the free market. Indeed what is perhaps more surprising is that the Race Relations Act was not repealed and the CRE abolished. For a dominant strand of thought during this period – evident in both the writings of the New Right and much of the tabloid press – pictured 'the uniqueness of Englishness . . . being diluted by the emerging multiculturalism' (Solomos 1993: 231). In a context where minority ethnic groups were 'increasingly presented . . . as a threat to the way of life of the majority white community and as a group which is difficult to integrate into the mainstream of British society' (Solomos 1993: 193), it might have been anticipated that a populist government would disband an organisation which sought to represent minority interests. Pragmatism, however, remained the order of the day. The Race Relations Act remained on the statute book, with its scope restricted, and the CRE survived, albeit on limited resources. At the same time the thrust of government policy took, as we saw in Chapter 5 in relation to education, an increasingly assimilationist turn.

We should not assume, however, that no progress was made towards equal opportunity during the long period of Conservative hegemony. In the aftermath of the urban unrest of the early 1980s, some local authorities woke from their slumbers and began developing policy in this area. Section 71 of the 1976 Race Relations Act, which enjoined local authorities to eliminate discrimination and promote equal opportunity, provided the legal basis for a series of initiatives. These included measures to advance equality of access to council housing, improve the representation of minority ethnic groups within local authority departments and ensure that service delivery took account of cultural diversity. The first measure entailed ethnic monitoring; the second the setting of targets; and the third the development of new training programmes and policies.

The priority given to racial equality in some local authorities stemmed from three factors. The 1981 riots, which involved confrontations between Black youth and the police, put the issue of racial inequality on the political agenda. At the same time, representatives of minority communities started to 'break into the local political system' and sought to keep the issue firmly on the agenda. And finally, in view of 'the unwillingness of both the Thatcher and Major administrations during the period from 1979 to 1997 to introduce new national initiatives in this field', the Left turned their attention to the local arena and sought to mobilise support around the issue of equal opportunities (Solomos 1998: 209).

Some local authorities signalled the significance which they attached to racial equality by engaging in positive action including contract compliance initiatives. The latter required, for example, contractors to provide evidence that they were implementing an equal opportunities policy. Whatever gains resulted from these initiatives tended to be short-lived, however. The pursuit of racial equality was vilified in much of the press as an example of 'loony left' politics and put local authorities on the defensive. At the same time the role of the local authorities was steadily diminished by the national government. The Greater London Council, which pioneered many initiatives, was abolished; privatisation meant that the role of local authorities in the delivery of services such as housing and education was eroded; contract compliance was effectively outlawed; and, with rate capping, fiscal constraints tightened and left local authorities with little room for manoeuvre. In this context, even the most radical authorities have subsequently adopted a lower profile on the issue of racial equality. Ironically, some of the measures used by local authorities to promote racial equality have since been given public endorsement.

It is now widely recognised that an organisation intent on preventing or detecting racial discrimination needs to undertake both 'ethnic monitoring and the setting of targets' (Sanders 1998: 38). Although these measures were initially resisted by employers and trade unions, over time even the national government recognised their value as part of good management practice and gave them official backing. Progress was made on the first when the CRE's Code of Practice was approved in 1983 by

Norman Tebbit as Secretary of State for Employment and progress was made on the second with the launch in 1991 by the then Secretary of State for Employment, Michael Howard, of the Department's *Equal Opportunities Ten Point Plan for Employers.* While no statutory force was given to ethnic monitoring and the setting of targets, at least these measures, which were consonant with the 'new managerialism' (Luthra 1997: 47), were given public endorsement.

While European Community law has had a significant impact in the area of sex discrimination, it has until recently had little impact on race relations law. The reason for this is that the original Treaty of Rome setting up the EC provided safeguards against discrimination on the grounds of sex (and indeed nationality) but not on other invidious grounds such as race. The result is that the CRE has not had the same opportunities as the Equal Opportunities Commission (EOC) to use European law 'to remedy the defects in the laws that they are charged to administer and enforce' (Lester 1998: 29). Anxious not to grant new powers to the Community, the Conservative Government consistently resisted the increasing calls by EC governments for a Treaty amendment and a Directive against racial discrimination.

Confronted by the government's refusal, until very recently, to strengthen the law and with European Community law unable to come to the rescue, the CRE meanwhile 'shifted away from law enforcement towards promotional work, and within law enforcement it has shifted away from formal investigations to complaints work and voluntary agreements' (Sanders 1998: 50).

Some achievements have none the less been made in law enforcement. The publicity consequent on the formal investigations, which discovered racial discrimination both in the allocation of housing by the London Borough of Hackney in 1984 and in the selection of students at St George's Hospital Medical School in 1988, had a significant impact on other organisations. In addition, there has been a substantial increase in the number of individual complaints and, of those which get as far as a tribunal hearing, an increase in the proportion that are successful. In 1993–94 'almost a third of applicants were successful' and 'compensation was awarded in almost four-fifths of cases' with 'the median award [being] £3500' (Blakemore and Drake 1996:

124–5). While the courts tended at one stage to defend 'the private rights of the individual, including the right to discriminate on the ground of the colour of a man's skin', over time there has been a greater willingness to regard 'racial discrimination not as an individual right but as a social wrong' and for the courts to be 'more willing than hitherto to grant judicial review against public bodies' (Griffith 1997: 177, 180) and indeed 'respect differences without violating the principle of equality' (Parekh 1997b: 129). What is more, the government, following a judgement of the European Court of Justice that financial compensation needed to be sufficient to deter employers from discriminating on the grounds of sex, agreed in 1993 to lift the upper limit on compensation for victims of racial discrimination as well as sexual discrimination. The costs therefore for employers now found to be discriminating are potentially much higher, with the average compensation award in 1999 rising to £9948.

Despite some success in the field of law enforcement, the CRE has increasingly turned to persuasion in order to advance racial equality. Research has been commissioned and campaigns have been mounted to promote equal opportunities. One example of such promotional work is *Racial Equality Means Business* which urges employers to provide equal opportunities not only because of their moral and legal obligations but also out of self-interest: an innovative organisation needs to be characterised by fair employment practices and made up of diverse groups. A lot still needs to be done. While 88 per cent of the largest 168 companies in 1995 had statements committing them to racial equality, only 45 per cent had a serious plan for implementing racial equality (Ousley 1995).

It is now over 25 years since the 1976 Race Relations Act was passed. The hopes that a number of commentators invested in the Act have in many ways been dashed. Racial discrimination has certainly not been eliminated and indeed according to most studies has not even diminished (Brown and Gay 1985; Simpson and Stevenson 1994; CRE 1996; Karn 1997). The failure of this legislation to make significant inroads in combating racial discrimination is not altogether surprising when we bear in mind the following points.

Firstly, the late 1970s and indeed the succeeding decades have been characterised by intermittent recessions and such economic instability has not been the most propitious time to develop equal opportunities (Rhodes and Braham 1989). Indeed it is conceivable that, in the absence of legislation, racial discrimination might have risen. Secondly, the dominance for much of this period of a government wedded to the market and committed to diminishing the role of the public sector has not helped since, as we have seen, it was local authorities and other public bodies that, in the absence of central government leadership, led the way on initiatives to promote racial equality. Thirdly, 'there are definite limits to the effectiveness of the law' (Jenkins and Solomos 1989: 210). While legislation 'can set standards of acceptable behaviour and provide redress for those who have suffered injustice at the hands of others', by itself, it 'cannot create good relations and change attitudes' (Lester 1998: 23). What is more, the emphasis within British common law on the individual, when it comes to the settlement of disputes, makes it difficult to grapple with issues which concern discrimination against groups. Fourthly, governments have lacked the political will to prioritise either equal opportunities in general or racial equality in particular, despite the fact that leadership in this area was a key part of the strategy behind the 1976 Act. Indeed 'instead of equal opportunity impinging upon every aspect of every government's business, the issue has, by virtue of the creation of [a] specialist [body, namely the CRE] . . . been successfully compartmentalised, isolated and marginalised' (Jenkins and Solomos 1989: 213). Fifthly, the increasing reliance on a voluntary approach in this area has failed to acknowledge the many obstacles in the way of a successful equal opportunities strategy such as 'the lack of support within . . . employing organisations for the concept . . . the characteristic informality and lack of accountability of many organisational procedures . . . [and] the weak position of the personnel function in most organisations' (Jenkins and Solomos 1989: 215).

A new era? The 2001 Race Relations (Amendment) Act

The advent of a new Labour Government in 1997 has entailed a series of initiatives which signal a renewed seriousness of approach to the promotion of equal opportunities. In their first term, two pieces of legislation were passed which its advocates claim have the potential to make serious inroads in combating racial discrimination: the 1998 Human Rights Act and the 2000 Race Relations (Amendment) Act. In their second term, further legislation is promised to give effect to two Directives (the Employment and Race Directives) which result from Britain's membership of the European Union.

Prior to the Human Rights Act, the European Convention on Human Rights was not incorporated into British law. Individuals therefore had to seek redress through the European Court in Strasbourg. Through this means, as we noted above, the EOC was able to remedy defects of legislation designed to promote gender equality. The Human Rights Act, which applies to public authorities and private organisations with public functions, incorporated the European Convention on Human Rights into British law and thereby for the first time explicitly identified people's positive rights. While judges cannot strike out laws, they can point to their incompatibility with human rights and strike out secondary legislation. Article 14 of the Act is particularly pertinent to racial equality since it grants people protection against discrimination in relation to the rights it guarantees. While the provisions of the Race Relations Act mean that the Human Rights Act is unlikely to be used to seek redress for racial discrimination, it could be used to challenge any suspected racial bias of courts and tribunals (issues outside the scope of the Race Relations Act) and has already been used by asylum seekers who claimed that their detention contravened human rights.

More significant for racial equality is the Race Relations (Amendment) Act, which came into force in 2001. In passing this Act, the government responded positively to some of the points made by the CRE in its review of the Race Relations Act in 1998. The Act extends the scope of the 1976 Act by covering public bodies which had been previously exempt and making it unlawful for public authorities to discriminate in carrying out any of their functions. While the 'underlying principle' of this Act, like previous race relations legislation, 'remains "a negative prohibition on discrimination"' (PIU 2002: 147), a new approach is also evident. For the first time, a general statutory duty is placed on all public authorities, and specific duties on some authorities, not only to prevent racial discrimination (including indirect discrimination) but also to promote racial equality. To help public authorities meet their duty and ensure that it is fulfilled, the Act gives the CRE the power not only to issue statutory codes of practice but also to conduct audits. By enjoining public bodies in this way to develop plans which promote racial equality, the Act is adopting a somewhat different approach to that embodied in previous race relations legislation: public authorities are now being required to take a pro-active stance to racial equality and thus take the lead in promoting equal opportunities.

At the European level, action has also recently been taken to combat discrimination. The Amsterdam Treaty, which was ratified in 1997, included a non-discrimination clause under Article 13 empowering the Council of Ministers to 'take appropriate action to combat discrimination based on sex, racial or ethnic origin, religion or belief, disability, age or sexual orientation' (Dummett 2000: 118). This formed the legal basis for the Employment and Race Directives proposed by the European Commission in 2000 and subsequently agreed by the Council of Ministers in 2001. The Directives require EU member states to introduce legislation to outlaw unfair discrimination in the fields of employment and training. The Race Directive also applies to areas such as education and goods and services. While Britain's race relations legislation is already broadly compatible with these Directives, the government recognises that it will need to introduce legislation to prohibit discrimination in employment and training on the grounds of sexual orientation, age and religion. Given the resurgence of Islamophobia and evidence that Pakistanis and Bangladeshis (who are typically Muslims) are much more likely to be disadvantaged than other minority groups, the advent of legislation outlawing religious discrimination will address the concerns of many Muslims and may play a part in helping to combat the severe disadvantage faced by some minority ethnic groups.

These legislative initiatives, coupled with new mainstream (and a few targeted) programmes which are designed to help people move from welfare to work, to regenerate deprived communities and raise the levels of educational attainment and skills, signal a renewed concern on the part of the government to promote equal opportunities. While it is not possible at this stage to gauge how successful these initiatives and programmes will be, a word of caution is in order.

In so far as data has been collected on the impact of mainstream programmes on minority ethnic groups, the evidence indicates that these 'have not been as successful for ethnic minorities when compared with Whites' (PIU 2002: 129). As for policies, which have been targeted at minority ethnic groups, 'evidence consistently points out that ethnic minorities are either unaware or are not participating on initiatives designed for them' (PIU 2002: 172). The main reasons for the lack of success of mainstream and targeted policies are twofold: a failure of past policy 'to reach out to ethnic minorities and target them to get the messages across' and the inability of past policy 'to meet the specific needs of ethnic minorities' (PIU 2002: 172). It is too early to say whether this acknowledgement, by a body located in the Cabinet Office, of the lack of success of previous measures from which minority groups theoretically had the most to gain will lead to more sophisticated policies. There is already evidence, however, that the government has abandoned its earlier colour and culture blind approach and recognises the need for mainstream programmes, such as neighbourhood renewal, both to incorporate a race equality strategy and involve community groups (Parekh 2000).

Of the legislative initiatives discussed above, the Race Relations (Amendment) Act is the one which is likely to have the most impact in ensuring that public authorities develop effective race equality plans. While the Act adopts a more proactive approach to the promotion of race equality, its effectiveness will depend on how seriously it is implemented. The Act itself does not apply to the private sector, which currently tends not to be convinced of the business case for race equality. The experience of anti-discrimination law in the United States and Northern Ireland suggests that the government and other public bodies will need to engage in contract compliance in order to effect significant change in the private sector. It may also be necessary for the government to take more heed of the advice of the CRE, embodied in its reviews of the 1976 Race Relations Act, if the implementation of the new legislation is to be effective in promoting racial equality. Extending legal aid to cover applicants before Employment Tribunals and shifting the burden of proof against organisations accused of discrimination may be necessary to generate bottom-up pressures to implement equal opportunity policies more effectively. In addition, removing some of the legal impediments to investigations by the CRE into organisations where there is suspicion that discrimination is occurring may also be necessary for the CRE to perform its law enforcement role effectively. The Race Relations (Amendment) Act signals a renewed commitment to racial equality. We shall have to wait and see if the implementation of this piece of legislation fares better than its predecessors.

To conclude that the measures governments have devised to combat racial disadvantage have so far proved relatively ineffective is not to claim that they were merely symbolic gestures, cynically designed 'in terms of giving the impression [of] something . . . being done' (Ben-Tovim and Gabriel 1987: 152). Organisations, such as the Campaign Against Racial Discrimination, which first put forward these proposals, genuinely wished to end racial discrimination and the government, in making a positive response to this demand, acted in line with liberal principles. In contrast to the 'use of the law in the imperial age to sanction formal differential treatment', race relations legislation has been developed to enable all citizens to enjoy 'equal rights and opportunities irrespective of racial or ethnic differentiation' (Goulbourne 1998a: 100).

Immigration policy and race relations legislation: racism and liberalism

Having examined both aspects of government policy in the field of race and ethnicity, what conclusions can we come to? Government policy has exhibited the influence of two contradictory traditions, racism and liberalism. While immigration policy and administration have tended to exemplify the first tradition, the measures designed to combat racial disadvantage have tended to exemplify the second tradition. The contradictory nature of government policy is well brought out by Parekh:

> The immigration policy rested on the assumption that black immigrants were less desirable than white, and were to be allowed in only when Britain could not dispense with their services. The anti-discrimination legislation rested on the opposite assumption. Furthermore, the immigration policy assumed that Britain was a homogeneous nation that could not integrate people of different 'stocks' and races, whom it must keep out if it was to

preserve its national 'identity'. By contrast, the anti-discrimination legislation assumed that it was a *state*, an inherently open institution based on little more than collective subscription to a common authority and capable of
responding to people of all races and cultures (Parekh 1991a: 23).

The rationale for the bipartisan policy, which emerged in the
early 1960s, was the belief shared by both the main political
parties that tight control on Asian and Black immigration was
a necessary prerequisite for racial harmony. 'While the US
strategy emphasised the need for greater consistency between
anti-discrimination policies and immigration, the British government argued that restrictions on immigration were the *sine
qua non* for a successful equal opportunity strategy at home'
(Stone and Lasus 1998: 224). In the event, immigration policy
'has not succeeded . . . in reassuring the public that immigration is under control' and, though we cannot be sure what attitudes would have been in the absence of such an immigration
policy, it is doubtful that it has led 'to more positive attitudes
toward black and Asian people than existed thirty years ago'
(S Spencer 1998: 76). This is not altogether surprising. For as
Roy Hattersley now acknowledges, immigration policy has created 'the impression that we "cannot afford to let them in".
And if we cannot afford to let them in, those of them who are
here already must be doing harm' (Roy Hattersley, 1996,
quoted in S Spencer 1998: 77).

The coexistence of laws which embody contrary principles
means that 'the positive impact of race equality law continues to
be diminished by the negative impact of unfair and discriminatory immigration and asylum law' (Lester 2000: 27). Indeed,
the most recent race equality law embodies both liberal and racist
principles. On the one hand, the Race Relations (Amendment)
Act, as we saw above, widens the scope of previous race relations
legislation by including public bodies which were previously
exempt in order to promote racial equality. On the other
hand, it expressly excludes from its coverage one such body,
notably the immigration service in relation to nationality or eth-
nic/national origin when authorised by a government minister
or legislation/rules in the area of immigration, asylum and
nationality law. This exemption allows immigration officers to
discriminate against a class of persons, such as Kurds and Roma,
whose identification will often be made 'on little more than their

personal appearance' (H Young 2001). The formulation of state policy continues to embody contrary principles.

Of the two strands of government policy, the government has shown a greater commitment to immigration control. A mainstream government department – the Home Office – has been responsible for the administration of immigration policy and vigorously enforced control. By contrast, the enforcement of race relations legislation has been delegated to regulatory agencies such as the CRE and the judicial system. The result is that 'instead of equal opportunity impinging upon every aspect of every department's business, the issue has, by virtue of the creation of the CRE, been successfully compartmentalised, isolated and marginalised' (Solomos 1989: 130). In the light of this, it is scarcely revealing to discover that immigration policy has proved more effective than race relations legislation.

Government policy in this field does not have to take the form which it has done. It is not determined in some mechanistic way by public opinion any more than it is by the needs of capital. 'Far from the state simply responding to pressures from outside' it has 'played a central role in defining both the form and content of policies' (Miles and Solomos 1987: 105). This is evident both in the persistence of a shared racialised discourse among policy makers – a discourse which has governed post-war (and indeed earlier) immigration policy – and the willingness, despite the lack of pressure from outside to do so, to pass anti-discrimination legislation. The promotion of racial equality needs to build on the existing race relations legislation and extinguish the racist elements of immigration policy.

Citizenship and the national community

A necessary condition for minority ethnic groups to be integral members of the national community is for them to enjoy effective citizenship rights. According to T H Marshall, citizenship comprises three elements: civil, political and social. The civil element consists 'of the rights necessary for individual freedom – liberty of the person, freedom of speech, thought and faith, the right to own property and to conclude valid contracts, and the right to justice'; the political element consists of 'the right to participate in the exercise of political power' either as a representative or a voter; and the social element consists of 'the whole range from the right to a modicum of economic welfare and security to the right to share to the full in the social heritage and to live the life of a civilised being according to the standards prevailing in the society' (Marshall and Bottomore 1992: 8).

In Marshall's view these rights have gradually been extended in Britain to cover the vast mass of the population. The seventeenth and eighteenth centuries witnessed the emergence of civil rights; the nineteenth century saw a significant expansion of political rights; and, with the advent of the welfare state, the twentieth century has seen the development of social rights. The development of citizenship rights entails the creation of a society in which class inequality coexists with status equality. While the capitalist market results in persistent inequalities between social classes which, if left unchecked, undermine social order, the extension of citizenship allows all members of all social classes to enjoy a 'single, uniform status' and as a result provides the basis of social solidarity (Marshall and Bottomore 1992: 21).

Marshall's classic formulation of citizenship focuses on British society and in particular the extension of rights to the working class. His critics argue that the development of citizenship rights in other societies has not followed the same trajectory as Britain's and that the emphasis on the incorporation of the working class underplays the continuing exclusion of other social groups (Bulmer and Rees 1996). Women, for example, not only acquired citizenship rights later than men but according to some commentators still find that their 'eligibility to many social rights is as a dependant of her husband or the man with whom she lives' (Williams 1989: 129). Our concern here is with minority ethnic groups in Britain. Do they enjoy full citizenship rights? We shall begin by exploring the impact of post-war immigration on citizenship within the wider European context.

Citizenship, nationality and migration in Western Europe

Immigration, which entails the movement of people across states, challenges Marshall's conception of citizenship 'as expanding categories of rights (but not duties), equally bestowed on expanding categories of persons, without consideration of their inherent characteristics' (Joppke 1999: 629). For it reveals that citizenship is not only a set of rights but also a mechanism of social closure: only citizens of a particular state have the right to enter the territory of that state and non-citizens who do gain entry do not automatically qualify for citizenship of that state. What is more, immigration uncovers the pretence that the state (even a liberal state) is culturally neutral. It is often apparent to immigrants that the state's 'official language, holidays, or church relations cannot but privilege the ethnic majority population over the immigrant minorities'. In this context, demands may grow not only for individuals to have equal rights in the public sphere but also, given the importance of wider community affiliations to people's identity, for the public sphere to be modified 'to accommodate the distinctive needs of culturally excluded groups' (Joppke 1999: 630).

Increasing migration in the post-war period has resulted in 'a form of civic stratification, an emerging form of inequality in which groups of people are differentiated by the legitimate claims they can make on the state' (Morris 1998: 251). Three broad groups can be distinguished: 'citizens whose rights are extensive, an intermediate group (the denizens) . . . comprising privileged aliens often holding multiple citizenship, but not having the citizenship of or the right to vote in the country of their residence' and 'helots', consisting of illegal migrants and asylum seekers, 'who have been granted only limited rights' (Cohen 1994: 187–9). The relative proportion of different groups varies from country to country and depends at least in part on the model of the nation which prevails in each nation state.

Three types of state policy towards immigrants and ethnic communities can be distinguished – differential exclusion, assimilation and pluralism (Castles 1995). Differential exclusion is characterised by a set of policies which allow incorporation into limited sectors such as the labour market but prohibit access to full citizenship rights. The presence of foreigners within the nation state is perceived to be a temporary phenomenon, involving either the 'recruitment of workers to meet [a] transitory labour [shortage] or [the] admission of refugees for temporary protection' (Castles 1995: 294). Since the nation is defined in terms of the shared ancestry of its members, the state is neither willing to tolerate the permanent settlement of foreigners nor grant citizenship to foreigners who do not share this ancestry.

Assimilationism is characterised by a set of policies which incorporate 'migrants into society through a one-sided process of adaptation: immigrants are expected to give up their distinct-ive . . . characteristics and become indistinguishable from the majority population' (Castles 1995: 297–8). Since the nation is defined in terms of the adherence of its members to a shared national culture, permanent immigration is permitted and newcomers granted citizenship so long as they subscribe to the national culture. Multiculturalism is envisaged as a temporary phenomenon which will evaporate as minority groups assimilate.

Pluralism is characterised by a set of policies which involve immigrants being 'granted equal rights in all spheres of society, without being expected to give up their diversity, although usually with an expectation of conformity to certain key values' (Castles 1995: 295). The nation is defined in terms of residence, with the result that immigrants, as long as they recognise the authority of the state, are granted citizenship relatively easily. In contrast to differential exclusion and assimilationism, pluralism recognises multiculturalism as a persistent feature of the nation.

None of these types can be found in a pure form in the real world. Rather countries approximate more or less closely to one or other type. Let us take the three countries which in absolute terms have the largest immigrant populations in Europe: Germany, France and Britain (Geddes 1996). While we need to acknowledge that in all three cases there have been significant changes over time in the state's response towards immigrants and ethnic communities, Germany, France and Britain have tended to approximate most closely to differential exclusion, assimilationism and pluralism, respectively.

Germany approximates most closely to differential exclusion. Despite recruiting many guestworkers and other temporary workers (predominantly from other European countries), and despite admitting a large number of asylum seekers, Germany does not see itself as a country of immigration. The dominant conception of the nation – a conception which preceded the establishment of a German state in 1871 (Brubaker 1996) – is one based on common descent. The result is a state policy which is markedly preferential towards ethnic Germans. 'People of

German origin (often dating back several centuries, and with individuals unable even to speak German)' emanating from various parts of Central and Eastern Europe have been granted immediate access to citizenship and, with reunification in 1990, people who have been separated for almost fifty years have been 'brought together under an umbrella definition of unified citizenship' (White 1999: 225). In marked contrast to the favourable treatment of those of German 'origin', there has been an extreme reluctance to grant full citizenship rights to foreign migrants and their descendants even when they have settled in Germany and increasingly been born and brought up in the country (Wilpert 1993). Frequently 'permanently settled foreigners . . . have acquired legal and social rights of citizenship which stop short of the entitlement to vote' (Mitchell and Russell 1996: 65).

A paradox – evident in the 1949 Basic Law or constitution of West Germany – lies at the heart of German policy. The Basic Law, on the one hand, 'retained a remarkably ethnic concept of citizenship', but, on the other hand, sought to atone for past racism 'by uniquely generous asylum policies'. This meant 'that while it was extremely hard to acquire rights of citizenship and political representation, it was comparatively easy to enter Germany as a refugee seeking political asylum' (Fulbrook 1996: 88, 101). Recently the state has sought to deal with this paradox by amending the Basic Law to reduce its obligation to accept refugees and relaxing the rules under which long-term residents can gain German nationality and citizenship. Aware that foreigners cannot be expected to identify with Germany if they do not have an opportunity to acquire citizenship and fearful that they will otherwise form a dangerous underclass (Lash 1994), the state in the early 1990s relaxed German naturalisation law, permitting access to 'citizenship on the basis of residence (effectively *ius domicilii* in place of the traditional *ius sanguinis* through bloodlines)' (White 1999: 225). The 1999 Nationality law went even further by not only again easing naturalisation rules but also granting citizenship to children whose parents had been legally resident for eight years or more (Brubaker 2001). While applicants for naturalisation are required to demonstrate that they are able to maintain themselves without recourse to public funds, and children of legal residents born abroad who want to be citizens are obliged to choose sole German nationality when they are 23 years old, there is little doubt that Germany has moved a long way from its earlier ethnic conception of citizenship.

What enabled 'a re-orientation of national self-understanding' were the end of the Cold War, reunification and the gradual decline of ethnic Germans in Eastern Europe (Koopmans 1999: 643). Despite this, the old definition of Germanness is difficult to break down and still has its adherents. The Christian Democrats, who fiercely resisted the move away from an ethnic conception of citizenship, initiated 'the most massive signature campaign (five million signatures) in post-war Germany' as part of their campaign against the introduction of the new Nationality law. Although this did not prevent the legislation being passed, it is likely that 'immigrants in Germany, and particularly their descendants who will now grow up as Germans . . . will start to demand equal treatment' which in turn 'might, as in France, provide opportunities for the extreme right to profile itself as the one remaining guardian of "'the national cause"'' (Koopmans 1999: 644). As it is, residues of the ethnic conception of citizenship still survive in Germany's refusal to accept dual citizenship. The ideal still remains sole citizenship, although dual citizenship of children of legal residents born abroad is tolerated for a transitional period. Although relaxation of the naturalisation rules has resulted in a dramatic increase in the naturalisation rate of Turks and other original guestworkers, it still remains the case that the population contains a high proportion of non-citizen residents, albeit in some cases with entitlement to some of the rights of citizenship (Morris 2000).

France approximates most closely to assimilationism. 'Of all European countries, [it] has the longest tradition of being an immigration-country' (Seifert 1997: 445). The current immigrant population stems predominantly from countries in Southern Europe and former colonies in North Africa, with the state exhibiting a marked preference towards immigrants willing to assimilate. The dominant conception of the nation – a conception which emerged after the establishment of the state (Brubaker 1996) and has its origins in the Revolution of 1789 – is one which visualises 'France not as a community of descent but as a territorial community' (Bryant 1997: 163). Citizenship is therefore granted not only to all who are born in France (the principle of *jus soli*) plus their descendants but also to many who migrate there. The expectation is, however, that all will assimilate to French cultural norms with the presumption of *la France, une et indivisible* entailing an intolerance of diverse cultural identities.

Aware that some immigrants granted citizenship do not wish to be French and that others are unwilling to assimilate to French cultural norms, the state has not only sought to restrict immigration but also in 1993 took the historic step of passing a law removing the automatic right to citizenship held by children born in France of foreign parents. Henceforth these children had to affirm between the ages of 16 and 21 their willingness to become French. While 'new laws passed in 1998 reinstated an automatic attribution of ius soli to second genera- tion migrant children' (Favell 2001: xv), assimilationism contin- ues to hold sway in France. Although the extreme right flirts with the possibility of differential exclusion and the state has found it necessary to develop special measures to further the integration of minority ethnic groups, significant pluralism remains across the political spectrum virtually inconceivable.

Of the three countries under consideration, Britain appears to be the closest to pluralism (Melotti 1997). While the dominant conception of the nation in Britain, as in France, is that of 'a ter- ritorial community with a civic conception of nation', British society is much more 'capable of accommodating a large amount of difference' and recognises that there are different ways of being British (Bryant 1997: 166–7). The emergence of the British state, with the Treaty of Union between England and Scotland in 1707, necessitated the construction of an overarching but not exclusive national identity. For Englishness and Scottishness constituted alternative ways of being British. The subsequent creation of the United Kingdom and the British Empire reinforced the need for 'a flexible category of belonging' and for a long time this was served by that of 'British subjects' (Cesarani and Fulbrook 1996: 7). Post-war immigration to Britain took place therefore at a time when there already were recognisably different ways of being British. Such a context has been less inimical to the 'ideas of multiculturalism' and a recog- nition of 'the legitimacy of ethnic difference' (White 1999:

228). In this respect Britain differs from both France and Germany, which, for different reasons, find more difficulty envisaging either a multicultural or a multi-ethnic nation.

We must not exaggerate, however, the differences between Britain and her European partners. British immigration policy has to some extent been presaged on racist assumptions, with the 1981 British Nationality Act signalling a move from a civic to an ethnic conception of the nation. And integration policy has, despite some moves towards pluralism, alternated on the whole between 'assimilationist and integrationist approaches' (Parekh 1991b: 191). What is more, state policy in the three countries has exhibited some convergence over time. Despite the fact that there have been occasions when policies have become more restrictive (for example in France in 1993 and Britain in 1981), 'the general trend in Western Europe is towards liberalised citizenship regimes [which] provide the right of citizenship to second-generation immigrants, attributed either at birth or available at majority age' (Joppke 1999: 645–6). While, in contrast to the United States, there has been a reluctance within Western Europe to grant special group rights to immigrants, the general trend is to accommodate their demands for a more equitable approach to integration and move away from an insistence upon assimilation to the majority culture towards what one writer has called 'multicultural citizenship' (Kymlika 2000).

Among member states of the EU, the trend towards liberalised citizenship regimes and multicultural citizenship has been accompanied by concerted efforts, on the one hand, to develop tough immigration controls and, on the other hand, to facilitate the integration of minority groups by addressing the issue of racism. To recognise some common responses among Western European countries should not blind us, however, to continuing differences between them. 'In contrast to the degree of convergence which characterises immigration policy across the New Europe, moves towards convergence in citizenship policies have been [more] limited, with few signs of serious movement towards transnational citizenship' (Mitchell and Russell 1996: 72). State policy to immigrants and ethnic communities in Germany, France and Britain continues to reflect to some extent different nationhood traditions.

Citizenship and minority ethnic groups in Britain

Access to political rights and to a lesser extent social and civic rights is largely dependent upon citizenship status in Germany, France and Britain. The position of minority ethnic groups in Britain compares favourably in this respect to that of their counterparts in Europe. For Britain's minority groups are more likely to enjoy citizenship status (D Smith and Wistrich 1997). We do need, however, to distinguish 'the formal possession of citizenship rights' from 'their substantive availability' (Mason 2000: 123), move on from an examination of citizenship as a legal status and explore the question of whether members of minority groups, including those granted citizenship, enjoy *effective* civil, political and social rights. Here we shall focus on the experience of minority groups in Britain. Since we have already noted the way immigration policy has adversely impacted on the social rights of resident minority groups, we shall concentrate on the other two elements of citizenship: civil and political rights.

Civil rights, ethnicity and the criminal justice system

Of central significance to civil rights are the practices and procedures of the criminal justice system. Initially little concern was evident that they might entail systematic ethnic bias. Indeed, in the early phase of migration, according to a major investigation into police–immigrant relations in 1972, 'black people were more law abiding than the general population' and 'there were few public manifestations of violence towards black [and Asian] immigrants' (Layton-Henry 1992: 125, 138). During the following ten years, however, relations between the police and the Black community deteriorated and evidence mounted of increasing racist attacks.

Two reports published in November 1981 signalled official concerns. The Scarman report into the Brixton disorders emphasised how the riots earlier in the year were essentially an outburst of anger and resentment by young Caribbeans against perceived harassment by the police, and the Home Office report into racial attacks revealed that South Asians were 50 times, and Afro-Caribbeans 36 times, more likely to be the victims of racially motivated attacks than Whites. Evidence 'documenting the differential involvement of black [and Asian] people with the criminal justice system, whether as suspects, victims or general customers [was by now] undeniable' (Reiner 1993: 2). Two issues in particular have given rise to concern: the racist violence and harassment experienced by minority ethnic groups and the criminalisation of Black people.

Although racist violence and harassment is by no means a new phenomenon in Britain and is at least as serious in France and Germany (Bjorgo and Witte 1993), where extreme right-wing parties enjoy more popularity and fan the flames of racism, mounting evidence indicates the scale of the problem (Virdee 1995). The 1992 British Crime Survey 'estimated that nationally there had been a total of 130,000 racially motivated crimes against South Asians and Caribbeans in 1991' of which approximately 10,000 were reported to the police (Modood *et al.* 1997: 263). The police statistics – though they cover the majority of the most serious cases – represent the visible tip of an iceberg, which stretches far below the surface if we include all racially motivated crimes and even deeper if we also incorporate 'forms of racially insulting and threatening behaviour which are not seen as criminal events in themselves' (Modood *et al.* 1997: 263). The 1994 PSI Survey provides an estimate of such low-level racist harassment and on that basis concludes 'that over a quarter of a million people were subjected to some form of racial harassment in a 12-month period' (Modood *et al.* 1997: 267). The consequences of such racist harassment, which are predominantly experienced by members of minority ethnic groups and often form an on-going process of victimisation, are extremely damaging. A range of studies confirms how they can create a climate of continual insecurity for victims and their families (Chahal and Julienne 1999). Such everyday harassment provides the backdrop to racist violence of which the murder of a Black teenager, Stephen Lawrence, by five White youths in 1993 is the most notorious example.

The issue which has attracted most attention from criminologists concerns the criminalisation of Black people. At the end of the criminal justice process, 'black people . . . are about six times as likely to be in prison as white people or South Asians' (D Smith 1997: 749). Two broad explanations have been put forward for this. The first sees the criminal justice system as racist and discriminating against Black people. The second sees Black people as disproportionately criminal. Although the debate between these two positions is extremely contentious, some analysts have tried to move beyond the 'either/or of racist criminal justice vs. black criminality' (Reiner 1993: 3).

A recent review of the research points to 'evidence of bias' against Black people at various stages in the criminal justice system: in the use of stop and search powers; in the decision to prosecute juvenile offenders; and in sentencing by the Crown Courts (D Smith 1997: 749). In some cases this bias stems from direct discrimination but more typically it arises from 'apparently race-neutral legal factors' such as charge and plea which are open to discretion and have an adverse impact on Black suspects (Fitzgerald 1998: 171). At the same time the review argues that 'in large part the difference in rate of arrest and imprisonment between black and white people arises from a difference in the rate of offending' (D Smith 1997: 751), a phenomenon also found among 'second- and third-generation immigrants' who experience 'a marginal social position' in other societies (I Marshall 1997: 238).

In short, both discrimination in the criminal justice system and the greater involvement of young Black men in street crime contribute to the criminalisation of Black people (Hudson, 1993). Their role in generating an over-representation of Black people in crime statistics cannot, however, 'be captured in a snapshot picture' and needs 'to be seen in terms of a dynamic relationship' (Fitzgerald 1998: 176), whereby 'discrimination on the one hand, and black crime on the other, reinforce and feed off one another in a vicious circle of amplification' (Reiner 1993: 14). Lea and Young (1982) illustrate how this vicious circle develops.

> For there to be policing by consent, a community must act as a source of information to the police so that the latter can 'catch and/or deter individual lawbreakers'. As unemployment generates an increasing crime rate in inner cities, however, the police begin to adopt a more aggressive policing policy and turn to operations which involve the 'random stopping of "suspicious" youth'. This inevitably results in large numbers of innocent people being stopped and searched. Once this happens, the community 'begins to become alienated from the police'. It 'comes to see any attempt

at an arrest by officers as a symbolic attack on the community' and ceases to provide the police with any information which can help them identify individual offenders. Faced with this situation, the police adopt an even more aggressive policing policy and so the vicious circle continues. In this context, 'whatever racist sentiments exist within the police force are reinforced'. If the drift towards 'military' policing is to be counteracted, the authors argue that the conditions which generate crime need to be attacked and that the police need to be made more accountable to the community (A Pilkington 1984: 170–1).

The 1999 Macpherson report on the police investigation into the murder of Stephen Lawrence addresses both the issue of racist violence and harassment, and police discrimination. Its overall conclusion is quite startling and goes far beyond any previous official inquiry in detecting in the police 'institutional racism'. While the report recognises that 'racism, institutional or otherwise, is not the prerogative of the Police Service' (Macpherson 1999: para. 6.54) and is a characteristic feature of other agencies both within and outside the criminal justice system, the primary focus is on the police. Such an emphasis is warranted given 'the key role [they] play as gatekeepers to the criminal justice system for the vast majority of citizens' (Mason 2000: 119).

For Macpherson, the failure of the police investigation into the murder of Stephen Lawrence was not attributable to overt acts of discrimination by individual officers acting out their personal prejudices, but stemmed instead from the occupational culture of the police. In an occupation that may entail danger, great emphasis is placed on teamwork, with jokes and banter being used to cement solidarity. Given the prevalence of derogatory stereotypes about minority ethnic groups among police officers, such jokes and banter often take a racist form and reinforce within the force a negative perception of Black and Asian people (Holdaway 1996). This in turn can lead to discriminatory policing as evident, for example, in Stephen Lawrence's companion on the night of his murder, Dwayne Brooks, being regarded by the police as a suspect rather than a witness (Bowling and Phillips 2002). Alongside 'racial categorisations of black youth', which result in systematic bias in the use of stop and search, is a tendency within the occupational culture of police officers to discount the relevance of racism 'to incidents that require its recognition' such as racially motivated attacks (Holdaway 1999: para. 8.2). Macpherson considered this to be a very serious failing and concluded his report by making 70 recommendations, of which 34 related to the handling of racist incidents.

While disappointment has been expressed at the lack of progress made in implementing some of these recommendations (CRE 2001), there is evidence of progress in the handling of racist incidents. A code of practice on reporting and recording racist incidents has been produced by the Home Office (2000); the Association of Chief Police Officers (ACPO 2000) have produced a guide to identifying and combating hate crime; and, after two blistering critiques evident in their first two reports (HMIC 1997; HMIC 1999), the third report of Her Majesty's Inspectorate of Constabulary (HMIC) on community and race relations has expressed cautious 'optimism that the Service is at last on the road to recovery' (HMIC 2001: 6). Despite such evidence that the police are at last taking more seriously race and community relations in general, and racist incidents in particular, research on a force commended by the HMIC as exemplifying good practice in dealing with racist incidents, and making progress in recruiting and retaining minority ethnic officers, reveals that much still needs to be done (A Pilkington *et al.* 2001). Ideas about race were still central to the occupational culture, with minority ethnic officers continuing to be subject to racist jokes and banter from their colleagues. As another writer confirms, 'there appears to be little evidence of underlying change in police organisational culture' (Loveday 2000: 26). In addition, a survey of victims of racist incidents pointed to a very high level of dissatisfaction with the way the police dealt with racist incidents (A Pilkington *et al.* 2001). More than half the respondents were dissatisfied with the police response, a much higher level of dissatisfaction than that of victims overall, and one comparable to that found by the 1994 PSI survey (Modood *et al.* 1997). We are still some way off being able to claim that members of minority ethnic groups have equality before the law.

Political rights and ethnicity

In turning to the question of political rights, attention needs to be given to the participation of minority ethnic groups in British politics. Here we can distinguish three forms of political activity: spontaneous protest; pressure group activity; and participation in the electoral system (Goulbourne 1998b).

The two most dramatic examples of 'spontaneous action bred of frustration with the relevant authorities' were a series of riots in inner city areas, the most serious of which (at least in the eyes of the media) occurred in 1981, 1985 and 2001, and the demonstrations in response to the publication of Salman Rushdie's *The Satanic Verses* which took place in 1988 (Goulbourne 1998b: 182).

According to Scarman 'the riots [in 1981] were essentially an outburst of anger and resentment by young black people against the police' (Scarman 1981, quoted in Benyon 1987: 35). Although the trigger events in each case revolved around a specific instance of perceived police harassment of black people, five underlying factors can be distinguished which precipitated the riots: the extensiveness of 'racial disadvantage and discrimination'; the high level of 'unemployment'; the widespread experience of 'deprivation'; a sense of 'political exclusion and powerlessness'; and general 'mistrust of, and hostility to, the police' (Benyon 1987: 33–5). While the 1981 riots may not have had a lasting impact, they did temporarily wake up some local authorities to the issue of racial equality and provided an opportunity 'to place black representation on the mainstream political agenda' (Shukra 1998a: 117–18).

The 1981 riots took most people by surprise, with many people shocked by the sight of nightly confrontations during April and July between youth and the police, accompanied by extensive property destruction and some looting (A Pilkington 1986). The recurrence of riots, however, in subsequent years has entailed a degree of desensitisation. While young Black men were again at the forefront of riots in 1985, the demographic composition of rioters changed in the early 1990s, with young White men at the fore (Power and Tunstall 1997), and again in 2001, with young Pakistani and Bangladeshi young men at the fore (Home Office 2001). In all cases, however, the trigger for the riots was either an incident of perceived police harassment or 'an unusual level of police intervention in response to a threatened breakdown in order' (Power and Tunstall 1997: x). The riots also shared other features. The rioters comprised (often unemployed) young men, living in deprived areas where the crime rate was high and police–community relations were poor. Experiencing relative deprivation, the young men involved felt excluded from mainstream society and powerless to improve their situation through acquiring educational qualifications and work. In this context, a common response was to reject the norms of mainstream society by signalling their potency through aggression and by breaking the law. Such behaviour eventually attracted abnormal police intervention, thus triggering the riots. In the case of the 1985 and 2001 riots, the underlying factors precipitating the riots were compounded by significant racial discrimination and racial disadvantage.

While the post-war riots, which have involved members of minority ethnic groups, share a number of common features, there are significant differences between the riots of 1981 and 1985 on the one hand, and those of 2001 on the other hand. The ones in the 1980s involved both Black and (to some extent) White young men in confrontation with the police, but they did not entail conflict between ethnic groups. Those that took place from April to July 2001 in the northern towns of Oldham, Burnley and Bradford, however, took place in areas where there was significant segregation between different communities and mounting conflict between Muslim and White young men, with the presence of extreme right-wing organisations often inflaming the situation. While significant economic deprivation, consequent upon the collapse of the textile industry, lies at the root of the riots, the different communities have fragmented and vented their frustrations on each other as well as the police (Kundnani 2001). There is an urgent need in this context to develop policies which deal with the roots of urban unrest and build cohesive communities. The recurrence of riots in the post-war period indicates, however, that previous policies have so far not proved to be very successful in arresting the serious deprivation characteristic of some areas.

A precursor to the involvement of Pakistani and Bangladeshi young men in the 2001 riots was the participation of their communities in an earlier campaign. The publication of *The Satanic Verses* was seen by many Muslims as deeply offensive and it 'became the focus around which many British Muslims, particularly in Bradford, mobilised to express their feelings about the perceived status of Islam in society' (Goulbourne 1998b: 184). Although the Rushdie affair raises a number of issues which we do not have time to explore here, reference does need to be made to one, namely the notion of citizenship which is being espoused by some Muslims (and indeed many other excluded groups). It is an ideal of equality which is not just based on 'the right to assimilate to the majority/dominant culture in the public sphere . . . and toleration of "difference" in the private sphere' but also includes 'the right to have one's "difference" . . . recognised and supported in the public and private spheres' (Modood and Werbner 1997: 20). The Rushdie affair represented for them a slight on their faith and community. In the light of this, Muslims campaigned not only to outlaw religious discrimination (already outlawed in Northern Ireland) but also to gain public funding for Muslim schools on the same basis as Christian and Jewish schools. Prior to the advent of the EU Directives, the government resisted the call for new legislation, but has recently, and for the first time, accepted applications for public funding of two Muslim schools.

Within minority ethnic communities, 'self-organisation . . . was quick to appear soon after arrival in Britain' (Goulbourne 1998a: 64). On this basis, a variety of organisations have subsequently emerged to voice concerns over particular issues and represent the interests of minority groups. In some cases they have organised on the basis of colour, using the signifier of 'Black' to represent their unity. More commonly they have organised on the basis of ethnicity, utilising existing community organisations to further their interests. In both cases this has usually 'involved working with . . . other groups from the majority society' (Goulbourne 1998a: 64). According to one writer, 'British minority activism is very much the product of British race relations politics' (Statham 1999: 620). While Caribbeans have tended to mobilise on racial lines under a Black identity and framed their demands in terms of racial equality, South Asians have tended to mobilise in different ways. Pakistanis and Bangladeshis have tended to mobilise on religious lines as Muslims and framed their demands in terms of 'extending the principle of racial equality to their non-racial group' (Statham 1999: 597) and Indians, who as a group have been more successful in socio-economic terms, have tended to have less incentive to mobilise. Although it is difficult to gauge the success of such pressure group activity, there is little doubt that it has helped place some issues, such as the underachievement of Caribbean children and the public funding of Muslim schools, on the political agenda.

The form of political activity which has received most attention from political scientists is the participation of minority ethnic groups in the party political and electoral systems. During the 1950s and 1960s the main political parties took little interest in the votes of Asian and Caribbean voters. In 1974, however, a report by the CRC analysed the general election results of that year and pointed to the significance of so-called 'ethnic marginals', that is, 'seats where local minority groups outnumber the scale of existing MPs' majorities' (Saggar 1997: 148). Since then the main political parties have sought to woo minority voters. The Labour Party has been much more successful than the Conservative Party in attracting such voters.

In the 2001 election, four in every five minority voters backed Labour as they have done in virtually every general election. While there has been a slight shift away from Labour of Black and particularly Asian voters, which means that 'the need to attract Black and Asian voters is likely to remain on the agendas of the parties (Saggar 1998: 28), what is more remarkable is the resilience of support for the party among minority ethnic voters. This cannot simply be explained by the class position of minority voters because they are much more inclined to support Labour than White voters in similar class positions (Saggar 1995). More plausible is the hypothesis that they 'share considerable political interests' which are at least partially articulated by the Labour Party (Messina 1998: 50).

Over time their faith in the party has paid some dividends in terms of minority representation. During the 1980s the Labour Party was much more open than the Conservative Party to minority ethnic interests and 'there was an increase in ethnic representation at local and national level' (Geddes 1998: 170). Building on some success in gaining increased representation at the local level, minority ethnic politicians used the unofficial forum of Black Sections in the Labour Party to demand the nomination of minority candidates for winnable seats (Shukra 1998b). The election of four minority candidates in the 1987 general election represented something of a breakthrough. While subsequent general elections have witnessed a further increase in minority representation, with 6 candidates (5 Labour and 1 Conservative) in 1992, 9 (all Labour) in 1997 and 12 (all Labour) in 2001, it cannot be said that a new era of ethnic representation has arrived. While there is evidence that 'the collective effort of the six MPs [elected in 1992] ensured that race issues have not been neglected at Westminster' (Nixon 1998: 219), at the same time the influence of ethnic minorities in Parliament remains minimal (Saggar 1993). Members of minority ethnic groups continue to be significantly under represented in Parliament and, to a lesser extent, on local councils. In view of the fact that their voices are scarcely to be heard within mainstream party politics, it cannot be said that their political rights have yet entailed political equality. Britain's minority ethnic communities may enjoy formal citizenship rights but we have some way to go before these become effective citizenship rights.

Conclusion

For most of the post-war period successive British governments have sought to depoliticise the issue of race and ethnicity by pursuing a two-pronged strategy. This has involved, on the one hand, measures designed to restrict immigration, especially non-White immigration and, on the other hand, measures designed to combat racial disadvantage and integrate ethnic minorities who have settled in the country. While immigration policy has been presaged on racist assumptions, integration policy has rested on liberal assumptions.

Over time some convergence has been evident in the responses of West European governments to issues surrounding migration. Such convergence, however, has been more evident in relation to immigration policy than integration policy. All three countries that we have examined now have strict immigration controls, but, in contrast to Germany, Britain has been more willing to grant immigrants formal citizenship rights while, in contrast to France, Britain has been less wedded to assimilationism. We should not, however, exaggerate these differences. There is evidence that Britain's minority groups do not always enjoy effective citizenship rights and an examination of state policy indicates that only hesitant moves have been made towards pluralism.

Recognising continuing racial disadvantage should not blind us, however, to the efficacy of agency. A central theme of this book has been to challenge the dominant stress on structural forces in much of the literature on race and ethnicity, and to highlight the diverse ways minority ethnic communities draw on their resources to resist exclusion and disadvantage. An examination of diverse forms of political activity serves to illustrate this.

8 Conclusion: the future of multi-ethnic Britain

Marx's famous dictum that history is made by human beings but not under conditions that they choose is widely accepted by social scientists. Its attraction stems from the fact that it succinctly expresses the need to give due weight to both agency and structure. Social change is only possible because of human action, but such action is in turn constrained by social forces. And yet when we examine much of the research on issues relating to race and ethnicity in Britain, we find that all too often it has tended either to highlight the structural forces which result in disadvantages for racialised groups or (more rarely) to celebrate the actions of human beings in seeking to sustain distinct ethnic cultures. Marx's dictum seems to have been forgotten.

For much of the post-war period, a particular framework has tended to underpin sociological understanding of issues relating to race and ethnicity. This framework has been characterised as that of 'racial dualism'. Two categories, distinguished by the colour of their skin, are identified, with White people envisaged as in a markedly more powerful structural position than Black people. While it is acknowledged that neither of these categories is homogeneous, the overriding emphasis is on racial oppression, with the primary task of researchers being to delineate and account for the disadvantages shared in common by Black people.

This framework was never completely hegemonic and coexisted for a long time with what has been characterised as 'the ethnic approach'. In contrast to racial dualism, this highlighted the importance of people's ethnic affiliations and the need to take account of culturally determined preferences in understanding the behaviour of ethnic minorities (C Ballard and Driver 1977). The ethnic approach was not un-influential and indeed provided the rationale for some of the multicultural initiatives discussed (and critiqued) in Chapter 5. Within Sociology, however, it tended to be pilloried for at best focusing on less fundamental issues (relating to culture rather than power) and at worst for legitimising a victim-blaming discourse (whereby cultural differences are deemed responsible for racial disadvantage).

Two developments prompted sociologists to reconsider the importance of ethnicity. The first was the cultural turn in social theory, which entailed recognising that the binary opposition between White and Black was too crude to capture the multiple and shifting identities characteristic of a global age. The second was the discovery within social research of significant ethnic diversity between minority groups previously pictured as sharing a comparable socio-economic position.

While many commentators are struck by the plethora of competing theoretical perspectives to issues relating to race and ethnicity (Back and Solomos 2000), it is possible to detect in the work of leading scholars such as Stuart Hall, Bhikhu Parekh and Tariq Modood the emergence of a new framework guiding research and policy formulation in this area. This framework, which entails synthesising features of racial dualism and the ethnic approach, can be characterised as that of 'racial disadvantage and ethnic diversity'. It acknowledges, in line with racial dualism, the continuing need to delineate and explain the common disadvantages faced by minority ethnic groups. At the same time and, in tune with the ethnic approach, it highlights the diversity among minority ethnic groups and emphasises that the socio-economic positions and identities of their members are not structurally determined but are, at least in part, formed by their actions. This framework thus seeks to give due weight to both agency and structure. In drawing upon this framework to explore issues relating to race and ethnicity in contemporary Britain, this book has attempted to remain loyal to Marx's dictum.

The Parekh report

While the primary concern of this book has been to provide an overview of research on issues relating to race and ethnicity in Britain and thereby to clarify the nature of multi-ethnic Britain at the start of a new millennium, it is not possible to pretend that the analysis has no policy implications. While these will be evident to the reader at various points in the text, they are expertly drawn together in a recent report (Parekh 2000).

In January 1998 the Runnymede Trust, an independent organisation set up in the late 1960s to provide informed comment on race and ethnicity, and promote racial equality, set up a Commission on the future of multi-ethnic Britain. This culminated on 11 October 2000 in the launch and publication of a major report, *The Future of Multi-Ethnic Britain* (Parekh 2000). In contrast to previous reports, such as those of Scarman (1981) and Macpherson (1999), it was not borne out of crisis and was not the product of an official inquiry. The purpose of the report was to analyse the current state of Britain and propose ways of combating racial disadvantage and enabling Britain to become a vibrant multicultural society. Chaired by Lord Parekh, the Commission

> consisted of six internationally respected professors, two peers and two knights of the realm, the master of a Cambridge college, a QC who advised the South African government on labour law, a senior fellow of an Oxford college and expert on criminology, a chief constable and a chief inspector of police, three prominent human rights experts, two senior policy researchers, one popular broadcaster who is also the chair of the Greater London Assembly and, until April [2000] . . . the political editor of the BBC (Alibhai-Brown 2000b).

While the composition of the Commission reflected the importance attached to bringing together distinguished people with specific expertise, care was also taken to ensure a gender balance and to include members from different communities. The report itself was unanimously agreed, being the product of extensive consultations with a host of organisations, a range of seminars on key issues and commissioned research. It was designed to be an authoritative report and a key contribution both to public debate and government policy formulation.

The report highlights six tasks that need to be urgently addressed. These comprise the following:

- the need to rethink the national story and national identity;
- the need to recognise that Britain comprises a range of 'majority' and 'minority' communities which are internally diverse and which are changing;
- the need to strike a balance between the need to treat people equally, the need to respect differences and the need to maintain shared values and social cohesion;

- the need to address and remove all forms of racism;
- the need to reduce economic inequalities;
- the need to build a pluralist human rights culture.

It is on the basis of this vision of what needs to be done that specific policy recommendations are made. Let us deal with each of these tasks in turn.

While all of these tasks are interrelated, the first two are so indissolubly connected that later in the report they are presented as one task. Britain, it is argued, is an imagined community and needs to be imagined in new ways in order to ensure that it is ethnically inclusive. The report suggests that it is helpful to think of Britain as 'a community of communities and a community of citizens' (Parekh 2000: 56). Thinking of Britain as a community, it is argued, alerts us to the importance of a common sense of belonging and the need for shared values and social cohesion. Thinking of Britain as a community of communities challenges the conventional view of Britain as divided into two seemingly homogeneous groupings, a White majority and ethnic minorities, and urges us instead to recognise that Britain comprises a number of fluid, overlapping and internally diverse national, regional and ethnic communities which cut across any simple majority/minority division. This means that treating people with due regard to respect for differences is not an issue only of concern to minority ethnic groups. At the same time, the report emphasises that it would be inappropriate to think of Britain purely in these terms since we are not only members of distinct communities but are also individuals who deserve to be treated equally. We need therefore to think of Britain not only as a community of communities but also as a community of citizens.

Conceptualising Britain, and its constituent communities, in these terms entails, it is argued, a need to strike a balance between cohesion, equality and difference. The report is unwilling to embrace any of the dominant models – nationalism, liberalism or communitarianism – in their pure forms because each of them is exclusively concerned to promote one of these values. Nationalism prioritises social cohesion and argues that people need to assimilate to a single national culture in order to bring about a common sense of belonging. Liberalism prioritises equality and argues that individuals, as bearers of rights, should be entitled to citizenship rights in a neutral public sphere. Communitarianism prioritises difference and argues that people's community affiliations are so fundamental to their identities that members of different communities warrant being treated differently.

The problems with each of these models become apparent when they are juxtaposed. Nationalism entails the imposition of the values of one group on to others and fails to recognise the legitimacy of alternative ways of life. Liberalism does not recognise that the public sphere inevitably bears the cultural imprint of the dominant ethnic group and fails to acknowledge the centrality of communal affiliations to people's cultural identities. Communitarianism glosses over the fact that communities are fluid, overlapping and internally diverse and fails to embrace 'the right of individuals . . . to dissent from, exit from and oppose if necessary their communities of origin' (S Hall 2000: 236).

By visualising Britain as a community of communities and a community of citizens, the report expresses support for the three principles of cohesion, equality and difference. 'They must be held together, qualifying and challenging each other, yet also mutually informing and enriching' (Parekh 2000: 105). This raises a conundrum, however, since these principles are, at least in part, at odds with each other. How do we reconcile these contrary values? While this tension 'may not be amenable to resolution in the abstract' (S Hall 2000: 235), the report presents some pointers, which enable a balance to be struck between these values.

Some 'common values are necessary to hold [Britain] together and give it cohesion' (Parekh 2000: 53). These are of two forms: procedural and substantive. Procedural values are those such as tolerance, mutual respect and rationality, which provide 'the basic preconditions for democratic dialogue'. Substantive values are those enshrined in international human rights standards which 'underpin any defensible conception of the good life . . . On the basis of such values it is legitimate to ban female circumcision, forced marriages, cruel punishment of children, and repressive and unequal treatment of women, even though these practices may enjoy cultural authority in certain communities' (Parekh 2000: 53–4). While these values set limits to permissible differences, the report argues that people should otherwise be free to pursue their own conceptions of the good life, and these may of course differ profoundly. We are still left therefore with the question of how the competing claims of difference and equality can both be recognised. Here the report emphasises the need for the public sphere to be more pluralistic and for disputes to be resolved through inter-cultural dialogue and negotiation.

Three further tasks need to be undertaken in order to realise the report's vision of Britain as a community of communities and a community of citizens. The first two are fundamental and have been addressed on a number of occasions in this book: the need to address and combat all forms of racism; and the need to reduce inequalities. Both are critical preconditions if people from all communities are to have equal citizenship rights and an equal sense of belonging to Britain. The third and final one relates to the 'ground rules that provide a minimum of protection for individuals and a framework for handling conflicts of interest' and comprises the need to build a pluralist human rights culture (Parekh 2000: 90). The report argues that, while race equality issues in the UK have tended not to be addressed within a human rights framework, it is important that they are so 'that racial discrimination [is no longer] seen as a comparatively minor problem [but] as a challenge for society as a whole' (Parekh 2000: 100). Since 'human beings are not only individuals but also culturally embedded', it 'is essential to recognise the rights that people have as members of religious, cultural and linguistic groups' (Parekh 2000: 91). It is important in short not to restrict human rights to ones defined in narrowly individualistic terms but to develop a pluralistic human rights culture.

The media's response to the Parekh report

Of critical importance to any report that seeks to inform public debate and influence policy making is the reception by the media. For it is primarily though the media that people gain information, and political parties and other major organisations are increasingly sensitive to media coverage. The initial response of the media seemed encouraging, with coverage a few days before the launch of the report being positive or at least factual and neutral. On 8 October the *Observer* ran a small news item with the headline, 'Labour "has failed to root out racism"', which outlined one of the report's conclusions that there was still much to do in order to address and remove all forms of racism in Britain. On the same day, the *Sunday Telegraph,* taking a somewhat different tack, ran a story with the headline, 'Critics of a "racist" Britain are misguided, says report', which picked up on a comment in the report that, in comparison to many countries, Britain is a multi-ethnic society relatively at ease with itself. While it is instructive to note how two newspapers, with very different political positions, selected very different aspects of the report to highlight, the early signs seemed to indicate that the report would be fairly, and even favourably, reported. All this changed the day before the report's launch.

The *Daily Telegraph* led the way with its main story on the front page headlined, 'Straw wants to rewrite our history', with the subheading '"British" is a racist word, says report'. This was accompanied by a scathing critique of the report in its editorial, headed, 'The British race' and an equally damning commentary entitled 'Thinkers who want to consign our island story to history'. Other newspapers took their cue from the *Daily Telegraph,* with both the *Daily Mail* and the *Sun* changing their later editions on 10 October to reproduce the same line. The *Daily Mail* headlined its story 'British is racist, says peer trying to rewrite our history', while the *Sun* under the heading, '"British" is race slur', carried a story which began: 'The word "British" is RACIST, according to a new report that has been welcomed by the government. And it says British history should be rewritten because it takes no account of ethnic minorities'. Later that day, the *Evening Standard,* published in London, reiterated the same message under the headline, 'The word "British" is racist – report'.

The following day, when the report itself was launched, coverage became more extensive but the overriding emphasis had been set the day before. The *Daily Mail* included an essay entitled, 'In praise of being British' and an equally damning editorial headed, 'What an insult to history and our intelligence'. The *Daily Telegraph* followed up its earlier condemnation of the report with an essay entitled, 'They met at Runnymede – to boss us all around'. Other newspapers latched on to a new story but generally followed the way that the *Daily Telegraph* had initially defined the story. *The Times* headlined its story: 'Drop the word "British" says race trust', while both the *Guardian* and the *Daily Mirror* took a similar line with their respective headlines, 'British tag is "coded racism"' and 'British is "just another word for prejudice"'. It is true that articles appeared that day, especially in the *Guardian* and *Independent*, which were more sympathetic to the report, but the overriding impression given by the headlines in the press was extremely negative.

On 11 October the report was officially launched, with the Home Secretary, Jack Straw, welcoming the overall thrust of the report, including the need for Britishness to 'become an inclusive plural' identity (Straw, 2000, quoted in *Runnymede Bulletin*, no.324)), while at the same time distancing himself from the tendency (in his view) for people on the left not to be proud of being English and/or British. The coverage the following day ignored the Home Secretary's welcome for the report and concentrated instead on his defence of Britishness. The *Daily Telegraph* again set the tone, 'Straw beats a very British retreat over race report' and reiterated its message in another editorial, 'Don't diss Britannia'. Other newspapers tended to take the same line. *The Times* was particularly scathing of the report supplementing its lead story headlined, '"Proud to be British" Straw raps race report' with two essays headed respectively, 'Whatever being British stands for, it will not be imposed by a bureaucratic, quasi-State commission' and 'Who do these worthy idiots think they are?' and an editorial with the heading, 'Nation and Race: a report that will be shelved, a debate that will not'. Headlines in the *Guardian, Independent* and *Financial Times* adopted the same overall framework in their lead stories, 'Be proud to be British, Straw tells left'; 'Straw launches scathing attack on "unpatriotic" left'; and 'Britishness defended after race report'. And the same was true of the tabloids, with the *Daily Express* announcing in its headline, 'Race report angers "proud Briton" Straw' and the *Daily Mirror* 'Straw backs Britain', while the *Daily Mail* took the same tack, albeit without the sympathy evident to Labour of the other two papers, 'Labour in retreat on race'. Other tabloids put things more graphically, with the *Daily Star* announcing 'This stuff gets on my Brits' and the *Sun* stating 'The Sun hits back at fools who say the word "British" is racist'. There were some more considered articles on the day of publication, including editorials in the *Independent* and *Daily Express* and essays in the *Guardian* and *Evening Standard*. The bulk of media coverage tended to drown out such voices so that the overwhelming message across the media tended to present the report in a highly negative way.

After 12 October the report received increasingly less explicit coverage in the daily newspapers. The advent of the Sunday papers temporarily gave it new life but, needless to say, the existing framework tended to be reproduced. The tabloids included essays that made their vehement opposition to the report very clear. The *News of the World:* 'It's stupid to brand True Brits as racist'; the *People:* 'Tough on pot but so weak on pottiness'; the *Mail on Sunday:* 'These race "warriors" simply stir up hatred'. Although the odd article appeared, for example in the *Observer,* sympathetic to the report, the overriding message in the broadsheets was just as critical as that in the tabloids. The *Sunday Times:* 'They are doing their level best to destroy Britain's identity' and the *Sunday Telegraph:* 'We know in our hearts what Britain means'. Thereafter, the report was no longer news and the story ran out of steam. It is true that, for a brief period, stories which related to race and ethnicity tended to make allusions to the report and its purported critique of Britishness as racist. This is evident in news items which appeared in the month following publication of the report, including a story prompted by a rather offhand comment by one of the commissioners about Prince Charles marrying a Black woman and what this would signal. As time passed, however, the report was forgotten and within a few months had become history.

What does media coverage of the report reveal? In line with the code of practice issued by the Press Complaints Commission, factual news was to some extent separated from commentaries and editorial opinions, and to some extent across the media can be detected a range of opinions. However, the coverage was highly selective, with the focus overwhelmingly being on the issue of national identity. While it is true that the report does emphasise the need to rethink the national story and national identity, it also, as we have seen, highlights five further tasks which need to be urgently addressed.

More important than the highly selective coverage, which might be justifiable in terms of news values, was the inaccuracy of much of the coverage. Three forms of inaccuracy can be identified (Richardson 2000): the use of false quotations from the report; quoting the report without contextualising the quotation appropriately; and misrepresentation of key arguments in the report. In many ways, the most serious is the first of these forms of inaccuracy. By claiming that the report said that the word British has 'racist connotations', the *Daily Telegraph* set the tone for much of the subsequent coverage, much of which reproduced this claim. In point of fact, the report does not say this; rather, it says that 'Britishness . . . has racial connotations'. This is very different, involving the claim that typically the word conjures up an image of a White society. By misquoting the report and substituting racist for racial, the *Daily Telegraph,* and newspapers which took the same line, gave readers the impression that the report was insulting them.

A second form of inaccuracy did not arise from false quotations but rather from the use of quotations out of context. The *Daily Telegraph* again took the lead when it represented the report as saying the following: 'The nation's very history should be rethought and certain aspects "jettisoned, revised or reworked"'. The impression given by this passage is that the authors of the report are somewhat like Stalinists who wish to rewrite history to suit their favoured ideology. Little or no acknowledgement is given to the fact that history is continually subject to reinterpretation and that such reinterpretation does not entail fabricating facts. What is more, the quotation from the report neglects to include the word 'preserved', despite the fact that the question the report asked about the nation's history related to what should be 'preserved . . . jettisoned . . . revised or reworked'. In addition there is a failure to point out that the report acknowledges that there is much in the nation's history of which citizens can feel pride.

The final form of inaccuracy involved misrepresentation of key arguments in the report. Again, we shall use an influential example from the *Daily Telegraph* where it was claimed that the Commission 'defines the UK as a community of communities rather than a nation'. The report on a number of occasions does indeed suggest that it is helpful to think of

Britain as 'a community of communities', although it does add that this needs to be allied to a recognition that Britain also needs to be thought of as 'a community of citizens'. While the report uses this conceptualisation of Britain to argue for a balance to be struck between cohesion, equality and difference, their argument is clearly open to challenge. Some liberals for example may consider treating people from different communities differently contravenes the paramount importance of treating individuals equally, while some conservatives may believe that recognising and responding to alternative community identities to that of the nation may undermine the social cohesion of the nation. And from a different perspective, some communitarians may feel that the value placed on treating individuals equally undermines community affiliations. Clearly the report raises an important issue that warrants serious public debate. Unfortunately, the presentation in the *Daily Telegraph,* and other newspapers, of the report's argument on this issue trivialised what was being put forward, by implying that the report thought that Britain should be renamed.

While close analysis of media coverage of the report reveals a range of opinions, with the range becoming somewhat wider over time, partly because of the intervention of some of the commissioners, there is no doubt that the terms of the debate were set early by the *Daily Telegraph* and that set limits to the range of opinions expressed in most newspapers. The consequence of this media coverage was that that public understanding of this major report was skewed and that the efficacy of the report both in terms of contributing to public debate and influencing key institutions was thwarted.

The report clearly touched a nerve. The hostile media coverage indicated the existence of considerable anger towards the idea that Britain needed to change in fundamental ways. In some respects the report served as 'a proxy target' for the resentment felt towards the earlier Macpherson report, which had pictured the police and other organisations as characterised by institutional racism. It had been difficult to voice such resentment because the latter 'was accepted by the government and is associated with the senseless murder of a promising young man' (Parekh 2001: 6). The Parekh report, which shared many of the same assumptions as the Macpherson report, thus constituted a convenient target for the articulation of strongly felt grievances. It is tempting, when faced by such hostile media coverage, to conclude that the likelihood of realising the report's vision is extremely slim. We need, however, to recognise contrary tendencies at work in British society. While some features provide grounds for optimism, others are less encouraging. What we need to do is to adopt an attitude of cautious optimism and seek through our actions to reinforce those tendencies that promote racial equality. We shall below identify an example of each of these tendencies.

Britishness and the 2001 general election

While the report's focus was much wider than that of national identity, it is significant that this formed the primary focus of media coverage. This aspect of the report struck a chord because it rekindled anxieties about who we are by reminding us that, at a time when there is pressure for us to acknowledge that we are a multi-ethnic society, develop closer ties with Europe and grant devolved powers to the constituent parts of the United Kingdom, there is indeed deep uncertainty as to what Britishness now comprises.

Issues relating to race and ethnicity were not central during the 2001 election campaign. Although the leader of the Conservative Party at one stage sought to fuel fears about an influx of asylum seekers, this fell on fallow ground and the Labour Party was returned to power with an increased majority. None the less, during the campaign, the issue of Britishness did arise, with the Labour Foreign Secretary, Robin Cook, and a backbench Conservative MP presenting to the electorate very different conceptions of Britishness.

In his speech, Robin Cook sought to rethink Britishness to take account of the fact that Britain is now a multi-ethnic society. It is worth quoting extracts from his speech at some length:

> It is not their purity that makes the British unique but the sheer pluralism of their ancestry . . . Chicken Tikka Massala is now a true British national dish, not only because it is the most popular, but because it is a perfect illustration of the way Britain absorbs and adapts external influences.

Chicken Tikka is an Indian dish. The Massala sauce was added to satisfy the desire of British people to have their meat served in gravy . . . Coming to terms with multiculturalism as a positive force for our economy and society will have significant implications for our understanding of Britishness. . . . The modern notion of national identity cannot be based on race and ethnicity, but must be based on shared ideals and aspirations. Some of the most successful countries in the modern world, such as the United States and Canada, are immigrant societies. Their experience shows how cultural diversity, allied to a shared concept of equal citizenship, can be a source of enormous strength. We should draw inspiration from their experience. . . . It is natural for every nation to be proud of its identity. We should be proud to be British. But we should be proud of the real Britain of the modern age. . . . Proud that the strength of the British character reflects the influences of the many different communities who have made their home here over the centuries. Proud that openness, mutual respect and generosity of spirit are essential British values. . . . .We should be proud that those British values have made Britain a successful multi-ethnic society. We should welcome that pluralism as a unique asset for Britain in a modern world where our prosperity, our security and our influence depend on the health of our relations with other peoples around the globe. . . . .Tolerance is important, but it is not enough. We should celebrate the enormous contribution of the many communities in Britain to strengthening our economy, to supporting our public services, and to enriching our culture and cuisine. And we should recognise that its diversity is part of the reason why Britain is a great place to live (Cook 2001).

What is interesting about this speech is that it echoes a number of themes highlighted by the Parekh report. Cook does try to re-imagine Britishness and, at least implicitly, acknowledges the need to seek a balance between the need to treat people equally, respect different cultures and ensure social cohesion. The speech inevitably contains Labour buzz words such as 'modern' and emphasises the pride we should feel in being British, but none the less it does represent an attempt to develop a more inclusive representation of Britishness with which we are asked to identify.

By contrast, John Townend's speech, which was partially a riposte to Cook's, represented an attempt to shore up an older and ethnically exclusive notion of Britishness:

Our homogeneous Anglo-Saxon society has been seriously undermined by the massive immigration – particularly Commonwealth immigration – that has taken place since the war. . . . Illegal immigrants have got a new ploy, they call themselves asylum seekers. In my view, the only way to deal with the problem is to send them back quickly. Many come from violent societies and inevitably crime is already beginning to rise in the areas where they are. . . . .I believe the concept of a multi-cultural, multi-ethnic, multi-lingual society is a mistake and will inevitably cause great problems. . . . .Mr Cook and many of his colleagues challenge the very concept of our nation. . . . .Presumably he considers us a mongrel race. I can tell him my Yorkshire constituents are insulted by such comments (Townend 2001).

While this speech shares a Little Englander position with the one of his quoted earlier in Chapter 6, it is interesting to note the shift in tone. Times have changed and even a maverick like Townend partially has to abide by new norms of acceptability. Although Townend seeks to exploit the issue of asylum seekers and on this issue was not at odds with the leader of the Conservative Party, his speech proved an embarrassment to William Hague. Like the other party leaders, he had not only signed, at the instigation of the CRE, a pledge not to exploit the issue of race and ethnicity for party gain, but also was keen to make his party attractive to members from minority communities. Townend's speech in fact was roundly condemned in most newspapers. While, as we have seen earlier, there is evidence that a Little Englander position has increasing adherents, it is interesting that within mainstream politics it is on the retreat. Here are some grounds for optimism.

11 September and its aftermath

It has been emphasised throughout this book that it is impossible to understand issues relating to race and ethnicity in Britain without taking account of the global context. The coordinated attacks on the World Trade Center in New York and the Pentagon in Washington illustrate this in dramatic fashion. Coverage of these attacks was conveyed across the world and led to the formation of an American-led coalition to fight terrorism. A massive bombing campaign ensued, with the Taliban regime in Afghanistan, believed to be harbouring the terrorist network responsible for the attacks, being removed from power. At the same time the representation of the events on 11 September 2001 as the responsibility of fundamentalist Muslims has generated a racist backlash directed at Muslims in most Western countries, including Britain.

In Britain the government and the media have been at pains to point out that the enemy is terrorism and not Islam, and Muslim organisations have condemned the attacks as un-Islamic. Despite this, British Muslims have been subject to increasing racist harassment and have felt intimidated about voicing their opposition to the bombing campaign in Afghanistan for fear of reprisals. Since 11 September 'to be a Muslim is to be under suspicion, under threat and, given the huge increase in racial violence, under attack' (Younge 2001).

Respect for fundamental human rights is deemed a luxury in this context. A new law, the Anti-Terrorism Crime and Security Act was passed in December 2001 which permits the unlimited detention of suspected terrorists and gives the police new powers. The fear within minority ethnic communities is that in the current climate they will be especially targeted by the police and the security services. At the same time the official response to the riots in northern cities has been to lay much (but not all) of the responsibility for them on to Muslims. The emphasis, three years after publication of the Macpherson report, is no longer on institutional racism but on a range of other factors, including self-imposed segregation. The discourse of a new Home Secretary, David Blunkett, signals this shift. '"We have norms of acceptability," he said shortly before December's reports into [the 2001] disturbances, "And those who come into our home – for that is what it is – should accept those norms just as we would have to do if we went elsewhere"' (Younge 2002). To present members of minority ethnic communities in this way is to present them as visitors rather than integral members of the nation and to forget that most, including the rioters, were born in this country. Their right to be British is not unqualified within this discourse but has to be demonstrated. We are a long way from re-imagining Britain as a community of communities and a community of citizens. Muslims are neither finding that their difference is being given public recognition nor being treated as citizens with equal rights. The opportunities for inter-cultural dialogue are being missed.

Any complacency we might have felt from noting the advent of the first race relations legislation for 25 years or from reading

Robin Cook's speech disappears. There are still contrary tendencies at work in British society, and there is no inevitability that the progress evident in the late 1990s will continue. We need in this context to ensure through our actions that the dominant tendency becomes one which entails promoting racial equality so that Britain indeed becomes a community of communities and a community of citizens.

Bibliography

Abercrombie, N (1996) *Television and Society,* Polity, Cambridge.

Ackroyd, J and Pilkington, A (1998) 'New dramas for new identities', *Multicultural Teaching,* vol.16, no.1.

ACPO (Association of Chief Police Officers) (2000) *A Guide to Identifying and Combating Hate Crime,* ACPO, London.

Adonis, A and Pollard, S (1997) *A Class Act: The Myth of Britain's Classless Society,* Hamish Hamilton, London.

Ahmad, W (ed.) (1993) *'Race' and Health in Contemporary Britain,* Open University Press, Buckingham.

Alcock, P (1997) *Understanding Poverty,* 2nd edn, Macmillan, London.

Aldrich, H, Cater, J, Jones, T and McEvoy, D (1981) 'Business development and self-segregation: Asian enterprise in three British cities' in C Peach, V Robinson and S Smith (eds) *Ethnic Segregation in Cities,* Croom Helm, London.

Alibhai-Brown, Y (1998) 'The media and race relations' in T Blackstone, B Parekh and P Sanders (eds) *Race Relations in Britain,* Routledge, London.

Alibhai-Brown, Y (1999) *True Colours: Public Attitudes to Multiculturalism and the Role of Government,* IPPR, London.

Alibhai-Brown, Y (2000a) *Who Do We Think We Are?* Allen Lane, London.

Alibhai-Brown, Y (2000b) 'Why does questioning the nature of Britishness raise so much fury?', *The Independent,* 18 October.

Amin, K with Oppenheim, C (1992) *Poverty in Black and White: Deprivation and Ethnic Minorities,* CPAG, London.

Andersen, J (1999) 'Social and system integration and the underclass' in I Gough and G Olofsson (eds) *Capitalism and Social Cohesion,* Macmillan, London.

Anderson, B (1983) *Imagined Communities: Reflections on the Origin and Spread of Nationalism,* Verso, London.

Anthias, F (1990) 'Race and class revisited – a reconceptualising of race and racisms', *Sociological Review,* vol.38, no.1.

Anthias, F (2001) 'New hybridities, old concepts: the limits of culture', *Ethnic and Racial Studies,* vol. 24, no.2.

Anthias, F and Yuval-Davis, N (1992) *Racialised Boundaries: Race, Nation, Gender, Colour, Class and the Anti-Racist Struggle,* Routledge, London.

Anwar, M (1998) *Between Cultures: Continuity and Change in the Lives of Young Asians,* Routledge, London.

Appignanesi, L and Maitland, S (eds) (1989) *The Rushdie Affair,* Fourth Estate, London.

Auletta, K (1982) *The Underclass,* Random House, New York.

Back, L (1996) *New Ethnicities and Urban Culture,* UCL Press, London.

Back, L and Solomos, J (eds) (2000) *Theories of Race and Racism,* Routledge, London.

Balibar, E (1991) 'Is there a "neo-racism"?' in E Balibar and I Wallerstein (eds) *Race, Nation, Class,* Verso, London.

Ball, S (1993) 'Education markets, choice and social class', *British Journal of Sociology of Education,* vol.14, no.1.

Ballard, C and Driver, G (1977) 'The ethnic approach', *New Society,* 16 June.

Ballard, R (1992) 'New clothes for the emperor? The conceptual nakedness of the race relations industry in Britain', *New Community,* vol.13, no.3.

Ballard, R (ed.) (1994) *Desh Pardesh: The South Asian Presence in Britain,* Hurst, London.

Ballard, R (1996) 'The Pakistanis: stability and introspection' in C Peach (ed.) *Ethnicity in the 1991 Census, Volume 2. The Ethnic Minority Populations of Great Britain,* HMSO, London.

Banks, M (1996) *Ethnicity: Anthropological Constructions,* Routledge, London.

Banton, M (1972) *Racial Minorities,* Fontana, London.

Banton, M (1985) *Promoting Racial Harmony,* Cambridge University Press, Cambridge.

Banton, M (1987) *Racial Theories,* Cambridge University Press, Cambridge.

Banton, M (1991) 'The race relations problematic', *British Journal of Sociology,* vol.42, no.1.

Banton, M (1997) *Ethnic and Racial Consciousness,* 2nd edn, Longman, London.

Barke, M and Fuller, D (2001) 'Race and ethnicity' in R Pain (ed.) *Introducing Social Geographies,* Arnold, London.

Barker, C (1997) *Global Television,* Blackwell, Oxford.

Barker, C (1999) *Television, Globalisation and Cultural Identities,* Open University Press, Buckingham.

Barker, M (1981) *The New Racism,* Junction, London.

Barker, P (1999) 'All things to all accusers', *New Statesman,* 26 March.

Barratt Brown, M (1970) *After Imperialism,* Heinemann, London.

Barry, A (1988) 'Black mythologies: representation of Black people on British television' in J Twitchin (ed.) *The Black and White Media Book,* Trentham, Stoke on Trent.

Baumann, G (1996) *Contesting Culture,* Cambridge University Press, Cambridge.

Beishon, S, Modood, T and Virdee, S (1998) *Ethnic Minority Families,* Policy Studies Institute, London.

Ben-Tobin, G and Gabriel, J (1987) 'The politics of race in Britain, 1962–79: a review of the major trends' in C Husband (ed.) *'Race' in Britain,* 2nd edn, Hutchinson, London.

Benyon, J (1987) 'Interpretations of civil disorder' in J Benyon and J Solomos (eds) *The Roots of Urban Unrest,* Pergamon, Oxford.

Berthoud, R (1998) *The Incomes of Ethnic Minorities,* Institute for Social and Economic Research, University of Essex.

Berthoud, R (1999) *Young Caribbean Men and the Labour Market,* YPS, York.

Berthoud, R (2000) 'Ethnic employment penalties in Britain', *Journal of Ethnic and Migration Studies,* vol.26, no.3.

Bhabba, H (1990) 'The third space' in J Rutherford (ed.) *Identity, Culture, Difference,* Lawrence & Wishart, London.

Bhattacharyya, G, Gabriel, J and Small, S (2002) *Race and Power,* Routledge, London.

Billig, M (1995) *Banal Nationalism,* Sage, London.

Bindman, G (1981) 'Positive action' in P Braham, E Rhodes and M Pearn (eds) *Discrimination and Disadvantage in Employment,* Harper & Row, London.

Bindman, G (1996) 'When will Europe act against racism?' *New Law Journal,* February.

Bindman, G (2000) 'Law enforcement and the lack of it' in M Anwar, P Roach and R Sondhi (eds) *From Legislation to Integration?* Macmillan – now Palgrave Macmillan, Basingstoke.

Bjorgo, T and Witte, R (eds) (1993) *Racist Violence in Europe,* Macmillan, London.

Blackburn, R, Dale, A and Jarman, J (1997) 'Ethnic differences in attainment in education, occupation and life-style' in V Karn (ed.) *Ethnicity in the Census, Volume 4,* HMSO, London.

Blair, M and Arnot, M (1993) 'Black and anti-racist perspectives on the National Curriculum and government educational policy' in A King and M Reiss (eds) *The Multicultural Dimension of the National Curriculum,* Falmer, Lewes.

Blair, M and Woods, P (1992) *Racism and Education,* Open University, Milton Keynes.

Blakemore, K and Drake, R (1996) *Understanding Equal Opportunity Policies,* Prentice Hall, London.

Bloch, A (1997) 'Ethnic inequality and social policy' in A Walker and C Walker (eds) *Britain Divided,* Child Poverty Action Group, London.

Bonner, J (1983) 'Out of the labyrinth – a clear and enduring scheme of citizenship', *Journal of Social Welfare Law.*

Bonnett, A (2000) *Anti-Racism,* Routledge, London.

Bowling, B and Phillips, D (2002) *Racism, Crime and Justice,* Longman, Harlow.

Bradley, H (1996) *Fractured Identities,* Polity, Cambridge.

Brah, A (1996) *Cartographies of Diaspora,* Routledge, London.

Braham, P, Rattansi, A and Skellington, R (eds) (1992) *Racism and Antiracism,* Sage, London.

Brake, M (1985) *Comparative Youth Culture,* Routledge, London.

Breugel, I (1989) 'Sex and race in the labour market', *Feminist Review,* no.32.

Brittan, E (1976) 'Multiracial education 2 – teacher opinion on aspects of school life: pupils and teachers', *Educational Research*, vol.18, no.3.

Brown, C (1984) *Black and White Britain: The Third PSI Survey*, Heinemann, London.

Brown, C and Gay, P (1985) *Racial Discrimination: 17 Years after the Act*, Policy Studies Institute, London.

Brubaker, R (1996) 'Civic and ethnic nations in France and Germany' in J Hutchinson and A Smith (eds) *Ethnicity*, Oxford University Press, Oxford.

Brubaker, R (2001) 'The return of assimilation? Changing perspectives on immigration and its sequels in France, Germany and the US', *Ethnic and Racial Studies*, vol.24, no.2.

Bryant, C (1997) 'Citizenship, national identity and the accommodation of difference: reflections on the German, French, Dutch and British cases', *New Community*, vol.23, no.2.

Bulmer, M and Rees, A (eds) (1996) *Citizenship Today: The Contemporary Relevance of T H Marshall*, UCL Press, London.

Bulmer, M and Solomos, J (eds) (1999) *Ethnic and Racial Studies Today*, Routledge, London.

Burden, T and Hamm, T (2000) 'Responding to socially excluded groups' in J Percy-Smith (ed.) *Policy Responses to Social Exclusion*, Open University Press, Buckingham.

Butler, C (1995) 'Religion and gender: young Muslim women in Britain', *Sociology Review*, vol.4, no.3.

Byrne, D (1999) *Social Exclusion*, Open University Press, Buckingham.

Cabinet Office (2000) *Minority Ethnic Issues in Social Exclusion and Neighbourhood Renewal*, Cabinet Office, London.

Calhoun, C (ed.) (1994) *Social Theory and the Politics of Identity*, Blackwell, Oxford.

Callinicos, A (1993) *Race and Class*, Bookmarks, London.

Campion, T (1996) 'Internal migration and ethnicity in Britain' in P Ratcliffe (ed.) *Ethnicity in the Census, Volume 3. Social Geography and Ethnicity in Britain: Geographical Spread, Spatial Concentration and Internal Migration*, HMSO, London.

Carter, B, Harris, C and Joshi, S (1993) 'The 1951–55 Conservative Government and the racialisation of Black immigration' in W James and C Harris (eds) *Inside Babylon*, Verso, London.

Cashmore, E and Troyna, B (1990) *Introduction to Race Relations*, Falmer, Lewes.

Castells, M (1997) *The Power of Identity*, Blackwell, Oxford.

Castles, S (1995) 'How nation-states respond to immigration and ethnic diversity', *New Community*, vol.21, no.3.

Castles, S and Kosack, G (1985) *Immigrant Workers and Class Structure in Western Europe*, Oxford University Press, Oxford.

Castles, S and Miller, M (1998) *The Age of Migration*, 2nd edn, Macmillan, London.

Cater, J and Jones, T (1989) *Social Geography*, Arnold, London.

Cesarani, D and Fulbrook, M (eds) (1996) *Citizenship, Nationality and Migration in Europe,* Routledge, London.

Chahal, K and Julienne, L (1999) *'We Can't all be White!': Racist Victimisation in the UK,* York Publishing Services, York.

Cheng, Y and Heath, A (1993) 'Ethnic origins and class destinations', *Oxford Review of Education,* vol.19, no.2.

Chitty, C (1993) 'The education system transformed', *Sociology Review,* vol.2, no.3.

Cohen, R (1994) *Frontiers of Identity: The British and Others,* Longman, London.

Cohen, R (1997) *Global Diasporas,* UCL Press, London.

Coleman, D and Salt, J (eds) (1996) *Ethnicity in the Census, Volume 1. Demographic Characteristics of the Ethnic Minority Populations,* HMSO, London.

Colley, L (1992) *Britons: Forging the Nation, 1707–1837,* Pimlico, London.

Colley, L (1999) 'This country is not so special', *New Statesman,* 3 May.

Connolly, P (1998a) *Racism, Gender Identities and Young Children,* Routledge, London.

Connolly, P (1998b) '"Dancing to the wrong tune": ethnography, generalisation and research on racism in schools' in P Connolly and B Troyna (eds) *Researching Racism in Education,* Open University Press, Buckingham.

Cook, R (2001) Extracts from a speech by the foreign secretary to the Social Market Foundation in London, *www.guardianunlimited.co.uk,* 19 April.

Cornell, S and Hartmann, D (1998) *Ethnicity and Race: Making Identities in a Changing World,* Pine Forge Press, London.

Cottle, S (1993) *TV News, Urban Conflict and the Inner City,* Leicester University Press, Leicester.

Cottle, S (2000) 'Media research and ethnic minorities: mapping the field' in S Cottle (ed.) *Ethnic Minorities and the Media,* Open University Press, Buckingham.

Craig, G (2001) *An End in Sight?* CPAG, London.

CRE (Commission for Racial Equality) (1996) *We Regret to Inform You: Testing for Racial Discrimination in Youth Employment in the North of England and Scotland,* CRE, London.

CRE (Commission for Racial Equality) (2001) 'Reforms fall short of Macpherson recommendations', *Connections,* Spring.

Crewe, I (1993) 'How Labour was trounced all round', *Guardian,* 14 June.

Cross, M (1991) 'Editorial', *New Community,* vol.17, no.3.

Cross, M (2000) 'Review symposium: ethnic minorities in British social science', *Journal of Ethnic and Migration Studies,* vol.26, no.2

Culley, L and Dyson, S (1993) '"Race", inequality and health', *Sociology Review,* vol.3, no.1.

Curtice, J and Heath, A (2000) 'Is the English lion about to roar? National identity after devolution' in R Jowell, J Curtice, A Park,

K Thomson, L Jarvis, C Bromley and N Stratford (eds) *British Social Attitudes: Focusing on Diversity, The 17th* Report, Sage, London.

Daniel, W (1968) *Racial Discrimination in England*, Penguin, Harmondsworth.

Daniels, T (1996) 'Programmes for Black audiences' in J Corner and S Harvey (eds) *Television Times*, Arnold, London.

Daniels, T (1998) 'Television studies and race' in C Geraghty and D Lusted (eds) *The Television Studies Book*, Arnold, London.

Dean, H (1991) 'In search of the underclass' in P Brown and R Scase (eds) *Poor Work*, Open University Press, Milton Keynes.

Demack, S, Drew, D and Grimsley, M (2000) 'Minding the gap: ethnic, gender and social class differences in attainment', *Race, Ethnicity and Education*, vol.3, no.2.

Denscombe, M (1997, 1998) *Sociology Update*, Olympus, Leicester.

DES (Department of Education and Science) (1965) *The Education of Immigrants, Education Survey 13*, HMSO, London.

Devine, F (1997) *Social Class in America and Britain*, Edinburgh University Press, Edinburgh.

Donald, J (1992) *'Race', Culture and Difference*, Open University Press, Milton Keynes.

Dorling, D (1997) 'Regional and local differences in the housing tenure of ethnic minorities' in V Karn (ed.) (1997) *Ethnicity in the Census, Volume 4. Employment, Education and Housing among the Ethnic Minority Populations of Britain*, HMSO, London.

Drew, D (1995) *'Race', Education and Work: The Statistics of Inequality*, Avebury, Aldershot.

Drew, D and Demack, S (1998) 'A league apart: statistics in the study of "race" and education' in P Connolly and B Troyna (eds) *Researching Racism in Education*, Open University Press, Buckingham.

Drew, D, Gray, J and Sporton, D (1997) 'Ethnic differences in the educational participation of 16–19-year-olds' in V Karn (ed.) *Ethnicity in the Census, Volume 4. Employment, Education and Housing among the Ethnic Minority Populations of Britain*, HMSO, London.

Drury, B (1991) 'Sikh girls and ethnic culture', *New Community*, vol.17, no.3.

Duffy, K (1998) 'Combatting social exclusion and promoting social integration in the European Union' in C Oppenheim (ed.) *An Inclusive Society*, IPPR, London.

Dummett, A (1998) 'British race relations in a European context' in T Blackstone, B Parekh and P Sanders (eds) *Race Relations in Britain*, Routledge, London.

Dummett, A (2000) 'Tackling racism: Britain in Europe' in M Anwar, P Roach and R Sondhi (eds) *From Legislation to Integration?* Macmillan, Basingstoke.

Eade, J (1996) 'Ethnicity and the politics of cultural difference: an agenda for the 1990s?' in T Ranger, Y Samad and O Stuart (eds) *Culture, Identity and Politics*, Avebury, Aldershot.

Egerton, M and Halsey, A H (1993) 'Trends by social class and gender in access to higher education in Britain', *Oxford Review of Education*, vol.19, no.2.

Elliot, F (1996) *Gender, Family and Society*, Macmillan, London.

Eysenck, H (1971) *Race, Intelligence and Education*, Temple Smith, London.

Fainstein, N (1992) 'The urban underclass and mismatch theory re-examined' in M Cross (ed.) *Ethnic Minorities and Industrial Change in Europe and North America*, Cambridge University Press, Cambridge.

Fainstein, N (1996) 'A note on interpreting American poverty' in E Mingione (ed.) *Urban Poverty and the Underclass*, Blackwell, Oxford.

Fainstein, S and Harloe, M (1992) 'Introduction: London and New York in the Contemporary World' in S Fainstein, I Gordon and M Harloe (eds) *Divided Cities: New York and London in the Contemporary World*, Blackwell, Oxford.

Favell, A (2001) *Philosophies of Integration: Immigration and the Idea of Citizenship in Britain and France*, 2nd edn, Palgrave, Basingstoke.

Fenton, S (1996) 'Counting ethnicity: social groups and official categories' in R Levitas and W Guy (eds) *Interpreting Official Statistics*, Routledge, London.

Fenton, S (1999) *Ethnicity, Racism, Class and Culture*, Macmillan, London.

Ferguson, R (1998) *Representing 'Race'*, Arnold, London.

Field, S (1986) 'Trends in Racial Inequality', *Social Studies Review*, vol.2, no.4.

Field, S, Mair, G, Rees, T and Stevens, P (1981) *Ethnic Minorities in Britain: A Study of Trends in their Position Since 1961*, HMSO, London.

Fischer, C, Hout, M, Lucas, S, Swidler, A and Voss, K (1996) *Inequality by Design: Cracking the Bell Curve Myth*, Princeton University Press, Princeton, NJ.

Fitzgerald, M (1998) '"Race" and the criminal justice system' in T Blackstone, B Parekh and P Sanders (eds) *Race Relations in Britain*, Routledge, London.

Flew, A (1986) 'Clarifying the concepts', in F Palmer (ed.) *Antiracism – An Assault on Education and Value*, Sherwood, London.

Flynn, J (1987) 'Massive IQ gains in 14 nations: what IQ tests really measure'. *Psychological Bulletin*, vol.101, no.2.

Foner, N (1979) *Jamaica Fairwell*, Routledge, London.

Foot, P (1969) *The Rise of Enoch Powell*, Penguin, Harmondsworth.

Foster, P (1990) *Policy and Practice in Multicultural and Antiracist Education*, Routledge, London.

Foster, P (1991) 'Case still not proven: a reply to Cecile Wright', *British Educational Research Journal*, vol.17, no.2.

Foster, P (1992) 'Teacher attitudes and Afro/Caribbean educational attainment', *Oxford Review of Education*, vol.18, no.3.

Foster, P (1993a) 'Some problems in establishing equality of treatment in multi-ethnic schools', *British Journal of Sociology*, vol. 44, no.3.

Foster, P (1993b) '"Methodological purism" or "A defence against hype"? Critical research in "race" and education', *New Community*, vol.19, no.3.

Foster, P, Gomm, R and Hammersley, M (1996) *Constructing Educational Inequality*, Falmer, Lewes.

Fryer, P (1984) *Staying Power: The History of Black People in Britain*, Pluto, London.

Fulbrook, M (1996) 'Germany for the Germans? Citizenship and nationality in a divided nation' in D Cesarani and M Fulbrook (eds) *Citizenship, Nationality and Migration in Europe*, Routledge, London.

Gabriel, J (1998) *Whitewash: Racialised Politics and the Media*, Routledge, London.

Galbraith, J (1992) *The Culture of Contentment*, Sinclair-Stevenson, London.

Gallie, D (1988) 'Employment, unemployment and social stratification' in D Gallie (ed.) *Employment in Britain*, Blackwell, Oxford.

Gans, H (1996) 'From "underclass" to "undercaste": some observations about the future of the post-industrial economy and its major victims' in E Mingione (ed.) *Urban Poverty and the Underclass*, Blackwell, Oxford.

Gardner, H (1995) 'Cracking open the IQ box' in S Fraser (ed.) *The Bell Curve Wars*, Basic, New York.

Gates, H (1996) 'Thirteen ways of looking at a Black man' in J Arthur and A Shapiro (eds) *Colour Class Identity*, Westview, Oxford.

Geddes, A (1996) *The Politics of Immigration and Race*, Baseline, Manchester.

Geddes, A (1998) 'Inequality, political opportunity and ethnic minority parliamentary candidacy' in S Saggar (ed.) *Race and British Electoral Politics*, UCL Press, London.

Ghuman, P (1999) *Asian Adolescents in the West*, BPS, Leicester.

Giddens, A (1973) *The Class Structure of the Advanced Societies*, Hutchinson, London.

Giddens, A (1981) *The Class Structure of the Advanced Societies*, 2nd edn, Hutchinson, London.

Giddens, A (1982) *Sociology: A Brief but Critical Introduction*, Macmillan, London.

Giddens, A (1990) *The Consequences of Modernity*, Polity, Cambridge.

Giddens, A (1997) *Sociology*, 3rd edn, Polity, Cambridge.

Giddens, A (1998) *The Third Way*, Polity, Cambridge.

Gillborn, D (1990) *'Race', Ethnicity and Education*, Unwin Hyman, London.

Gillborn, D (1995) *Racism and Antiracism in Real Schools*, Open University Press, Milton Keynes.

Gillborn, D (1998) 'Racism and the politics of qualitative research: learning from controversy and critique' in P Connolly and B Troyna (eds) *Researching Racism in Education*, Open University Press, Buckingham.

Gillborn, D and Gipps, C (1996) *Recent Research on the Achievement of Ethnic Minority Pupils*, OFSTED, London.

Gillborn, D and Mirza, H (2000) *Educational Inequality: Mapping Race, Class and Gender*, OFSTED, London.

Gillborn, D and Youdell, D (2000) *Rationing Education*, Open University Press, Buckingham.

Gillespie, M (1995) *Television, Ethnicity and Cultural Change*, Routledge, London.

Gilroy, P (1987) *There Ain't No Black in the Union Jack*, Hutchinson, London.

Gilroy, P (1992) 'The end of antiracism' in J Donald and A Rattansi (eds) *'Race', Culture and Difference*, Sage, London.

Gilroy, P (1993) *Small Acts*, Serpent's Tail, London.

Ginsburg, N (1992) *Divisions of Welfare*, Sage, London.

Glazer, N and Moynihan, D (1970) *Beyond the Melting Pot*, 2nd edn, MIT Press, London.

GMG (Glasgow Media Group) (1997a) *'Race', Migration and Media*, GMG, Glasgow.

GMG (Glasgow Media Group) (1997b) *Ethnic Minorities in Television Advertising*, GMG, Glasgow.

Goldberg, D (1993) *Racist Culture*, Blackwell, Oxford.

Goodman, A, Johnson, P and Webb, S (1997) *Inequality in the UK*, Oxford University Press, Oxford.

Gordon, P and Rosenberg, D (1989) *The Press and Black People in Britain*, Runnymede Trust, London.

Goulbourne, H (1998a) *Race Relations in Britain since 1945*, Macmillan, London.

Goulbourne, H (1998b) 'The participation of new minority ethnic groups in British politics' in T Blackstone, B Parekh and P Sanders (eds) *Race Relations in Britain*, Routledge, London.

Green, A (1997) 'Patterns of ethnic minority employment in the context of industrial growth and decline' in V Karn (ed.) *Ethnicity in the Census, Volume 4*, HMSO, London.

Green, D (ed.) (2000) *Institutional Racism and the Police*, Institute for the Study of Civil Society, London.

Griffin, J (1972) 'The experience of being Black' in P Worsley (ed.) *Problems of Modern Society*, Penguin, Harmondsworth.

Griffith, J (1997) *The Politics of the Judiciary*, 5th edn, Fontana, London.

Grinter, R (1985) 'Bridging the gulf: the need for anti-racist multicultural education', *Multicultural Teaching*, vol.3, no.2.

Grosvenor, I (1997) *Assimilating Identities*, Lawrence & Wishart, London.

Guiberneau, M and Goldblatt, D (2000) 'Identity and nation' in K Woodward (ed.) *Questioning Identity: Gender, Class, Nation*, Routledge, London.

Hakim, C (1996) *Issues of Women's Work*, Athlone, London.

Hall, K (1995) '"There's a time to act English and a time to act Indian": the politics of identity among British-Sikh teenagers' in

S Stephens (ed.) *Children and the Politics of Culture,* Princeton University Press, Princeton, NJ.

Hall, S (1991) 'Old and new identities, old and new ethnicities' in A King (ed.) *Culture, Globalization and the World-System,* Macmillan, London.

Hall, S (1992a) 'The question of cultural identity' in S Hall, D Held and T McGrew (eds) *Modernity and its Futures,* Polity, Cambridge.

Hall, S (1992b) 'Our mongrel selves', *New Statesman,* 19 June.

Hall, S (1992c) 'The West and the rest: discourse and power' in S Hall and B Gieben (eds) *Formations of Modernity,* Polity, Cambridge.

Hall, S (1995) 'The Whites of their eyes' in G Dines and J Humez (eds) *Gender, Race and Class in Media,* Sage, London.

Hall, S (1996) 'New ethnicities' in H Baker, M Diawara and R Lindeborg (eds) *Black British Cultural Studies,* University of Chicago Press, London.

Hall, S (1997a) 'The centrality of culture: notes on the cultural revolutions of our time' in K Thompson (ed.) *Media and Cultural Regulation,* Sage, London.

Hall, S (1997b) 'The spectacle of the "other" in S Hall (ed.) *Representation: Cultural Representations and Signifying Practices,* Sage, London.

Hall, S (2000) 'The multi-cultural question' in B Hesse (ed.) *Un/settled Multiculturalisms,* Zed, London.

Hall, S, Critcher, C, Jefferson, T, Clarke, J and Roberts, B (1978) *Policing the Crisis,* Macmillan, London.

Halsey, A (1977) 'Towards meritocracy? The case of Britain', in J Karabel and A Halsey (eds) *Power and Ideology in Education,* Oxford University Press, Oxford.

Halsey, A (1995) *Change in British Society,* 4th edn, Oxford University Press, Oxford.

Halsey, A, Heath, A and Ridge, J (1980) *Origins and Destinations: Family, Class and Education in Modern Britain,* Oxford University Press, Oxford.

Hannaford, I (1996) *Race: The History of an Idea in the West,* Woodrow Wilson Centre Press, Washington, DC.

Hartmann, P and Husband, C (1974) *Racism and the Mass Media,* Davis-Ponter, London.

Harvey, D (1989) *The Condition of Post-Modernity,* Oxford University Press, Oxford.

Heath, A and Clifford, P (1996) 'Class inequalities and educational reform in twentieth century Britain', in D Lee and B Turner (eds) *Conflicts About Class,* Longman, London.

Heath, A and McMahon, D (1997) 'Education and occupational attainments: the impact of ethnic origins' in V Karn (ed.) *Ethnicity in the Census, Volume 4. Employment, Education and Housing among the Ethnic Minority Populations of Britain,* HMSO, London.

Heath, A and McMahon, D (2000) 'Ethnic differences in the labour market: the role of education and social class origins', *Oxford Sociology Working Papers.*

Heath, A, Mills, C and Roberts, J (1992) 'Towards meritocracy? Recent evidence on an old problem' in C Crouch and A Heath (ed.) *Social Research and Social Reform*, Oxford University Press, Oxford.

Heisler, B (1991) 'A comparative perspective on the underclass: questions of urban poverty, race and citizenship', *Theory and Society*, vol.20, no.4.

Held, D (1992) 'The development of the modern state' in S Hall and B Gieben (eds) *Formations of Modernity*, Polity, Cambridge.

Hernstein, R and Murray, C (1994) *The Bell Curve: Intelligence and Class Structure in American Life*, Free Press, New York.

Hewitt, R (1990) 'Youth, race and language in contemporary Britain: deconstructing ethnicity' in L Chisholm, P Buchner, H Kruger and P Brown (eds) *Childhood, Youth and Social Change: A Comparative Perspective*, Falmer, London.

Hickman, M and Walter, B (1997) *Discrimination and the Irish Community: A Report for the Commission for Racial Equality*, CRE, London.

Higson, A (1998) 'National identity and the media' in A Briggs and P Cobley (eds) *The Media: An Introduction*, Longman, Harlow.

Hills, J (1995) *Inquiry into Income and Wealth, Volume 2. A Summary of the Evidence*, Joseph Rowntree Foundation, York.

HMIC (Her Majesty's Inspectorate of Constabulary) (1997) *Winning the Race: Policing Plural Communities*, Home Office, London.

HMIC (Her Majesty's Inspectorate of Constabulary) (1999) *Winning the Race Revisited: Policing Plural Communities. A Follow Up*, Home Office, London.

HMIC (Her Majesty's Inspectorate of Constabulary) (2001) *Winning the Race: Embracing Diversity*, Home Office, London.

Hobsbawm, E (1969) *Industry and Empire*, Penguin, Harmondsworth.

Hobsbawm, E and Ranger, T (eds) (1983) *The Invention of Tradition*, Cambridge University Press, Cambridge.

Holdaway, S (1996) *The Racialisation of British Policing*, Macmillan, London.

Holdaway, S (1999) 'Understanding the police investigation of the murder of Stephen Lawrence: a mundane sociological analysis', *Sociology Research Online*, vol.4, no.1.

Home Office (2000) *Code of Practice on Reporting and Recording Racist Incidents*, Home Office, London.

Home Office (2001) *Building Cohesive Communities. A Report of the Ministerial Group on Public Order and Community Cohesion*, Home Office, London.

Home Office (2002) *Secure Borders, Safe Haven – Integration with Diversity in Modern Britain*, Home Office, London.

Hudson, B (1993) 'Racism and criminology: concepts and controversies' in D Cook and B Hudson (eds) *Racism and Criminology*, Sage, London.

Hudson, R and Williams, A (1995) *Divided Britain*, Wiley, Chichester.

Hunt, S (1995) 'The "race" and health inequalities debate', *Sociology Review*, vol.5, no.1.

Husband, C (ed.) (1987) *'Race' in Britain*, 2nd edn, Hutchinson, London.

Hutchinson, J and Smith, A (eds) (1994) *Nationalism*, Oxford University Press, Oxford.

Iganski, P and Payne, G (1996) 'Declining racial disadvantage in the British labour market', *Ethnic and Racial Studies*, vol.19, no.1.

Independent on Sunday (2001) 'Asylum changes must be both humane and efficient', Editorial, 28 October.

IPPR (Institute for Public Policy Research) (1997) *Racial Attitudes Survey*, IPPR, London.

James, W (1993) 'Migration, racism and identity formation: the Caribbean experience in Britain' in W James and C Harris (eds) *Inside Babylon*, Verso, London.

Jeffcoate, R (1984) *Ethnic Minorities and Education*, Harper & Row, London.

Jencks, C (1991) 'Is the American underclass growing?' in C Jencks and P Peterson (eds) *The Urban Underclass*, Brookings Institution, Washington, DC.

Jenkins, R (1997) *Rethinking Ethnicity*, Sage, London.

Jenkins, R and Solomos, J (eds) (1989) *Racism and Equal Opportunity Policies in the 1980s*, 2nd edn, Cambridge University Press, Cambridge.

Jensen, A (1969) 'How much can we boost IQ and scholastic achievement?', *Harvard Education Review*, vol.39, no.1.

Jones, S (1996) *In the Blood*, Collins, London.

Jones, T (1993) *Britain's Ethnic Minorities*, Policy Studies Institute, London.

Joppke, C (1999) 'How immigration is changing citizenship: a comparative view', *Ethnic and Racial Studies*, vol.22, no.4.

Karn, V (ed.) (1997) *Ethnicity in the Census, Volume 4. Employment, Education and Housing among the Ethnic Minority Populations of Britain*, HMSO, London.

Karn, V and Phillips, D (1998) 'Race and ethnicity in housing: a diversity of experience' in T Blackstone, B Parekh and P Sanders (eds) *Race Relations in Britain*, Routledge, London.

Katz, M (1993) 'The urban "underclass" as a metaphor of social transformation' in M Katz (ed.) *The "Underclass" Debate*, Princeton University Press, Princeton.

Kirp, D (1979) *Doing Good by Doing Little: Race and Schooling in Britain*, University of California Press, London.

Klein, G (1993) *Education towards Race Equality*, Cassell, London.

Kohn, M (1995) *The Race Gallery: The Return of Racial Science*, Vintage, London.

Koopmans, R (1999) 'Germany and its immigrants: an ambivalent relationship', *Journal of Ethnic and Migration Studies*, vol.25, no.4.

Kundnani, A (2001) 'From Oldham to Bradford: the violence of the violated' in Institute of Race Relations (ed.) *The Three Faces of British Racism*, IRR, London.

Kymlika, W (2000) 'Nationbuilding and minority rights: comparing West and East', *Journal of Ethnic and Migration Studies,* vol.26, no.2.

Kysel, F (1988) 'Ethnic background and examination results', *Educational Research,* vol.30, no.2.

Lash, S (1994) 'The making of an underclass: neo-liberalism versus corporatism' in P Brown and R Crompton (eds) *Economic Restructuring and Social Exclusion,* UCL Press, London.

Lattimer, M (1999) 'When Labour played the racist card', *New Statesman,* 22 January.

Law, I (1996) *Racism, Ethnicity and Social Policy,* Prentice Hall, London.

Law, I (1997) *Privilege and Silence: 'Race' in the British News During the General Election Campaign, 1997,* University of Leeds.

Law, I (2002) *Race in the News,* Palgrave Macmillan, Basingstoke.

Layton-Henry, Z (1992) *The Politics of Immigration,* Blackwell, Oxford.

Lea, J and Young, J (1992) 'The riots in Britain 1981: urban violence and political marginalisation' in D Cowell, T Jones, and J Young (eds) *Policing the Riots,* Junction, London.

Leslie, D (1998) *An Investigation of Racial Disadvantage,* Manchester University Press, Manchester.

Lester, A (1998) 'From legislation to integration: twenty years of the Race Relations Act' in T Blackstone, B Parekh and P Sanders (eds) *Race Relations in Britain,* Routledge, London.

Lester, A (2000) 'The politics of the Race Relations Act 1976' in M Anwar, P Roach and R Sondhi (eds) *From Legislation to Integration?* Macmillan, Basingstoke.

Levitas, R (1999) *The Inclusive Society: Social Exclusion and New Labour,* Macmillan, London.

Lewis, P (1994) *Islamic Britain,* I B Tauris, London.

Lister, R (1990) *The Exclusive Society: Citizenship and the Poor,* CPAG, London.

Lister, R (1996) 'In search of the "underclass"' in C Murray (ed.) *Charles Murray and the Underclass: The Developing Debate,* IEA, London.

Littlewood, P (1999) 'Social exclusion', *Social Science Teacher,* vol.29, no.1.

Lockwood, D (1970) 'Race, conflict and plural society' in S Zubaida (ed.) *Race and Racialism,* Tavistock, London.

Loveday, B (2000) 'Must do better: the state of police race relations' in A Marlow and B Loveday (eds) *After Macpherson,* Russell House, Lyme Regis.

Luthra, M (1997) *Britain's Black Population,* Arena, Aldershot.

Mac an Ghaill, M (1988) *Young, Gifted and Black,* Open University Press, Buckingham.

Mac an Ghaill, M (1998) *The Making of Men: Masculinities, Sexualities and Schooling,* Open University Press, Buckingham.

Mac an Ghaill, M (1999) *Contemporary Racisms and Ethnicities,* Open University Press, Buckingham.

MacDonald, I (1989) *Murder in the Playground,* Longman, London.

MacDonald, R (ed.) (1997) *Youth, the 'Underclass' and Social Exclusion,* Routledge, London.

MacEwan, M (1994) 'Anti-discrimination law in Great Britain', *New Community,* vol. 20, no.3.

MacMaster, N (2001) *Racism in Europe,* Palgrave Macmillan, London.

Macpherson, W (1999) *The Stephen Lawrence Inquiry: Report of the Inquiry by Sir William Macpherson of Cluny,* HMSO, London.

Malik, K (1996) *The Meaning of Race,* Macmillan, London.

Mann, K (1992) *The Making of an English 'Underclass'? The Social Divisions of Welfare and Labour,* Open University Press, Milton Keynes.

Mann, M (1993) *The Sources of Social Power,* Cambridge University Press, Cambridge.

Marshall, I (1997) *Minorities, Migrants and Crime,* Sage, London.

Marshall, T and Bottomore, T (1992) *Citizenship and Social Class,* Pluto, London.

Mason, D (1994) 'On the dangers of disconnecting race and racism', *Sociology,* vol.28, no.4.

Mason, D (1995) *Race and Ethnicity in Modern Britain,* Oxford University Press, Oxford.

Mason, D (1996) 'Themes and issues in the teaching of race and ethnicity in Sociology', *Ethnic and Racial Studies,* vol.19, no.4.

Mason, D (2000) *Race and Ethnicity in Modern Britain,* 2nd edn, Oxford University Press, Oxford.

May, S (1999) 'Critical multiculturalism and cultural difference: avoiding essentialism' in S May (ed.) *Critical Multiculturalism,* Falmer, London.

McClintock, A (1995) *Imperial Leather,* Routledge, London.

McCrudden, C, Smith, D and Brown, C (1991) *Racial Justice at Work,* Policy Studies Institute, London.

McGrew, A (1992) 'A global society?' in S Hall (ed.) *Modernity and its Futures,* Polity, Cambridge.

McGuigan, J (1996) *Culture and the Public Sphere,* Routledge, London.

McKie, D and Brook, L (1996) 'A decade of changing attitudes' in B Taylor and K Thomson (eds) *Understanding Change in Social Attitudes,* Dartmouth, Aldershot.

Melotti, U (1997) 'International migration in Europe: social projects and political cultures' in T Modood, and P Werbner (eds) *The Politics of Multiculturalism in the New Europe,* Zed, London.

Mercer, K (1989) 'General introduction' in T Daniels and J Gerson (eds) *The Colour Black,* BFI, London.

Mercer, K (1990) 'Welcome to the jungle: identity and diversity in postmodern politics' in J Rutherford (ed.) *Identity: Community, Culture and Difference,* Lawrence & Wishart, London.

Messina, A (1998) 'Ethnic minorities and the British party system in the 1990s and beyond' in S Saggar (ed.) *Race and British Electoral Politics,* UCL Press, London.

Metcalf, H, Modood, T and Virdee, S (1996) *Asian Self-Employment: The Interaction of Culture and Economics in England,* Policy Studies Institute, London.

Miles, R (1982) *Racism and Migrant Labour,* Routledge, London.

Miles, R (1989) *Racism,* Routledge, London.

Miles, R (1990) 'Racism, ideology and disadvantage', *Social Studies Review,* vol.5, no.4.

Miles, R (1993a) *Racism After 'Race Relations',* Routledge, London.

Miles, R (1993b) 'The articulation of racism and nationalism: reflections on European history' in J Wrench and J Solomos (eds) *Racism and Migration in Western Europe,* Berg, Oxford.

Miles, R and Phizacklea, A (1984) *White Man's Country: Racism in British Politics,* Pluto, London.

Miles, R and Small, S (1999) 'Racism and ethnicity' in S Taylor (ed.) *Contemporary Sociology,* Macmillan, London.

Miles, R and Solomos, J (1987) 'Migration and the state in Britain: a historical overview' in C Husband (ed.) *Race in Britain,* 2nd edn, Hutchinson, London.

Miller, D (1995a) *On Nationality,* Oxford University Press, Oxford.

Miller, D (1995b) 'Reflections on British national identity', *New Community,* vol.21, no.2.

Milner, D (1983) *Children and Race Ten Years On,* Ward Lock Educational, London.

Mirza, H (1992) *Young, Female and Black,* Routledge, London.

Mitchell, M and Russell, D (1994) 'Race, citizenship and "Fortress Europe"' in P Brown and R Crompton (eds) *Economic Restructuring and Social Exclusion,* UCL Press, London.

Mitchell, M and Russell, D (1996) 'Immigration, citizenship and the nation-state in the new Europe' in B Jenkins and S Sofos (eds) *Nation and Identity in Contemporary Europe,* Routledge, London.

Model, S (1999) 'Ethnic inequality in England: an analysis based on the 1991 Census', *Ethnic and Racial Studies,* vol.22, no.6.

Modood, T (1992a) *Not Easy Being British: Colour, Culture and Citizenship,* Trentham, Stoke on Trent.

Modood, T (1992b) 'British Asian Muslims and the Rushdie affair' in J Donald and A Rattansi (eds) *'Race', Culture and Difference,* Sage, London.

Modood, T (1998) 'Ethnic diversity and racial disadvantage in employment' in T Blackstone, B Parekh and P Sanders (eds) *Race Relations in Britain,* Routledge, London.

Modood, T and Werbner, P (eds) (1997) *The Politics of Multiculturalism in the New Europe,* Zed, London.

Modood, T, Beishon, S and Virdee, S (1994) *Changing Ethnic Identities,* Policy Studies Institute, London.

Modood, T, Berthoud, R *et al.* (1997) *Ethnic Minorities in Britain,* Policy Studies Institute, London.

Moon, G and Atkinson, R (1997) 'Ethnicity' in M Pacione (ed.) *Britain's Cities: Geographies of Division in Urban Britain,* Routledge, London.

Moore, R (1977) 'Migrants and the class structure of Western Europe' in R Scase (ed.) *Industrial Society: Class, Cleavage and Control,* Allen & Unwin, London.

Moore, R (1989) 'Ethnic divisions in Western Europe' in R Scase (ed.) *Industrial Societies: Crisis and Division in Western Capitalism and State Socialism,* Unwin Hyman, London.

Moore, R (1996) 'Back to the future: the problem of change and the possibilities of advance in Sociology of Education', *British Journal of Sociology of Education,* vol.17, no.2.

Moore, R (1999) 'The underclass', *Social Science Teacher,* vol.29, no.1.

Morley, D and Robins, K (1995) *Spaces of Identity,* Routledge, London.

Morris, L (1994) *Dangerous Classes,* Routledge, London.

Morris, L (1998) 'Legitimate membership of welfare community' in M Langan (ed.) *Welfare: Needs, Rights and Risks,* Routledge, London.

Morris, L (2000) 'Rights and controls in the management of migration: the case of Germany', *Sociological Review,* vol.48, no.2.

Morrison, T (ed.) (1993) *Race-ing Justice, En-gendering Power,* Chatto & Windus, London.

Morrison, T and Lacour, C (ed.) (1997) *Birth of a Nation'hood,* Pantheon, New York.

Mortimore, P, Owen, C and Phoenix, A (1997) 'Higher education qualifications' in V Karn (ed.) *Ethnicity in the Census, Volume 4. Employment, Education and Housing among the Ethnic Minority Populations of Britain,* HMSO, London.

Murray, C (1984) *Losing Ground,* Basic, New York.

Murray, C (1996) *Charles Murray and the Underclass: The Developing Debate,* IEA, London.

Murray, C and Hernstein, R (1994) 'Race, genes and IQ – an apologia', *New Republic,* 31 October.

Mynott, E (2000) 'The asylum debate', *Runnymede Bulletin,* no.322.

Myrdal, G (1963) *Challenge to Affluence,* Pantheon, New York.

Nazroo, J (1997) *The Mental Health of Ethnic Minorities,* Policy Studies Institute, London.

Nixon, J (1998) 'The role of Black and Asian MPs at Westminster' in S Saggar (ed.) *Race and British Electoral Politics,* UCL Press, London.

Noon, M and Blyton, P (1997) *The Realities of Work,* Macmillan, London.

Nuttall, D, Goldstein, H, Prosser, R and Rasbash, J (1989) 'Differential school effectiveness', *International Journal of Educational Research,* vol.13.

OFSTED (Office for Standards in Education) (1999) *Raising the Attainment of Minority Ethnic Pupils,* OFSTED, London.

Omi, M and Winant, H (1994) *Racial Formation in the United States,* 2nd edn, Routledge, London.

ONS (Office for National Statistics) (1996) *Social Focus on Ethnic Minorities,* HMSO, London.

ONS (Office for National Statistics) (2001) *Social Trends 31,* HMSO, London.

Osgerby, B (1998) *Youth in Britain since 1945*, Blackwell, Oxford.

Osler, A and Morrison, M (2000) *Inspecting Schools for Racial Equality*, Trentham, Stoke on Trent.

Ousley, H (1995) 'Talent spotting', *The Guardian*, 25 February.

Owen, D (1997) 'Labour force participation rates, self-employment and unemployment' in V Karn (ed.) *Ethnicity in the Census, Volume 4*, HMSO, London.

Owen, D and Green, A (2000) 'Estimating commuting flows for minority ethnic groups in England and Wales', *Journal of Ethnic and Migration Studies*, vol.26, no.4.

Owen, D, Green, A, Pitcher, J and Maguire, M (2000) *Minority Ethnic Participation and Achievements in Education, Training and the Labour Market*, Department for Education and Employment, HMSO, London.

Pallister, D and Millar, S (1999) 'Lawrence Inquiry', *The Guardian*, 25 February.

Parekh, B (1983) 'Educational opportunity in multi-ethnic Britain' in N Glazer and K Young (eds) *Ethnic Pluralism and Public Policy*, Heinemann, London.

Parekh, B (1989) 'The Rushdie affair and the British press', *Social Studies Review*, vol.5, no.2.

Parekh, B (1991a) 'Law torn', *New Statesman and Society*, 14 June.

Parekh, B (1991b) 'British citizenship and cultural difference' in G Andrews (ed.) *Citizenship*, Lawrence & Wishart, London.

Parekh, B (1992) 'The hermeneutics of the Swann report' in D Gill, B Mayor and M Blair (eds) *Racism and Education*, Open University Press, Milton Keynes.

Parekh, B (1996) 'United colours of equality', *New Statesman*, 13 December.

Parekh, B (1997a) 'National culture and multiculturalism' in K Thompson (ed.) *Media and Cultural Regulation*, Sage, London.

Parekh, B (1997b) 'Equality in a multicultural society' in J Franklin (ed.) *Equality*, Institute for Public Policy Research, London.

Parekh, B (1998) 'Integrating minorities' in T Blackstone, B Parekh and P Sanders (eds) *Race Relations in Britain*, Routledge, London.

Parekh, B (2000) *The Future of Multi-Ethnic Britain*, Profile, London.

Parekh, B (2001) 'Reporting on a report', *Runnymede Bulletin*, no.326.

Parker, D (1994) 'Encounters across the counter: young Chinese people in Britain', *New Community*, vol.20, no.4.

Parkin, F (1979) *Marxism and Class Theory*, Tavistock, London.

Patterson, S (1965) *Dark Strangers*, Penguin, Harmondsworth.

Paul, K (1997) *Whitewashing Britain*, Cornell University Press, London.

Peach, C (1968) *West Indian Migration to Britain: A Social Geography*, Oxford University Press, Oxford.

Peach, C (1978/9) 'British unemployment cycles and West Indian immigrants – 1955–1974', *New Community*, vol.7, no.1.

Peach, C (1984) 'The force of West Indian island identities in Britain' in C Peach, C Clarke and D Ley (eds) *Geography and Ethnic Pluralism*, Allen & Unwin, London.

Peach, C (1992) 'Urban concentration and segregation in Europe since 1945' in M Cross (ed.) *Ethnic Minorities and Industrial Change in Europe and North America*, Cambridge University Press, Cambridge.

Peach, C (ed.) (1996) *Ethnicity in the 1991 Census, Volume 2. The Ethnic Minority Populations of Great Britain*, HMSO, London.

Peach, C and Rossiter, D (1996) 'Level and nature of spatial concentration and segregation of minority ethnic populations in Great Britain, 1991' in P Ratcliffe (ed.) *Ethnicity in the Census, Volume 3*, HMSO, London.

Peach, C, Rogers, A, Chance, J and Daley, P (2000) 'Immigration and ethnicity' in A Halsey (ed.) *Twentieth Century British Social Trends*, Macmillan, London.

Percy-Smith, J (2000) *Policy Responses to Social Exclusion*, Open University Press, Buckingham.

Peterson, P (1992) 'The urban underclass and the poverty paradox' in C Jencks and P Peterson (eds) *The Urban Underclass*, Brookings Institution, Washington, DC.

Phillips, D (1997) 'The housing position of ethnic minority group home owners' in V Karn (ed.) *Ethnicity in the Census, Volume 4. Employment, Education and Housing among the Ethnic Minority Populations of Britain*, HMSO, London.

Phillips, D and Sarre, P (1995) 'Black middle-class formation in contemporary Britain' in T Butler and M Savage (eds) *Social Change and the Middle Classes*, UCL Press, London.

Phizacklea, A (1992) 'Jobs for the girls: the production of women's outerwear in the UK' in M Cross (ed.) *Ethnic Minorities and Industrial Change in Europe and North America*, Cambridge University Press, Cambridge.

Phizacklea, A and Miles, R (1980) *Labour and Racism*, Routledge, London.

Pilkington, A (1984) *Race Relations in Britain*, University Tutorial Press, Slough.

Pilkington, A (1986) 'The state, the mass media and racial minorities' in L Cohen and A Cohen (eds) *Multicultural Education*, Harper & Row, Cambridge.

Pilkington, A (1993) '"Race" and ethnicity' in S Hall (ed.) *Social Structures and Social Divisions, Block 2*, Open University, Milton Keynes.

Pilkington, A (1997a) 'Is Sociology dead? Sociology, the Enlightenment and the challenge of the postmodernists', *Sociology Review*, vol.6, no.4.

Pilkington, A (1997b) 'Is there a British underclass?' in A Giddens (ed.) *Sociology: Introductory Readings*, Polity, Cambridge.

Pilkington, A (1997c) 'Ethnicity and education', *Developments in Sociology*, vol.13.

Pilkington, A (1999) 'The underclass revisited', *Social Science Teacher,* vol.29, no.1.

Pilkington, A and Sherratt, N (1993) 'The interacting dynamics of class, "race"/ethnicity and gender' in S Hall (ed.) *Social Structures and Social Divisions, Block 2,* Open University, Milton Keynes.

Pilkington, A, Leisten, R, Puwar, N and Armstrong, S (2001) *Macpherson and After,* UCN, Northampton.

Pilkington, E (1988) *Beyond the Mother Country: West Indians and the Notting Hill White Riots,* IB Tauris, London.

PIU (Performance and Innovation Unit) (2002) *Ethnic Minorities and the Labour Market Interim Analytical Report,* Cabinet Office, London.

Power, A and Tunstall, R (1997) *Dangerous Disorder: Riots and Violent Disturbances in Thirteen Areas of Britain, 1991–92,* Joseph Rowntree Foundation, York.

Pryce, K (1986) *Endless Pressure,* 2nd edn, Bristol Classical Press, Bristol.

Ram, M (1992) 'Coping with racism: Asian employers in the inner-city', *Work, Employment and Society,* vol.6, no.4.

Rampton, A (1981) *West Indian Children in our Schools,* HMSO Cmnd. 8273, London.

Ranger, T, Samad, S and Stuart, O (eds) (1996) *Culture, Identity and Politics,* Avebury, Aldershot.

Ratcliffe, P (ed.) (1996) *Ethnicity in the Census, Volume 3 Social Geography and Ethnicity in Britain: Geographical Spread, Spatial Concentration and Internal Migration,* HMSO, London.

Ratcliffe, P (1997) '"Race", ethnicity and housing differentials in Britain' in V Karn (ed.) *Ethnicity in the Census, Volume 4. Employment, Education and Housing among the Ethnic Minority Populations of Britain,* HMSO, London.

Ratcliffe, P (1999) 'Housing inequality and "race": some critical reflections on the concept of "social exclusion"', *Ethnic and Racial Studies,* vol.22, no.1.

Ratcliffe, P (2000) 'Is the assertion of minority identity compatible with the idea of a socially inclusive society?' in P Askonas and A Stewart (eds) *Social Inclusion: Possibilities and Tensions,* Macmillan, London.

Rattansi, A (1992) 'Changing the subject?' in J Donald and A Rattansi (eds) *'Race', Culture and Difference,* Sage, London.

Rees, P and Phillips, D (1996a) 'Geographical spread: the national picture' in P Ratcliffe (ed.) *Ethnicity in the Census, Volume 3 Social Geography and Ethnicity in Britain: Geographical Spread, Spatial Concentration and Internal Migration,* HMSO, London.

Rees, P and Phillips, D (1996b) 'Geographical patterns in a cluster of Pennine cities' in P Ratcliffe (ed.) *Ethnicity in the Census, Volume 3. Social Geography and Ethnicity in Britain: Geographical Spread, Spatial Concentration and Internal Migration,* HMSO, London.

Rees, T (1982) 'Immigration policies in the United Kingdom' in C Husband (ed.) *'Race' in Britain,* Hutchinson, London.

Reiner, R (1993) 'Race, crime and justice: models of interpretation' in L Gelsthorpe (ed.) *Minority Ethnic Groups in the Criminal Justice System*, Institute of Criminology, Cambridge.

Rex, J (1970) *Race Relations in Sociological Theory*, Weidenfeld & Nicholson, London.

Rex, J and Tomlinson, S (1979) *Colonial Immigrants in a British City: A Class Analysis*, Routledge, London.

Rhodes, E and Braham, P (1989) 'Equal opportunity in the context of high levels of unemployment' in R Jenkins and J Solomos (eds) *Racism and Equal Opportunity Policies in the 1980s*, 2nd edn, Cambridge University Press, Cambridge.

Richards, S (1999) 'NS interview: Gordon Brown', *New Statesman*, 19 April.

Richardson, R (2000) 'Children will be told lies', *Runnymede Bulletin*, no.324.

Roberts, K (2001) *Class in Modern Britain*, Palgrave Macmillan, Basingstoke.

Robinson, F and Grigson, N (1992) 'The "underclass": a class apart? *Critical Social Policy*, no.34.

Robinson, P (1998) 'Employment and social inclusion' in C Oppenheim (ed.) *An Inclusive Society*, IPPR, London.

Robinson, V (1980) 'Correlates of Asian immigration: 1959–1974', *New Community*, vol.8, no.1.

Robinson, V (1986) *Transients, Settlers and Refugees*, Clarendon, Oxford.

Robinson, V (1990a) 'Roots to mobility: the social mobility of Britain's Black population, 1971–87', *Ethnic and Racial Studies*, vol.13, no.2.

Robinson, V (1990b) 'Boom and gloom: the success and failure of Britain's South Asians' in C Clarke, C Peach and S Vertovec (eds) *South Asians Overseas: Migration and Ethnicity*, Cambridge University Press, Cambridge.

Robinson, V (1996) 'Inter-generational differences in ethnic settlement patterns in Britain' in P Ratcliffe (1996) (ed.) *Ethnicity in the Census, Volume 3. Social Geography and Ethnicity in Britain: Geographical Spread, Spatial Concentration and Internal Migration*, HMSO, London.

Ross, K (1996) *Black and White Media*, Polity, Cambridge.

Rowe, M (2000) 'Asylum seekers in the UK', *Politics Review*, vol.10, no.2.

Sachdev, D (1996) 'Racial prejudice and racial discrimination: whither British youth?' in H Roberts and D Sachdev (eds) *Young People's Social Attitudes*, Barnado's, Ilford.

Saggar, S (1992) *Race and Politics in Britain*, Harvester Wheatsheaf, London.

Saggar, S (1993) 'Black participation and the transformation of the "race issue" in British politics', *New Community*, vol.20, no.1.

Saggar, S (1995) 'The electoral behaviour of ethnic minorities in British politics', *Developments in Politics*, vol.7.

Saggar, S (1997) 'The dog that didn't bark? Immigration, race and the general election' in A Geddes and J Tonge (eds) *Labour's Landslide,* Manchester University Press, Manchester.

Saggar, S (1998) 'Party strategy and ethnic politics in the general election campaign', *Politics Review,* vol.7, no.4.

Said, E (1978) *Orientalism: Western Concepts of the Orient,* Penguin, Harmondsworth.

Said, E (1993) *Culture and Imperialism,* Vintage, London.

Sanders, P (1998) 'Tackling racial discrimination' in T Blackstone, B Parekh and P Sanders (eds) *Race Relations in Britain,* Routledge, London.

Sarre, P (1989) 'Race and the class structure' in C Hamnett, L McDowall and P Sarre (eds) *The Changing Social Structure,* Sage, London.

Sarup, M (1991) *Education and the Ideologies of Racism,* Trentham, Stoke on Trent.

Saunders, P (1996) 'A British Bell curve?' *Sociology Review,* vol.6, no.2.

Scarman, L (1981) *The Scarman Report: The Brixton Disorders,* HMSO, London.

Schlesinger, P (1991) *Media, State and Nation,* Sage, London.

Seifert, W (1997) 'Admission policy, patterns of migration and integration: the German and French case compared', *New Community,* vol.23, no.4.

Sewell, T (1997) *Black Masculinities and Schooling,* Trentham, Stoke on Trent.

Shukra, K (1998a) 'New Labour debates and dilemmas' in S Saggar (ed.) *Race and British Electoral Politics,* UCL Press, London.

Shukra, K (1998b) *The Changing Pattern of Black Politics,* Pluto, London.

Simpson, A and Stevenson, J (1994) *Half a Chance, Still?* Nottingham and District Racial Equality Council, Nottingham.

Sinclair, S (2000) '"Poverty", "social exclusion" and "citizenship"', *Social Science Teacher,* vol.30, no.1.

Sivanandan, A (1995) 'Le trahison des clercs', *New Statesman and Society,* 14 July.

Skellington, R (1996) *'Race' in Britain Today,* 2nd edn, Sage, London.

Sly, F (1995) 'Ethnic groups and the labour market: analyses from the spring 1994 Labour Force Survey', *Employment Gazette.*

Smith, A (1995) 'The formation of national identity' in H Harris (ed.) *Identity,* Oxford University Press, Oxford.

Smith, D (1977) *Racial Disadvantage in Britain,* Penguin, Harmondsworth.

Smith, D (ed.) (1992) *Understanding the Underclass,* Policy Studies Institute, London.

Smith, D (1997) 'Ethnic origins, crime, and criminal justice' in M Maguire, R Morgan and R Reiner (eds) *The Oxford Handbook of Criminology,* 2nd edn, Oxford University Press, Oxford.

Smith, D and Tomlinson, S (1989) *The School Effect,* Policy Studies Institute, London.

Smith, D and Wistrich, E (1997) 'Citizenship and social exclusion in the European Union' in M Roche and R van Berkel (eds) *European Citizenship and Social Exclusion*, Ashgate, Aldershot.

Smith, M (1986) 'Pluralism, race and ethnicity in selected African countries' in J Rex and D Mason (eds) *Theories of Race and Ethnic Relations*, Cambridge University Press, Cambridge.

Smith, S (1989) *The Politics of 'Race' and Residence*, Polity, Cambridge.

Smithers, R (2001) 'Punishment for Black pupils appears harsher', *The Guardian*, 1 March.

Solomos, J (1989) 'The changing politics of race', *Developments in Politics*, vol.1.

Solomos, J (1993) *Race and Racism in Britain*, 2nd edn, Macmillan, London.

Solomos, J (1998) 'Social policy and social movements: "race", racism and social policies' in N Ellison and C Pierson (eds) *Developments in British Social Policy*, Macmillan, London.

Solomos, J (1999) 'Social research and the Stephen Lawrence Inquiry', *Sociology Research Online*, vol.4, no.1

Solomos, J and Back, L (1996) *Racism and Society*, Macmillan, London.

Spencer, I (1997) *British Immigration Policy Since 1939*, Routledge, London.

Spencer, S (1998) 'The impact of immigration policy on race relations' in T Blackstone, B Parekh and P Sanders (eds) *Race Relations in Britain*, Routledge, London.

Srinivasan, S (1992) 'The class position of the Asian petty-bourgeoisie', *New Community*, vol.19, no.1.

Statham, P (1999) 'Political mobilisation by minorities in Britain: negative feedback of "race relations"', *Journal of Ethnic and Migration Studies*, vol.25, no.4.

Stepan, N (1990) 'Race and gender: the role of analogy in science' in T Goldberg (ed.) *The Anatomy of Racism*, University of Minnesota Press, Minneapolis.

Stewart, A (2000) 'Social inclusion: an introduction' in P Askonas and A Stewart (eds) *Social Inclusion: Possibilities and Tensions*, Macmillan, London.

Stone, J (1977) 'Race relations and the sociological tradition' in J Stone (ed.) *Race, Ethnicity and Social Change*, Duxbury, North Scituate, MA.

Stone, J and Lasus, H (1998) 'Immigration and ethnic relations in Britain and America' in T Blackstone, B Parekh and P Sanders (eds) *Race Relations in Britain*, Routledge, London.

Stopes-Roe, M and Cochrane, R (1990) *Citizens of this Country*, Multilingual Matters, Clevedon.

Swann, M (1985) *Education for All*, Cmnd. 9453, HMSO, London.

Taylor, M (1981) *Caught Between: A Review of Research into the Education of Pupils of West Indian Origin*, NFER Nelson, Windsor.

Taylor, P, Richardson, J, Yeo, A, Marsh, I, Trobe, K and Pilkington, A (1995) *Sociology in Focus,* Causeway, Ormskirk.

Taylor, S (1992) 'The politics of race and immigration in Britain', *Developments in Politics,* vol.4.

Thomas, J (1998) 'Job aspirations and ethnic minority unemployment in the UK: is there a connection? *Journal of Ethnic and Migration Studies,* vol.24, no.1.

Tomlinson, S (1990a) *Multicultural Education in White Schools,* Batsford, London.

Tomlinson, S (1990b) 'Effective schooling for ethnic minorities', *New Community,* vol.16, no.3.

Tomlinson, S (2000) 'Ethnic minorities and education: new disadvantages' in T Cox (ed.) *Combatting Educational Disadvantage,* Falmer, London.

Tomlinson, S and Craft, M (eds) (1995) *Ethnic Relations and Schooling,* Athlone, London.

Townend, J (2001) Extracts from his speeches, *www.guardianunlimited.co.uk,* 28 March and 26 April.

Townsend, P (1979) *Poverty in the United Kingdom: A Survey of Household Resources and Standards of Living,* Penguin, Harmondsworth.

Townsend, P, Davidson, N and Whitehead, M (1992) *Inequalities in Health,* Penguin, Harmondsworth.

Travis, A (2002) 'Ministers saw "racism" as defensible', *The Guardian,* 1 January.

Troyna, B (1984) 'Fact or artefact? The "educational underachievement" of Black pupils', *British Journal of Sociology of Education,* vol.5, no.2.

Troyna, B (1995) 'Beyond reasonable doubt? Researching "race" in educational settings', *Oxford Review of Education,* vol.21, no.4.

Troyna, B and Carrington, B (1990) *Education, Racism and Reform,* Routledge, London.

Troyna, B and Williams, J (1986) *Racism, Education and the State,* Croom Helm, London.

Van Dijk, T (1991) *Racism and the Press,* Routledge, London.

Van Dijk, T (1993) 'Denying racism: elite discourse and racism' in J Wrench and J Solomos (eds) *Racism and Migration in Western Europe,* Berg, Oxford.

Van Dijk, T (2000) 'New(s) racism: a discourse analytical approach' in S Cottle (ed.) *Ethnic Minorities and the Media,* Open University Press, Buckingham.

Virdee, S (1995) *Racial Violence and Harassment,* Policy Studies Institute, London.

Visram, R (1986) *Ayahs, Lascars and Princes,* Pluto, London.

Wallman, S (1986) 'Ethnicity and the boundary process in context' in J Rex and D Mason (eds) *Theories of Race and Ethnic Relations,* Cambridge University Press, Cambridge.

Walvin, J (1987) 'Black caricature: the roots of racialism' in C Husband (ed.) *'Race' in Britain,* 2nd edn, Hutchinson, London.

Ward, R and Cross, M (1991) 'Race, employment and economic change' in P Brown and R Scase (eds) *Poor Work: Disadvantage and the Division of Labour,* Open University, Milton Keynes.

Watson, J (ed.) (1977) *Between Two Cultures,* Basil Blackwell, Oxford.

Weber, M (1997) 'What is an ethnic group?' in M Guibernau and J Rex (eds) *The Ethnicity Reader,* Polity, Cambridge.

Werbner, P (1992) 'Social networks and the gift economy among British Pakistanis', *Sociology Review,* vol.1, no.3.

Werbner, P (1997) 'The dialectics of cultural hybridity' in P Werbner and T Modood (eds) *Debating Cultural Hybridity,* Zed, London.

Westergaard, J and Resler, H (1975) *Class in a Capitalist Society,* Heinemann, London.

Westwood, S and Bhachu, P (eds) (1988) *Enterprising Women,* Routledge, London.

White, P (1999) 'Ethnicity' racialisation and citizenship as divisive elements in Europe' in R Hudson and A Williams (eds) *Divided Europe,* Sage, London.

Willey, R (1984) *Race, Equality and Schools,* Methuen, London.

Williams, F (1989) *Social Policy: A Critical Introduction,* Polity, Oxford.

Wilpert, C (1993) 'The ideological and institutional foundations of racism in the Federal Republic of Germany' in J Wrench and J Solomos (eds) *Racism and Migration in Western Europe,* Berg, Oxford.

Wilson, W (1987) *The Truly Disadvantaged,* University of Chicago Press, Chicago.

Wilson, W (1991) 'Public policy research and the truly disadvantaged' in C Jencks and P Peterson (eds) *The Urban Underclass,* Brookings Institution, Washington, DC.

Wilson, W (1999) *The Bridge Over the Racial Divide,* University of California Press, London.

Woods, P (1992) 'Racism and inequality in education' in M Blair and P Woods (eds) *Racism and Education: Structures and Strategies,* Open University Press, Milton Keynes.

Woodward, K (ed.) (1997) *Identity and Difference,* Sage, London.

Wrench, J and Solomos, J (1993) 'The politics and processes of racial discrimination in Britain' in J Wrench and J Solomos (eds) *Racism and Migration in Western Europe,* Berg, Oxford.

Wright, C (1987) 'Black students – White teachers' in B Troyna (ed.) *Racial Inequality in Education,* Tavistock, London.

Wright, C (1992) 'Early education: multiracial primary school classrooms' in D Gill, B Mayor and M Blair (eds) *Racism and Education,* Sage, London.

Young, K (1992) 'Class, race and opportunity' in R Jowell, S Witherspoon and L Brook (eds) *British Social Attitudes: The 9th Report,* Dartmouth Publishing, Dartmouth.

Young, H (2001) 'Labour's law of ethnic punishment shames us all', *The Guardian,* 8 May.

Younge, G (2001) 'The right to be British', *The Guardian,* 12 November.

Younge, G (2002) 'Britain is again White', *The Guardian,* 18 February.

Yuval-Davis, N (1992) 'Fundamentalism, multiculturalism and women in Britain' in J Donald and A Rattansi (eds) *'Race', Culture and Difference,* Sage, London.

Index